AN AFFAIR WITH KOREA:

MEMORIES OF SOUTH KOREA IN THE 1960s

VINCENT S. R. BRANDT

Center for Korea Studies Publications

The Northern Region of Korea: History, Identity, and Culture
Edited by Sun Joo Kim

Reassessing the Park Chung Hee Era, 1961–1979:
Development, Political Thought, Democracy, and Cultural Influence
Edited by Hyung-A Kim and Clark W. Sorensen

Colonial Rule and Social Change in Korea, 1910–1945
Edited by Hong Yung Lee, Yong Chool Ha, and Clark W. Sorensen

An Affair with Korea: Memories of South Korea in the 1960s
By Vincent S. R. Brandt

This work was supported by the Academy of Korean Studies (KSPS) Grant funded by the Korean Government (MOE) (AKS–2011–BAA–2101).

이 저서는 2011년도 정부(교육부)의 재원으로 국학중앙연구원(한국학진흥사업단)의 지원을 받아 수행된 연구임 (AKS-2011-BAA-2101).

The Center for Korea Studies Publication Series is dedicated to providing excellent academic resources and conference volumes related to the history, culture, and politics of the Korean peninsula.

Clark W. Sorensen | Director & General Editor | Center for Korea Studies

An Affair with Korea: Memories of South Korea in the 1960s

VINCENT S. R. BRANDT

A CENTER FOR KOREA STUDIES PUBLICATION

UNIVERSITY OF WASHINGTON PRESS | SEATTLE & LONDON

An Affair with Korea: Memories of South Korea in the 1960s
By Vincent S. R. Brandt
Photographs by Vincent S. R. Brandt
© 2014 by the Center for Korea Studies, University of Washington
Printed in the United States of America
18 17 16 15 14   1 2 3 4 5

CENTER FOR KOREA STUDIES
Henry M. Jackson School of International Studies
University of Washington
Box 353650, Seattle, WA 98195-3650
http://jsis.washington.edu/Korea

UNIVERSITY OF WASHINGTON PRESS
P.O. Box 50096, Seattle, WA 98195 U.S.A.
www.washington.edu/uwpress

LIBRARY OF CONGRESS CATALOGING-IN-PUBLICATION DATA
Brandt, Vincent S. R.
  An affair with Korea / Vincent S.R. Brandt. — First edition.
      pages   cm
   Summary: "In 1966 Vincent S. R. Brandt lived in Sokp'o, a poor and isolated South Korean fishing village on the coast of the Yellow Sea, carrying out social anthropological research. At that time, the only way to reach Sokp'o, other than by boat, was a two hour walk along foot paths. This memoir of his experiences in a village with no electricity, running water, or telephone shows Brandt's attempts to adapt to a traditional, preindustrial existence in a small, almost completely self-sufficient community. This vivid account of his growing admiration for an ancient way of life that was doomed, and that most of the villagers themselves despised, illuminates a social world that has almost completely disappeared. Vincent S. R. Brandt lives in rural Vermont"—Provided by publisher.
   ISBN 978-0-295-99341-6 (pbk. : alk. paper)
   1. Brandt, Vincent S. R. 2. Villages—Korea (South)—Case studies. 3. Fishing villages—Yellow Sea Coast (Korea) 4. Fishers—Yellow Sea Coast (Korea) 5. Maritime anthropology—Yellow Sea Coast (Korea) 6. Yellow Sea Coast (Korea)—Description and travel. 7. Ch'ungch'ong-namdo (Korea)—Rural conditions—20th century. 8. Ch'ungch'ong-namdo (Korea)—Social life and customs—20th century. 9. Americans—Korea (South)—Korea (South)—Biography. 10. Anthropologists—United States—Biography. I. Title.
   HN730.5.A8B725 2013
   306.09519—dc23   2013032302

For Hi Kyung, my "North Korean refugee"

Contents

Preface | ix
List of Illustrations | x

Prologue | 1

1   Sŏkp'o 1965–1966 | 9

2   Settling In | 24

3   Patriotic Journey | 43

4   Settling In II | 62

5   Getting Involved | 74

6   Getting There | 87

7   Fathers and Sons | 103

8   Spirits: Familiar, Benign, and Malevolent | 122

9   Fishing I | 141

10   The Anthropologist at Work and Play | 160

11   Contraband | 174

12   Fishing II | 187

13   Go Peacefully; Stay Peacefully | 208

14   Re-encounter | 215

Preface

I spent most of 1966 in Sŏkp'o, a poor and isolated fishing village on the Yellow Sea coast of central South Korea, carrying out social anthropological research. At that time the only way to get to Sŏkp'o, except by boat, was to walk for two hours from where the bus line ended further down the coast. There were no roads, only foot paths. And, of course, there was no electricity, running water, or telephone. This book is an informal memoir of that experience.[1] The focus is not so much on the anthropological findings, as it is on my personal involvement—my attempt to adapt to a traditional, pre-industrial existence in a small, almost completely self-sufficient community. Further, it is an account of my growing admiration for an ancient way of life that was doomed, and that most of the villagers themselves, while still governed by its dictates, despised. It is also about how the residents of Sŏkp'o coped with the strange challenge of having a foreigner live in their midst. In the prologue I have tried to place Sŏkp'o in the social and economic context of contemporary South Korea, and finally in the final chapter titled Re-encounter, I have summarized my impressions of Sŏkp'o when I returned there for three months twenty-five years later. Today (2013) the rapid pace of development and change in South Korea continues. Living standards continue to climb. The social world of Sŏkp'o described in this book has almost completely disappeared.

NOTES

1. My anthropological monograph, entitled *A Korean Village: Between Farm and Sea*, was published in 1971 by Harvard University Press.

Illustrations

MAPS

Map 1.1   Map of South Korea 10
Map 1.2   Map of Sŏkp'o 12

FIGURES

Figure 2.1   The men repairing irrigation dikes. *Makkŏlli* will follow.
              (April 26, 1966) 25
Figure 4.1   Roof ceremony. Learning to enjoy ceremonial drinking. (1966) 68
Figure 4.2   My first ethnological experience of village-wide cooperation—
              house building. (1966) 68
Figure 4.3   My $300 house. A neighbor is harvesting soybeans. My thin straw
              roof is an indication of the newness of the house. (1966) 70
Figure 4.4   Looking northwest, threshing rice on an unirrigated rice field.
              (1966) 70
Figure 5.1   Mun lineage women returning from the well. Adolescent girl wears
              Western-style clothes. (1966) 79
Figure 6.1   A member of the Yi lineage singing (chanting) *sijo* into the tape
              recorder. (1966) 88
Figure 7.1   Making a new sail on my veranda; cheap family labor.
              (Kim and Richie, 1966) 104
Figure 7.2   One of the village's "weighty" men. (1966) 113
Figure 8.1   Women in white; Death anniversary of parent. Afterwards there
              will be feasting and drinking and sometimes dancing. (1966) 123
Figure 8.2   Pirate engaged in ceremonial activity. (1966) 123

Figure 8.3   I was kept busy supplying formal photographs of aging couples and individuals to serve as focal points at ceremonies after their death. (1966) 124

Figure 8.4   "Breakfast" after midnight ancestor ceremony. Village head (drinking) and fellow Yi lineage members at an ancestor worship ceremony. (1966) 124

Figure 9.1   Boat "play" (paennori); author at the helm. (1966) 145

Figure 9.2   Boat "play"; mixing it up. (1966) 145

Figure 11.1   Looking south across the salt pans down the coast from my house; Yellow Sea on the right. (1966) 175

Figure 11.2   Photo of the passengers on the Samhae Ho. This is the boat that we took to Inch'ŏn. (1966) 178

Figure 12.1   Low tide showing mud as far as one can see. (1966) 194

Figure 12.2   The roof was damaged in a southwest storm, and the men are hurrying to complete repairs before bad weather returns. (November, 1966) 203

Figure 12.3   Stone commemoration of author's time in Korea, photo taken in 1966. On my return to Sŏkp'o twenty-five years later in 1992, the stele was still upright but badly overgrown. 206

Figure 13.1   Looking east over the Big Hamlet. My house is in the clump of trees in the middle of the photo. (1966) 209

Figure 14.1   These are oyster racks, the source of contemporary prosperity. (1992) 219

Figure 14.2   Sŏkp'o's motorized fleet twenty-five years later. (1992) 225

Figure 14.3   Rice harvester/combine. (1992)   233

Figure 14.4   One of Sŏkp'o's "rich" men. He sent his son to college in Seoul.
(1992)   233

Figure 14.5   Impromptu makkŏlli party on path between Fourth and Fifth hamlets.
This one ended up with solo dancing by the woman at extreme left.
(1992)   235

Prologue

When visibility is good, the approach to Kimp'o Airport just outside Seoul provides spectacular scenery. It also brings back all sorts of wonderful memories that have piled up in the course of a great many trips to Korea since 1952. Seoul has always been for me both exotic and familiar, a place where unexpected adventures were usually lying in wait, but where I could also count on old friends to put me up for the night—or for a week—without advance notice.

During the Korean War, I was a young diplomat at the American Embassy, first in Pusan and then, from February of 1953, in Seoul. Those were the very worst of times for Koreans, but a halcyon period for me. In the Pusan area of the south I had a fascinating job, roaming through the most distant and isolated parts of a mountainous countryside with a Jeep and interpreter. My assignment was to check up on the distribution of relief grain and run down reports of rural starvation that appeared frequently in the Pusan newspapers. Perhaps halcyon isn't quite the right word to describe the experience of being shot at by guerillas. On one very memorable occasion we were driving along a deserted mountain road at dusk. One bullet hit the hood of the Jeep and another broke the windshield. The terrified driver whipped the Jeep around and headed back the way we had come without any orders from me. Combat police at the nearest town told us this only happened late in the day when the guerillas figured they were safe from pursuit by Army helicopters. After that we stopped driving well before suppertime and no longer spent the night in isolated villages.

In those towns and villages, my interpreter, who became a close friend, introduced me to rural life and entertainments. I learned to eat with chopsticks, sleep on the floor, and take baths out of a giant cauldron with a wood fire underneath. I learned to drink various homemade alcoholic beverages and to sing folk songs along with the local female entertainers. Because American officialdom firmly believed that all Korean food was dangerously unhealthy, each time we left Pusan the Jeep was loaded with C-rations. Instead of eating these, we benevolently distributed them to local farmers in return for information, directions, food, drink, and lodging. In place of canned pork and beans we ate fresh greens with hot bean paste sauce and kimch'i or tofu mixed with various vegetables and meat. On one occasion when the sub-county magistrate was being particularly hospitable, the meat turned out to be dog.

In the city of Pusan, between trips to the countryside, I fell in love with a North Korean refugee and sailed a small boat among wooded islands off what must be one of the most beautiful seacoasts in the world. I also met one of South Korea's most celebrated traditional artists, who was then a penniless refugee like nearly everyone else. He introduced me to the pleasures of painting bamboo leaves and rock orchids and plum blossoms on rice paper with ink and an oriental brush. More than that, he taught me how to sit cross-legged for long periods and compose my mind. Immersed in chaos and deprivation, the Koreans struggled to survive, while I reveled in my first encounter with a whole new civilization.

During the intervening years, I have always come back to Korea with agreeable anticipation, expecting fresh adventures and a renewal of warm associations. And I have usually not been disappointed. But this time—it is September 1992—I find myself for the first time wanting to postpone my encounter with Seoul, wishing that we could just keep making giant circles over the metropolitan area instead of landing. I know there are ten and a half million busy, determined people down there, and I will have to compete with them for limited space on sidewalks, buses, and subways, as well as for the chance to breathe some of the brownish, bad-tasting cloud that hangs over the city.

South Korea today is a prosperous, dynamic, industrial country, and most people are no longer interested in the past or in Americans. I know that my few dollars can no longer buy the fantastic luxuries that used to be easily available thirty years ago. Then, a Koryŏ celadon bowl was still within my reach in a tiny, cramped Insa-dong antique shop, or a sumptuous meal might be accompanied by young women in graceful, traditional dress who sang ancient love songs or flirted with the customers while pouring their drinks. Before, there were always certain coffee shops, restaurants, bars, curio stores, and one memorable barbershop where I was a *tangol sonnim*, that is, a regular (or in my case somewhat irregular) customer who had been patronizing the same place for many years. In the Far East, these long-continued relationships have a special luster, even a kind of sanctity, and for me this always meant a heart-warming welcome and the illusion, at least, of special treatment whenever I went back for a meal or a haircut or a cup of ginseng tea after a year or so away in America. But now I know that all the places where I used to be a tangol sonnim have been torn down, and I have no idea where their aging proprietors have gone. Instead of winding alleys with ramshackle shops, downtown Seoul is covered with enormous high-rise office buildings decorated with glossy granite facades.

As the plane banks steeply, I can look right down along the trailing edge of the wing to the mountains where I used to climb with members of the Korean Alpine Club forty years ago during my days as a diplomat. I see Ch'unch'uk-sa with its blue-tiled roof, the Buddhist temple where we climbers often spent the night and cooked our meals. Just beyond are the sheer rock faces that used to instill in me such strong feelings, both of terror and of soaring accomplishment.

Over the past forty years I have seen the city explode in every direction, even north into the mountains. Built-up areas now invade nearly every valley and ravine, pushing far up the steep slopes. The secluded pine woods and mountain ponds where as a young bachelor I used to take girlfriends for picnics have been overrun with roads, houses, and schools. In the distance, beyond these mountains close to Seoul, are more mountains and then still more mountains in every direction.

Now the plane swings northwest, and I can see all the way into forbidden, hostile North Korea. Airplane and missile bases are situated less than five minutes flying time across the Demilitarized Zone. Does the Democratic People's Republic of Korea have nuclear weapons yet, as the headline in my paper suggests?[1] Suddenly I see in my mind a horrible image of a dark missile hurtling up out of the northern dusk to destroy us. I suppress the awful fantasy, and we are spared.

The plane keeps turning toward the west and then south until the Yellow Sea appears, hazy and gleaming in the late afternoon sun. Here the mountains have become steep, black, silhouetted islands—hundreds of them. The plane banks again. This time I can see far down the jagged coast to the south, perhaps even as far as Sŏkp'o, the fishing village that is my immediate goal on this trip to South Korea.

Twenty-five years ago, in the process of shifting careers from diplomacy to anthropology, I lived in Sŏkp'o for almost a year to carry out a community study. Isolated, impoverished, and backward even by South Korean standards, Sŏkp'o seemed in 1966 to belong to another century. By the time I left in January 1967, the village was much more than just another research site. It had become a kind of spiritual home.

I found Sŏkp'o to be a spectacularly attractive place, where everyday behavior contrasted sharply with my own ego-centered, Western way of life. The more I learned about how people there worked together, helped each other out, and tolerantly settled their conflicts, the more admiration I felt for this small community on the Yellow Sea. That experience of participating, even if only briefly and partially, in an isolated, self-contained premodern world was one of the great adventures of my life.

After finishing my fieldwork in 1967, I returned home to the university to write it all up as a doctoral dissertation. There I had wonderful luck. A nice big, well-lit office, normally occupied by an associate professor, became available at the last minute. It was far grander than a graduate student, a mere teaching fellow, deserved. With lots of unobstructed wall space I was able to display an enormous amount of data from my fieldwork in Sŏkp'o. I spent my days surrounded by these visual reminders of the village. I put up three big maps. The first showed all the houses, the paths, the tombs, and the wells, color-coded according to the various kinship groups. Another map showed agricultural land, forest, salt pans, reservoirs, oyster-gathering areas, and the major fishing grounds.

The third map gave directions and distances from the village to nearby towns, the county seat, and various offshore islands. I pinned up cards for each household with information about property, lineage, and family reputation. On most of them I was able to paste a small photograph of the household head or his wife to jog my memory. Elaborate indexes and crossreferences to my field notes were tacked up just over my desk. Most evocative of all were the big enlargements of scenic photographs I had taken of the coast, the harbor, and the various hamlets of the village. For almost a year, while writing my dissertation, I could shut myself in that room, leave the city of Cambridge, and reenter my own fantasy version of Sŏkp'o.

Now, a generation later, as I look out of the plane that is about to land, I am anxious about the changes that I will encounter. Will I be able to find again the tranquil, easygoing place that I remember? Do the villagers still take their ancient code of ethics seriously? Will they welcome me with the same goodwill and warmth that existed before?

As the plane drops lower I see the six-lane expressway between Seoul and Inch'ŏn clogged with slowly moving rush hour traffic. It is September, and the ripening rice is turning yellow gold; but there are not many rice fields left in this megalopolitan area. Rows of suburban villas and apartment blocks encroach on the villages, and where farming is still going on, the fields are mostly covered with low, polyethylene greenhouses, not with ripening grain. Tall factory chimneys, crowned with strobe lights to warn pilots, sprout from the landscape.

Emerging from customs into the main lobby of the airport, I have to pass in a narrow lane through the tightly packed crowd that has come to meet incoming passengers from overseas. It is a lonely and intimidating moment. Indifferent faces stare at me, registering only the fact that I am not the one they want. Suddenly I see a large, handsomely lettered sign with my name on it. Someone has sent a car to meet me. I am back in Seoul. The driver who greets me is from a luxury hotel that belongs to one of my oldest and richest Korean friends. Ever since I first met him in Pusan in 1952, he has helped me in all sorts of ways whenever I have been in South Korea. I plan to stay at his hotel for a couple of days, luxuriously recovering from jet lag before moving to faculty housing at a nearby university for a few more days to catch up on academic developments. Then I will leave Seoul and start work in the village. After the long flight, it is comforting to be whisked away to a five-star palace high on the mountainside looking south over the Han River. For a half hour or so, sitting back in the plush comfort of the dark limousine, I once again have that old State Department illusion of being a person of consequence. The driver tells me that times are bad and he is having trouble paying his daughter's high school tuition. When I ask if things are better than three years ago, he replies, "Of course." He is noncommittal about politics and the government. I realize that almost unconsciously I have started interviewing an "informant." I try to relax instead and watch the city slide by. As usual, all sorts of new construction is going on: half-built skyscrapers, enormous apartment blocks, and streets torn up for new subways. Dazzling neon lights twist themselves everywhere into Chinese characters and phonetic Korean writing. Consumers crowd the sidewalks on this warm September evening.

There is a small network of friends I have known ever since the Korean War, and they all seem to have prospered. I am wined and dined in lavish style. From my middle-class, New England perspective this world of chauffeur-driven cars, expensive restaurants, and ornate bars where seductively groomed hostesses fill my glass and praise my Korean, is just as exotic as the fishing village I have come to study. I feel I should be taking ethnographic notes. Late at night when I return to the hotel, I stay away from its bars and nightclubs, eager to sleep. But in Seoul nightlife is intrusive. In the hotel corridor a lovely young woman in an evening dress implores me in broken English to let her into my room. She whispers that she is in trouble at the nightclub and evil men are after her. My chivalry is not up to this professional challenge, however, and I abandon her in the hall.

In the 1990s, although a quarter of South Korea's forty-five million people live in the Seoul metropolitan area, most of them were not born there. They have migrated from small villages during the past two or three decades, in response to the decline of agriculture and the creation of millions of new urban jobs in factories, offices, small shops, and service trades. Towns and smaller provincial cities have grown rapidly too. Only about half as many people still live in the countryside as in the 1960s. Every village has its abandoned houses, while on some isolated islands and in the distant mountains entire communities have disappeared. Because this massive exodus is so recent and continues, most Seoul residents still have close relatives in their ancestral villages. If there is one single generalization about Koreans that has held up well throughout the years of rapid modernization (and there aren't many), it is that they remain strongly kinship oriented. For this reason millions of people constantly travel back and forth between all of the nation's thirty-six thousand villages and the capital. Transportation facilities have improved enormously during the past thirty years. After all, South Korea is a very small country (about the same size as West Virginia), and it is possible to get anywhere in a single day. But the desire to visit relatives—in both directions, towards and away from Seoul—keeps outstripping the capacity of trains, buses, cars, and airplanes. On the major holidays there is pandemonium and a temporary breakdown of the system at the big express bus stations in Seoul. The rest of the time, from an American point of view, things are just badly overcrowded. But Koreans seem to like the hustle and bustle, the tension, and the satisfaction of running with heavy baggage to catch an overloaded bus just as it pulls out of the station. At least they smile and laugh while they are doing it. That is the way travel is; it is all part of the fun, along with drinking soju, eating hard-boiled eggs, and being reunited with close kin.

Leaving Seoul for Sŏkp'o, I find that I have a fair amount of baggage. It has not been easy getting from the university (on the west side of the city) to the southern bus terminal far from downtown Seoul. I have done a lot of hiking, ridden a city bus, and then changed subway lines twice. I am sweating and annoyed, mostly at myself for not taking a taxi. Ridiculously, I am still following an old fieldwork principle, without updating its application: I am trying to share the world of ordinary people and avoid the behavior of rich foreigners, long after Koreans have become rich themselves.

The bus is headed for Sŏsan, the county seat of the coastal area where the village of Sŏkp'o is located. There I will get in touch with Yi Byong Gi (Teacher Yi), who was my landlord, friend, best informant, and the principal and only teacher of the village school in Sŏkp'o twenty-five years ago.

Traffic is heavy and the bus is much too hot. The middle-aged passenger next to me in a suit and tie presses his thigh against mine mercilessly. The more I cringe, the more he spreads himself, taking advantage of the extra space. I try to relax and preach cultural relativism to myself, but it isn't easy. Inwardly I denounce what I have decided is the new breed of ill-mannered, materialistic, middle-class Korean. But then, after getting off to stretch at a rest stop, my fellow traveler comes back bringing me a cold beer. I accept gratefully, and we talk about the contrasts between life in Seoul and the provincial city of Taejŏn. I make a mental note to try and avoid hasty generalizations. When we finally leave the big, divided expressway, turning off to the west on smaller provincial roads, our speed picks up, the sun comes in on the other side of the bus, and I enjoy the endless pleasure of watching the countryside go by. During the past twenty-five years the appearance of rural South Korea has changed dramatically. Thatched roofs have disappeared, and the hills and mountains are almost entirely reforested. There are still a few ploughs and carts drawn by oxen, but mostly I see small tractors and pickup trucks.

I have clear memories of Sŏsan, the dusty, somnolent county seat where I always had to change buses and often spent the night when traveling from Seoul to the village in the past. But there is almost no link between those distant images and the Sŏsan I see today—a bustling city of one hundred thousand people—where I exit after four hours on the bus.

Standing disoriented with my bags in front of the bus station, I watch taxis and cars and crowds of people pass on the narrow streets, wondering what to do next. Then I look up from the square where the buses surge back and forth, disgorging and picking up passengers. I am amazed to see the same second-floor coffee shop I used to frequent twenty-five years ago. The name "Adam" (from *adam-hada*, cozy) is the same, and it seems doubtful that the windows or curtains have been washed in all this time. It had always been pleasant to relax upstairs by a window, drinking coffee and looking out to see when the next bus was getting ready to leave. I am elated; that's where I can rest and find a phone to call Teacher Yi.

I climb the narrow stairs, my rucksack and suitcase brushing heavily against the whitewashed wall, and stumble through swinging glass doors that weren't there before. A heavy older woman inside stares at me bluntly and without welcome, a foreigner out of place in provincial South Korea. She is familiar. Can this creature with mottled skin, wildly frizzy hair, and gleaming gold teeth be what has happened to the elegant and graceful young woman who managed the place a generation ago? I can see her wondering where she has seen me before. The Americans who used to be at a nearby missile base all went home a long time ago. Finally she recognizes me and waddles over, beaming with golden intensity. We sit by a window and reminisce, and I learn that she now owns the Cozy Coffee Shop. She shouts to a waitress who brings not only coffee but a small glass of amber liquid. "Now we make good whiskey in Korea," my old friend tells me. "We don't need to buy it from American soldiers like the old days." Then she makes me look out the window, pointing down to a shiny, black sedan in the street below. "There, that's my car; can you imagine! Even in my wildest dreams I never thought I would own my own car, when you were here before." I am filled with nostalgic affection and want to talk, but she is quickly gone, greeting other customers.

I have no trouble reaching Teacher Yi at his school. He tells me to wait at the coffee shop. He will join me in fifteen minutes.

NOTES

1. North Korea first tested a nuclear weapon device on October 9, 2006. [eds].

1

Sŏkp'o 1965–1966

I always had a sense of calm well-being waking up in Teacher Yi's guest room with its uncovered wooden beams and whitewashed mud walls. In addition to the wood smoke from the cooking and heating fires, I could smell the dried fish, garlic, sesame seeds, red pepper, and grain in the storage space next door. The guest room had no windows, but had four small paper-covered doors let in a soft, early morning light. Consciousness came gradually along with the low, rhythmic sound—more of a vibration—of the ox munching beyond the other side of the wall by my head. The morning fire that heated the ox's mash also warmed my floor through the system of stone flues that made old Korean farmhouses so wonderfully snug in cool weather. More warmth came in with the spring sunlight when I opened the doors. Then I would crawl out onto the wide, polished boards of the veranda, savoring the only real privacy of the day.

The guest room, or *sarangbang*, along with the unfinished storage space next to it, formed the southern side of the house. A fuller translation of *sarangbang* would be the outer room of a larger farmhouse that serves as an informal meeting place for influential or older men in the neighborhood. There was no furniture in this room. Thin reed mats were placed directly on the uneven, dried-mud floor. They served as cushions during the day and as a mattress at night. The *sarangbang* was the only room with direct access to the outside, and men could gather there without entering the courtyard of the house and disturbing (or being disturbed by) other members of the owner's family. My room continued to be the neighborhood *sarangbang*, and men would gather there without warning to talk and smoke and drink at any time from 10:00 a.m. until 10:00 p.m., staying on sometimes well past midnight. Although eventually I understood (and this took a few days) why my bedroom

Map 1.1 Map of South Korea

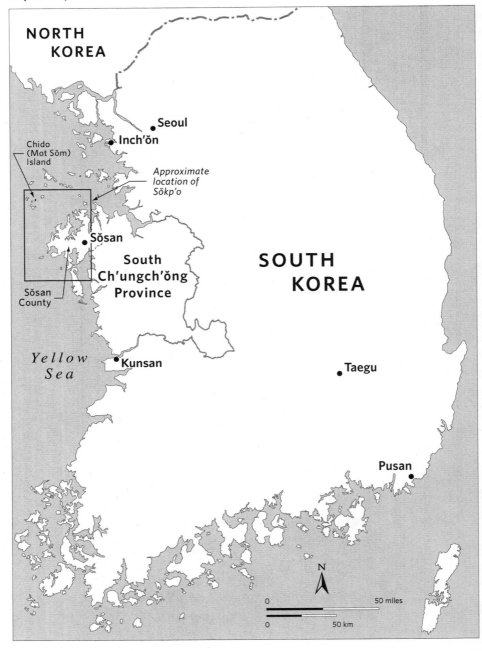

was being constantly invaded by elderly gentlemen who sat talking for hours about genealogies and tomb sites, I never really got used to it.

The other three sides of the house, comprising family quarters, the kitchen, toilet, chicken house, ox stall, and tool shed, all opened onto an enclosed courtyard, protected from the outside world by an imposing wooden gate. In back, against the hillside, was another small enclosed yard, the exclusive domain of the women.

On my side of the house, to the south, I looked out onto a broad, ochre-colored dirt threshing ground and a gently leaning thatched shed covering the night soil storage pit, which doubled as my private toilet. One hundred and fifty yards or so beyond the night soil pit, at the base of a steep wooded hill-side, was a clear stream where women gathered to wash clothes. To the east the land sloped down for a couple hundred yards past some other houses and then flattened out into terraced rice fields that stepped gradually down to the bay. An old stone dike separated the lowest fields from the mudflats that were covered by salt water at high tide.

I could get a pretty good idea of the outdoor activities of a substantial por-tion of Sŏkp'o's population just by standing outside Teacher Yi's house and looking out over the nearby fields and across the mud or water. By the time I was off the veranda brushing my teeth, Kim P'albong, Teacher Yi's live-in agricultural worker, would already be up and carrying heavy buckets of night soil out to the cabbage and pepper plants.

Teacher Yi's cousins and second cousins and third cousins and uncles and uncles once removed who lived nearby were also out working in their fields, even before their wives had lighted the kitchen fires for breakfast. Down on the mudflats, if it was low tide, there were usually a couple of men digging for octopus while children gathered snails and clams. A little later, work would start on the dike. The purpose of the dike was to seal off an arm of the bay and create new rice fields. Villagers with no other employment slowly carried their loads of rock and dirt on pack frames out to the wide unfinished portion of the dike and dumped them into the gap, only to have everything washed away by the next tide.

From my vantage point I could look north across the half mile of mudflats (at low tide) or water (when the tide came in) to the "Big Hamlet," a tightly packed cluster of forty-five houses by the harbor. If the gap in the dike were ever closed, these mudflats would become rice fields. When the fishing fleet was in,

Map 1.2 Map of Sŏkp'o

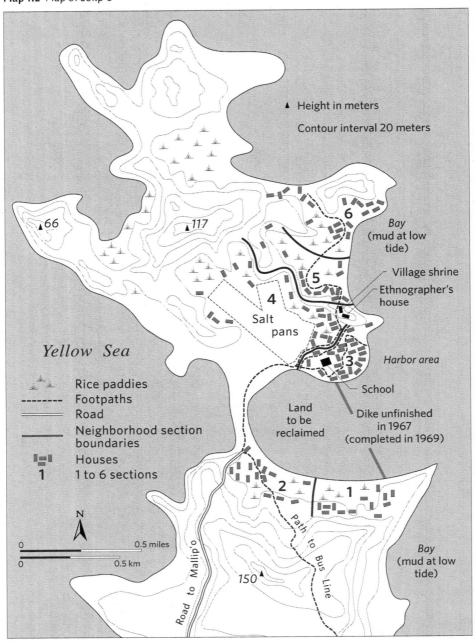

▲ Height in meters

Contour interval 20 meters

▲66

▲117

6

Bay
(mud at low
tide)

Village shrine

Ethnographer's
house

5

4

Salt
pans

Harbor area

3

Yellow Sea

School

Dike unfinished
in 1967
(completed in 1969)

Land
to be
reclaimed

Rice paddies
Footpaths
Road
Neighborhood section
boundaries
Houses
1   1 to 6 sections

2

1

N

0   0.5 miles

0   0.5 km

Road to Mallip'o

Path to Bus Line

150 ▲

Bay
(mud at low
tide)

I could usually see eleven or twelve sailing junks drawn up on the beach or bobbing around at anchor just offshore. The coming and going of the boats was mysteriously irregular, depending on the state of the tide, the weather, the season, and the whim of the fishermen. The Big Hamlet, along with the two smaller, dispersed hamlets at the northern tip of the peninsula, was connected to the mainland by a narrow grass-covered sandspit bordering the ocean. This sandspit was out of sight to my left behind a shoulder of the hill, but I could hear the waves breaking on it in rough weather. Beyond the Big Hamlet, the peninsula, now almost an island, spread out to encompass white-sand beaches alternating with rocky cliffs on the ocean side, while wooded bluffs or rice fields bordered the bay. More or less in the middle of this *presque isle* there was another towering hill or small mountain. The land rose gradually, with open fields giving way to pines as the slopes steepened. The villages across the bay to the east were so far off that I could just barely make out their boats and houses on a clear day. In that direction it was usually only possible to see hills and mountains, sharply silhouetted in the morning but turning to hazy purple as the day wore on.

I was in South Korea to carry out social anthropological research to decipher the customs, value system, and social structure of a small community using the "sympathetic participant-observation" method. Having already spent eleven years in the diplomatic service (two of them in Korea), I was now in a fishing village as an over-age graduate student, trying to earn a doctoral degree and launch a second career. My somewhat vague objective on the Korean Yellow Sea coast was to compare and contrast the experiences and personalities of farmers and fishermen. A number of studies throughout the world and my own previous experience in Japan had suggested that fishermen tend to be bold, swaggering risk takers, less bound than landsmen by the conventions and values of a society's mainstream ideology. Farmers, on the other hand, were, according to this simplistic hypothesis, more likely to be careful conservatives, concerned with preserving tradition and maintaining the status quo. Sŏkp'o, with its mixture of farming and fishing households, seemed an ideal place to test such a theory. My personal reasons for picking a village on the ocean were probably more compelling: I like the ocean, coastal scenery, boats, and seafood.

But it had taken me a long time to find the right place. South Korea has an enormously long coastline. For several weeks I roamed both the east and west coasts of the Korean peninsula by bus and on foot. I stayed in country inns where they were available and in farmhouses where they were not. There were exotic bugs, filthy toilets, stomach trouble, strange bedroom companions, and extremes of heat and cold. Privacy was almost nonexistent. In most places I was more than just a peculiar object of curiosity; I was the most entertaining event that had come along in weeks. In areas where American troops had once been stationed, children would crowd around yelling, "Hello!" and asking for candy and cigarettes. Almost always there was at least one high school student who wanted to practice his English. Old people would come very close to examine me, sometimes pulling at the blond hair on my forearm to see if it was real.

In Korea hospitality has always been a moral obligation, a matter of individual and community pride. Without fail someone would make sure that I was fed and had a place to sleep. And no one, except innkeepers, ever took money for a night's lodging. In return I was subjected to public scrutiny and intensive questioning about America and the outside world. There seemed to be no end to the villagers' desire to break out, even momentarily, from the constraints of rural life.

As a result of all my wandering, I finally narrowed the search for a research site to a portion of the Yellow Sea coast in South Ch'ungch'ŏng Province. This is the part of South Korea that sticks out the farthest into the Yellow Sea towards China. Here, there is fairly deep water right up to the rocky shore, so small boats have easy access to offshore fishing. At most other places along Korea's west coast, where the tidal range is over twenty feet, miles of mudflats extend far out from shore except at high tide. In 1966, the whole region, which has a wildly indented coastline, was isolated and undeveloped, with few roads. This appealed to my sense of adventure. I also hoped that the isolation would allow me to find a relatively traditional community.

A Korean friend in Seoul who had formerly been a minister in the government heard about my plans and offered to introduce me properly to the local county magistrate in Sosan, the county seat. My friend had a colleague, another former minister, and together they enthusiastically proposed a joint expedition to help me get started with my fieldwork. It was time, they said, to get away from Seoul and experience the "fresh, robust pleasures of country life." They told me that from ancient times men of good character and high position had periodically left the corrupting influences and materialistic temptations of the capital to seek spiritual refreshment in simple, rustic surroundings. Both of these men were cultivated, cosmopolitan members of the South Korean elite. At first I was doubtful about having such high-powered escorts. The last thing I wanted was any sort of official intervention in my work. On the other hand, it seemed like a good idea to square things away with the local authorities right from the start. And in any case, I was curious about those "robust pleasures."

So we set off in a handsome new Land Rover, complete with driver and baskets full of food and drink. As a rule it took six hours to get to Sosan by train and bus. In our private vehicle we should have been able to do it in three and a half hours. As things worked out, it took two days. On the first day, with only about an hour to go to reach Sosan, we turned off the main road and headed up into the mountains on a dirt track. After a long, rough climb we finally arrived at a handsome compound of several old wooden buildings that looked like the home of a Yi Dynasty (1392–1910) aristocrat. It was a hot spring resort, and it was obvious that we were expected. Two stylish women in traditional dress came out to greet us, flanked by maids and porters. The main building had heavy, curved-tile roofs and massive wooden pillars. Several smaller annexes angled off from it, with the whole compound laced together by paths and small gardens. Plaques with beautifully inscribed Chinese characters proclaiming ancient moral axioms hung over the doors or on corner posts.

We took off our shoes and went inside, where I was amazed to find that each of us had his own room. In the Far East the usual procedure at an inn is for all members of a group traveling together to sleep in the same room. Here, in my own room, the oiled-paper floor shone with a rich brown patina. The hanging landscape scroll and a screen decorated with calligraphy seemed to be of museum quality. In the corner on a delicate stand of persimmon wood, was a Koryo celadon bowl. Brocade cushions invited the tired traveler to take his ease. At the far end of the room was a small double door of intricate geometric lattice work covered with paper. The door opened onto a rock garden and just outside, underneath the broad eaves of the tiled roof, a platform of polished wood provided a place to sit and look at the garden and mountains in the distance. There was a pair of sandals on the ground below, in case the occupant might want to stroll outdoors.

It was all much more luxurious than the finest suite at an expensive international hotel in Hong Kong or Tokyo. The room and its garden had a kind of *Arabian Nights* quality, as if all the resources of an entire civilization had been dedicated just to pleasing my senses. And yet the dominant theme was restraint, with an emphasis on spare forms and rich, subdued colors. I was encountering an ancient, elite, cultural heritage—not as an exhibit in a museum, but as a welcoming personal environment.

While I was thinking about the extraordinary things that lots of money could still buy in a poor, "undeveloped" country, another elegant woman came in with tea and a registration slip. While she waited, I filled it out, finding considerable satisfaction in being able to decipher the characters and fill in the blanks, even though my writing looked like that of a fourth-grade student. Rising with the sighing sound of heavy silk skirts, she said, "Please go and join your friends in the bath and relax after your hard journey to this faraway place."

After nearly an hour of soaking, scrubbing, rinsing, and soaking again, we gathered in the room of my friend. It was larger and still more sumptuous than mine. On a low table in the center there were whiskey (real Johnny Walker Black Label), ice, and glasses, along with fifteen or twenty small dishes of hot and cold food. This was the *anju*, appetizers to accompany drinking. My friends demanded *yakchu*, the yellowish country beer that is entirely homemade and could no longer be found easily in Seoul. Its name means medicinal spirits, and we drank that instead of the whiskey.

Three attractive young women poured our *yakchu* and popped delicacies into our mouths. Maids kept bringing more dishes until the round table was completely covered. The drinking phase of the meal went on for quite a while. At first the women served us sedately, while we talked among ourselves. Gradually the mood became more cordial, even a little boisterous, until we finally were pouring reciprocal cupfuls for our female companions. Then the table was partially cleared and a whole new banquet of side dishes was brought in along with rice and soup. I couldn't help remarking ironically about "simple country pleasures." My friend answered, "You will find out all about those soon enough. Tonight we just enjoy ourselves. You may need some nice memories when you are sharing fishermen's food in a dirty hut."

After dinner we played a little poker, with the women joining in, and out of the fast, joking chatter I picked up a couple of references to strip poker. I was a little disappointed and confused when one of my friends suggested that it was time to "separate" since it had been a long day and we must be tired. It hadn't been a long day, and I wasn't particularly tired, but there was no way I could prolong the lively party on my own.

In my room bedding had already been spread out on the floor. The thick quilt was made of brightly colored silk with a clean white sheet sewn on the underside. There was a small lamp by the pillow and alongside it a pitcher of cold barley tea. Most of the room was in deep shadow. I was about to take off my clothes when the door opened after a discreet knock and one of the matrons who had originally welcomed us came in. She patted the bedding, rearranged the pillow, checked to make sure there was tea, and asked polite questions about America. She praised my Korean, although we both knew it was terrible. Then she asked me a number of different times in a number of different ways if there was anything else I wanted. Having been spoiled and catered to all evening, I couldn't think of a thing. She seemed to leave reluctantly, after making some more purely ritual conversation, and I wondered if perhaps I had been expected to make some sort of pass at her. But she just did not have the manner of someone in that line of work. In addition to poise and elegance, she had a certain managerial bearing. If not the owner, I was certain that she was at least running things at the inn.

As usually happens after a good deal of liquor, I was wide awake by two in the morning. The only thing that infallibly works on these occasions is to get up, do a few exercises, and drink some water. Then I can get back to sleep without any trouble. I pushed open the door to the garden to find an early full moon. It was cold in the mountains, but I had a bathrobe and the sandals were there waiting. I would exercise outdoors. The moonlight was so bright that I could read the Confucian mottos on the buildings. After some mild calisthenics I wandered along the path, soon reaching the building where my friends were lodged. On the stone step below the veranda of each of their rooms a pair of white women's slippers gleamed in the moonlight alongside the dark men's shoes. I returned to my room, now wide awake. So that was why the matron had lingered! I was supposed to order a companion for the night. Obviously I had failed my first test in "sympathetic participant observation."

The county magistrate in Sosan, who had been advised of our visit by the Ministry of Home Affairs in Seoul, was graciously attentive when we reached his office the next afternoon. He gave us a formal briefing complete with statistics on local population, rice production, fish catches, and the numbers of middle and high school graduates. He was even able to pinpoint the few coastal villages where a local boy had gone on to college. It was obvious that he was far more concerned with the educational attainments of the people under his jurisdiction than their economic prosperity. He also provided me with a written introduction to a Mr. Koo, who lived in Mohang, the village at the end of the road where it reached the coast.

My friends planned to spend the next night at another resort, but they insisted on first taking me two hours out of their way on a terrible road to reach Mohang and Mr. Koo. I could tell they were worried about just dropping me off in the middle of nowhere at dusk. For them the countryside meant clear air, picturesque villages, and good-hearted, simple people. But these were pleasures to be enjoyed only during the day and then usually from the seat of a car or Jeep. My friends brought their own food, and when they talked to villagers, it was as if they were graciously condescending to bridge an enormous gap between themselves and a slightly different species. Above all, they had no desire to experience the discomforts of rural life at night. By then I was eager to break loose and try getting along on my own, but my generous friends would not leave until they found Mr. Koo and made sure I would be fed and lodged.

At last the Land Rover disappeared, and I was alone in a small, very cold square room with a kerosene lamp for company. In the corner was a roll of bedding that only vaguely resembled the splendid comforter and gleaming white sheets of the night before. This was December, and I had the definite impression that at Mr. Koo's house they changed the sheets once a year, only at New Year's.

The floor of the room warmed up quickly after the fire was lit, and before long a woman brought in a tray with rice, a bowl of soup, a small dish of spicy pickled cabbage, oysters in hot sauce, and some sort of spinach-like vegetable. There were big chunks of fish in the soup, and I found myself enjoying this meal as much as I had the previous night's feast. After supper I went for a walk in the moonlight up over a long hill and down to the harbor, where about twenty fishing boats surged restlessly against each other behind a small break-water. The wind was bitter, out of the north, and I hurried back to my cubicle with its hot floor. Trying not to look at or think about the color and condition of the sheets, I spread out the bedding, lay down, and was quickly asleep.

Two days later I found Sŏkp'o. It was a long way off anything that resembled a beaten track, at the extreme northwestern tip of a jagged peninsula sticking far out into the Yellow Sea. For nearly two hours I had walked north from Mohang along a narrow path worn into steep, pine-covered slopes that fell away, on my left, to the ocean. Through the trees I could see the sparkle of the afternoon sun on the water, while the smell of warm pine needles was reassuringly familiar. A couple of miles out to sea a big, two-masted junk headed for dim islands on the horizon.

The trail climbed until it was a couple of hundred feet above the ocean and finally curved around the last shoulder of the mountain. There stretched out below me was one of the most beautiful places I had ever seen. Surrounded on all sides by water and connected to the mainland only by a narrow sandspit lay the village of Sŏkp'o. To the west a sunlit sea flashed with white caps. To the east a tranquil bay provided shelter for the fishing fleet and access by boat to other, only slightly less isolated villages. Small hamlets of thatched-roof houses nestled here and there against the hills and mountains where there was shelter from the sea wind.

As I followed the path down into the nearest hamlet, men stopped work and regarded me gravely, while women disappeared indoors. The children hid behind buildings, peering out and giggling among themselves. For me, it was ethnographic love at first sight. I felt transported through time into a bucolic, pre-industrial world. After wandering around for an hour or so, I stopped a teen-aged boy to ask if there was an inn where I could spend the night. It was already midafternoon and cold. I had no desire for a two-hour walk back to Mohang after dark. He laughed at the idea of an inn, saying, "This village isn't on the way to anywhere. No one visits Sŏkp'o unless he has relatives here to stay with." Finally the boy said, "I will take you to Teacher Yi. He will know what to do."

Sŏkp'o's primary school was in a small wooden building in the center of the largest hamlet. Yi Byong Gi, the only teacher, was still at his desk, although the children had all left. He was eager to show me around the school. "I started this tiny school ten years ago, and I am still the principal and only teacher. When I was a boy, we had to walk to Mohang to primary school. In April my first assistant is coming. It will be nice to have some help at last, but I am worried because he will be so much better educated than I." I explained that I wanted to come and live in the village, and I asked for Teacher Yi's help and advice. He said, "This village is very poor and backward, and the people have no learning. But they are good hearted. Please stay here and help us to develop our lives." This was the first of many similar statements that I was to hear during my stay in Sŏkp'o.

After our tour of the school, Yi Byong Gi invited me to his house. As we walked across the sandspit to the hamlet where all the Yi clan households were located, the sun was low over the ocean on our right. Fishermen were sitting on the steeply sloped beach still mending nets, while on the other side the mudflats were almost completely covered by the incoming tide. I tried to express my initial wonder at the beauty and calm of the village. To my lyrical comments Teacher Yi answered, "The soil is poor, and there is almost no flat land here for growing rice. Rain is very irregular in this part of Korea, and the salt air is bad for most crops."

When I remarked that people looked healthy and contented, he continued. "It takes two hours to get to the nearest middle school, so only a handful of boys can pursue their education beyond the sixth grade. This year there will be no girls from Sŏkp'o in middle school. The market is still farther away. None of the fishermen here has enough money to buy an engine for his boat, and each year there are fewer sailboats because fishing the old way no longer pays. There are too many people. Most of the village would like to leave, but they have no other place to go."

Even in an impoverished country, the village was terribly poor. By 1966, the South Korean economy was beginning to move ahead, but it would be many years before the effects of development trickled down to this coastal region. Because of the rugged terrain and deeply indented coastline of Ch'ungch'ŏng Province, villages there were isolated and backward, with Sŏkp'o even more inaccessible than most. Its six hamlets, of ten to forty households each, were strung out over a couple of miles of varied coastline. Steep hills rose up from the water in every direction leaving only a few small areas level enough to plant rice, the main source of rural wealth. Small terraced rice fields covered the gradual lower slopes near the hamlets, but as the land got steeper and the water supply more uncertain, they were replaced by barley. The higher slopes were covered with pines, a particularly gnarled, tough Korean variety that seemed determined to create poetic landscapes on every ridge and promontory but that contributed little to the local economy.

Fish catches were small and uneven, hardly enough to pay for the costs of maintaining the small junk-rigged sailboats. For protein the villagers depended mostly on oysters and other shellfish gathered by women and children. Except for an occasional stroke of exceptional luck, fishing, instead of being a consistently productive occupation, had for those villagers with little or no land, become a way to keep occupied, utilize their skills, and maintain their self-respect. It was also a training ground for young men of poor families, who could then go off to Inch'ŏn or some other port and get jobs as fishermen on big, oceangoing boats.

The villagers were well aware of their own poverty, illiteracy, and general lack of cultural refinement. Korea is a small country, and throughout its history elite prejudice against those who are unlettered and work with their hands has been great. In 1966, the traditionally enormous gap between rural and urban life was actually increasing. Sŏkp'o residents judged themselves harshly, sharing the contempt of townsmen who looked down on them as backward, uneducated peasants struggling to survive by "dirty" subsistence labor. But their humility was offset, at least on their own home ground, by a certain poise and confidence; perhaps self-respect is the right word. The village was a place where getting along well with other people was a constant preoccupation, and where sensitivity, tolerance, and the desire to preserve good feelings usually took precedence over individual ambition and material goals. In fact, the people of Sŏkp'o prided themselves on their reputation for "human heartedness"(insim). They were familiar enough with the outside world to know that being able to count on the relative honesty, lack of aggressiveness, tolerance, and cooperation of their neighbors was a valuable part of village life that city dwellers often had to do without. And yet, it was as if they valued these things in particular because there was nothing else in their lives to be proud of. Inhabitants of other villages in the area, even while speaking disparagingly about the "difficult" backwardness of Sŏkp'o, granted that its residents had insim.

Villagers dreamed of town life, not only because of the "clean" work and higher living standards, but because they deeply believed that education for their children was life's most worthy objective, as well as being the surest possible route to a better life. Young people, of course, wanted greater freedom and more opportunity for individual self-expression. Most Sŏkp'o residents lived in the village only because they had to, and as soon as conditions made it possible, they were likely to migrate to the city. Restlessness, ambition, and dreams of material glory simmered away constantly underneath the appearance of tranquil resignation.

I was to learn a lot during my year in the village, not just about an entirely different culture and way of life, but also about myself. Often I was pleasantly surprised, even dazzled, by what I found: a place where most people were consistently cheerful in adversity, generous in helping others as well as in making allowances for their faults, and dedicated to fulfilling their own obligations. It was not a bad recipe for social harmony. I was forced to rethink and reappraise a great deal about my own values and heritage that I had always taken for granted. Most notably, I came to realize that the quality we had made the cornerstone of the Western value system, individualism, would be rejected as gross selfishness by the residents of Sŏkp'o.

But that first evening in the village I was still a naïve and wondering new-comer. In the December dusk Teacher Yi's guest room seemed gloomy and cold at first, but a fire soon warmed the floor. A small oil lamp gave a dim but cozy light, with most of the room remaining in deep shadow. What bright-ened things up a great deal more was the same "medicinal" yellowish *yakchu* that I had drunk with my friends at the hot springs. Teacher Yi's wife served it with dried roasted eel. I had a flask of whiskey in my rucksack, and after a couple of rounds of *yakchu* in tiny cups, we switched to that. Yi Byong Gi drank moderately, since he had his reputation as schoolteacher to uphold. But he enjoyed liquor, and we got along well from the start.

Three months later, when I moved to the village permanently, most of the other villagers were, at first, intensely curious, and the *sarangbang* was often crowded. Then my entertainment value slacked off rather abruptly, partly I sup-pose, because the novelty wore off, and partly because my Korean was still lim-ited. But Teacher Yi quickly learned to tailor his language to fit my vocabulary, and he became my best informant, patiently trying to answer the endless stream of questions I asked about all the bewildering things I encountered every day.

During the next year I became close friends with a few individuals, thor-oughly disliked a few others, and managed to develop friendly relations with the rest of the people in Sŏkp'o. Much later I learned that there was a sizable group who regarded me in the beginning with considerable suspicion. This group developed two main theories to explain my presence, the reason I had given—a desire to study village life—being too absurd for serious consider-ation. The first theory was that I was some sort of American spy or agent collaborating with the South Korean CIA, and that this represented a provoca-tion to the North Koreans who might attack the village from the sea as a result. The second theory was that I was really looking for gold or oil. There were a few shell mounds along the coast, and I had been poking around in them looking unsuccessfully for neolithic artifacts. The random digging had, I was told, excited a good deal of interest, and there were even a few people who had gotten out their shovels and gone prospecting themselves.

2

Settling In

Diary Entry: April 26, 1966
After one month in the village:

To get here I have followed a narrow, curving, grassy path that separates the knee-high barley from the pine trees. It dips gently from the ridge behind Teacher Lee's [Yi] house and then makes a long, graceful, climbing turn around the headland some sixty feet above the ocean. I'm lying down in a sunny spot where a blinding streak of shining ocean framed by pine branches leads off to the western horizon. The night before last there was a moderate gale, and the dying remains of yesterday's big swells make gentle noises on the rocks below. What a place to savor solitude! With no appointments, no place to go, no demands, I do as I please. I've talked to at least fifteen people today. I'm pleasantly tired, and it's nice to be alone.

There is so much genuine cordiality here. I encounter smiles everywhere. As I walked up here, a man plowing with his ox stopped to ask when I had gotten back from Seoul, when my family will arrive, and how the new house is coming along. I was delighted because I understood almost everything and could answer. Women walking with babies strapped on their backs and huge, ungainly chunks of baggage balanced on their heads greeted me. Three men repairing dikes in a rice field stopped work and asked me to join them for a bowl of makkŏlli. Further up from the village, boys cutting wood on the mountain appeared suddenly out of the apparently deserted landscape and asked about life in America. A shy girl hanging back on the fringes of the group fiercely pretended she didn't want her picture taken and then got her brother to ask when it will be developed. My life here consists mostly of

Figure 2.1 The men repairing irrigation dikes. *Makkŏlli* will follow. (April 26, 1966.)

spectacular walks from one hamlet to another, punctuated by greetings and chatter and smiles.

At first, without even trying to do systematic fieldwork, I just wandered around the village soaking up impressions and meeting people. They were as curious as I was. I began to wonder about the real reasons that drive anthropologists out of the cozy security of academic life into lonely alienation and physical discomfort. I don't think many of us come clean in our accounts of these expeditions. Perhaps, in my case, the commitment to research, to getting a PhD, and to the advancement of learning was less pressing than a longing for adventure and a desire to reclaim the lost utopias of childhood. I experienced the pleasantly unsettling feeling during my first weeks in Sŏkp'o of being in touch again with some sort of half-forgotten, elemental, and sustaining reality. I had somehow managed to find my way back through a passage that had been closed off since the age of ten or eleven.

Diary Entry: April 27, 1966

Not since childhood have I been able to soak up all the precious trivial elements of the natural world the way I do now. Here everyone lives close to nature. There's nothing to spoil the simple harmony. All I have to do is conform to the villagers' way of life. I am finding a whole new, slow-paced way to enter this world. Each day things become more comfortably familiar. I recognize the way certain houses and trees reflect the light against a background of water or hills at different times of day, or how the whole panorama changes with the tide. There is movement, but no hurry.

A sailing junk entering the bay hasn't changed position much in fifteen minutes. Women bending over to weed sweet potatoes make almost imperceptible progress in the distance. My first impression of the village last December was touched with the usual melancholy of an idyllic landscape that is somehow always out of reach. But now all this tranquil beauty is mine to live in! Memories keep coming back of the intensity of childhood experience. Only then was there this same quality of timelessness, when nothing interrupted my direct and total involvement in climbing a tree, or hiding in the grass, or wading in tidal pools.

But something else sustained me in Sŏkp'o right from the start, in addition to the emotional satisfactions described in my journal: as an anthropologist I felt a compelling obligation not only to adopt the same living conditions as the villagers and share in whatever activities were going on around me but also to reject my own critical evaluations and try to see things from the villagers' point of view. It wasn't always easy, especially when the boards in a dark toilet shed were covered with freshly minted feces, or when I was sharing a bowl of makkŏlli with someone who had filthy hands and a consumptive cough, or when I was trapped for hours in dark, smoky rooms, listening to half-understood, interminable conversations. But even granted that the ability to think and feel like a villager was completely out of reach, the effort itself was all-important. I am convinced that this struggle to "sympathize" with a totally foreign point of view, allowing my own immediate judgments to be overruled or at least put in jeopardy, probably accounted more than anything else for whatever success I had in understanding what was really going on.

The area where I was living, among all the Yi households, was the upper-class neighborhood of the village. Koreans have a strong sense of continuity with the past, and detailed and accurate knowledge of illustrious ancestors (supported by authentic, ancient documents) has always been a necessary condition for prestige and rank. The Yis of Sŏkp'o have traced their origin back directly to the twelfth son (by a concubine) of King T'aejong (r. 1400–18), one of whose descendants, a former county magistrate, moved to Sŏkp'o in 1649. A member of the yangban or aristocratic class would never have voluntarily exiled himself in such a place, so presumably this ancestor had gotten into trouble at court or had been on the losing side in a factional struggle. The Japanese administration legally abolished hereditary upper-class status during the Colonial Period (1910–45), but family blood lines still had sociological importance in Sŏkp'o in the 1960s. Teacher Yi's family, while neither the wealthiest nor the most influential among the twenty-four Yi households, was nevertheless fairly well off and highly respected.

In terms of average household possessions, the Yis were not richer than other Sŏkp'o residents. And there were lazy drunkards among them, although perhaps not quite as many as among the Kims, the Muns, and the Kangs. There was, however, a subtle but discernable difference in the atmosphere of the Yi neighborhood, particularly in contrast to the Big Hamlet (K'un maul, or simply "over there"), with its sulchip[1] and idle fishermen. Houses were neater and better maintained, there was less noisy quarreling, and women were quieter, staying closer to home. In other words the rules of etiquette and of parŭn haengtong (proper Confucian behavior) were more closely observed in the Yi neighborhood.

In three other respects the differences were more obvious. The Yis held more elaborate ceremonies to commemorate their ancestors, they invested more in educating their children, and they did not engage in fishing. The prejudice against fishing has faded in South Korea, but it was still part of the yangban mentality in Sŏkp'o when I was there. Growing rice was a much more prestigious occupation than fishing. Teacher Yi explained it as follows: "Because a fisherman may drown each time he goes to sea, he risks dying before his parents. If that happens, he will neither be able to take care of them in their old age, nor perform the proper rituals after their death. There is no greater crime than this failure to perform in a filial manner towards one's parents."

Everyone in Teacher Yi's neighborhood was his relative. In Korean villages the daughters married out while the sons stayed behind, so every relative was named Yi. Korean names nearly all have three syllables, first the lineage name, second the generation name, and third an individual name chosen for personal or aesthetic reasons. The lineage name is always pronounced first and the personal name last. Since everyone in Teacher Yi's generation had the same second as well as first syllable in his name, there was little to distinguish one name from another. Most of the elderly visitors to my room in the evenings were also Yis, although they had a different generation name. I began keeping a card file for each individual, but still it was hard to remember who was called what. There were other problems as well. Except among close relatives, school classmates, and people the same age who grew up together, given names were almost never used in addressing adults. A personal name was a very private possession.

Because no foreigner had ever lived in the village before, my Yi neighbors had a hard time settling on a proper term of address for me. These matters are important in Korea, where every relationship involves some degree of superiority and inferiority and no one is comfortable unless the names and titles reflect the relative status of the people involved. Proper personal behavior and the proper treatment of others are directly related to what people call each other. Especially polite forms of speech and deeper bows are used when speaking to older or higher-ranking people, while superiors use blunt, familiar forms when they talk to those who are younger or inferior in rank. The system can be incredibly complex. In Sŏkp'o, where everyone's position was familiar and more or less fixed, the problem did not normally exist, but in dealing with an American "scholar" (a much loftier status in the Korean scheme of things than in America), villagers were worried about getting things right. When I talked to Teacher Yi at our very first meeting, I had explained that I wanted to share the life of the villagers and expected no special treatment. It wasn't always so pleasant, however, when this wish was granted. There were times during the transplanting of rice, building a house, or hauling nets, when I found myself engaged in heavy manual labor for many hours at a stretch. Even the simplest work required skills I had never learned. After forty it is too late to learn how to balance heavy loads on a pack frame, plant rice seedlings, tie knots in straw, or bait hundreds of fish hooks with any speed and dexterity. The villagers laughed, and I was often humiliated. Still, the rewards of such "participant observation" were considerable. In addition to the feelings of cooperation and conviviality that were generated at those times, there was always a lot of food and drink afterwards.

It was on such an occasion that the problem of finding the right name for me was finally solved. I had been in the village a little over a month and had spent a couple of days helping transplant rice. Instead of really helping, I probably interfered with the whole operation, but the fact that I had stayed with it all day and collected my share of leeches generated a lot of goodwill. At the collective feast afterwards, attended by some twenty-five or thirty Yi males, we worked out a system. They would all call me *sŏnsaeng* (teacher), and I would call them by the same kinship term used by Teacher Yi, as if he and I were brothers. A kind of high-spirited, impromptu oral examination took place at the meal, as one person after another called out to see if I knew the right word for his particular relationship to Teacher Yi. To everyone's delight, I got most of them wrong that first time, but it turned out to be a wonderful way to learn a complicated system of kinship nomenclature. I worked hard to get it right, and still today, whenever I remember a particular individual from the Yi Hamlet, I think of him as "uncle," "older brother," or "younger brother" (used also for cousins of the same generation), "nephew," or even "father." My informal adoption into Teacher Yi's household gave me a nice, secure feeling that helped a good deal during periods of doubt and uncertainty. The rest of the village also eventually adopted *sŏnsaeng* or *sŏnsaengnim* (still more honorific) as my title, and twenty-one years later, in 1987 when my daughter visited Sŏkp'o, the villagers still referred to me as "teacher."

Teacher Yi usually ate supper with me in the *sarangbang* and sometimes breakfast as well. He said it was to keep me from feeling lonely. It was an ideal arrangement that allowed me to practice Korean while asking him about all the fascinating and puzzling things that I was observing all around me every day. I would ask questions such as, "Why do so many people come to help put on the roof of the new house being built next door?" The site was below us towards the bay to the east, and as I stood outside in the morning, I could look down on the crowd of men and boys swarming over and around the white, freshly sawn wooden frame and rafters. It seemed to me that there were far more people than could usefully be employed all at once, and the hubbub and confusion was enormous. Shouts and laughter, including wildly sexual and scatological jokes, rang out in the calm and misty morning air. Frequent breaks to eat and drink further fueled the mood of animated and noisy goodwill. Over supper I asked Teacher Yi, "Are they all relatives of the house owner? Who is in charge of the work? How does the owner pay back so many people? Do all houses in Sŏkp'o get built this way? Are people here always this happy and noisy when they work together?"

And then Teacher Yi, who had always taken such ordinary, everyday matters for granted, would try to explain how things worked.

> No one is really in charge at this stage of construction. Everyone knows how to put on a roof. When someone tries to boss a job like this, people just laugh at him. Of course, Lee [Yi] Taryŏng's (the owner's) close relatives are all there, but his neighbors as well as friends from all over the village also join in. There are several who come because they have nothing to do and are happy to work for the food and drink. When a crowd gathers like this, we get a lot of work done quickly, and everyone feels good. If you don't help your neighbors, they won't help you.

It didn't all come out quite as neatly and concisely as this, partly because of language difficulties and partly because it was hard for Teacher Yi to realize how little I understood about communal effort and morale. But we had lots of time, and he was patient. During the following weeks I asked him about who was poor and who was rich, who was popular and who was not, and who had authority and influence and how much. I asked who married whom and why, and I tried to find out about conflict, envy, and suspicion as well as about cooperation and trust. Teacher Yi, although very reluctant to say anything derogatory about anyone, was unfailingly responsive to all these questions and tried to find words and phrases that I could understand. I wonder if any other ethnographer has ever had such a willing, gentle, and expert guide. In addition to Teacher Yi and his nearby relatives, the first villagers that I got to know more than casually were members of the group of elderly gentlemen whose regular meeting place had become my bedroom. The sarangbang is important in Korean villages. It is here that problems of the day are discussed by the yuji ("weighty" individuals) in each hamlet and an informal consensus is reached as to how to deal with them. The *sarangbang* is as much a part of local government as it is a place of recreation. It is also a center of moral and ritual authority. I was trying to bed down in the midst of an ongoing socio-political institution.

Diary Entry May 8, 1966

Each evening from before supper until bedtime, my room is more or less crowded with older men of the neighborhood. Sometimes men from other hamlets stop by out of curiosity. I still don't get more than about half of what is being said during these long sessions, and it's aggravating because I'm sure I'm missing all sorts of valuable information. The old men have a thick local accent, totally unlike what we learned at language school in Seoul; and besides, most of them are missing a lot of teeth.

I tried using a tape recorder, hoping to put these conversations on tape for further study. No one had ever seen a tape recorder before, and it was an enormous success. But as things turned out, it never became part of the ethnographic process. Most of the villagers developed an insatiable desire to hear themselves sing, and as soon as the tape recorder appeared, someone would send for makkŏlli, and the music would start. The machine wore out in a few months. What I remember most vividly of the *sarangbang* evenings was my total mental exhaustion. After a whole day of concentrated grappling with the language, my brain would function less and less effectively until finally it would turn off with an almost audible click. I would continue to sit cross-legged in a kind of meditative trance, waiting for the "guests" to leave. The small kerosene lamp provided more shadows than light. The atmosphere was warm and close, with abundant pipe smoke and the sweet, ripe smell of unwashed bodies.

Diary Entry May 15, 1966

Last night's debate was entirely devoted to death, burial rites, and finding the correct spot for one's grave. I have never seen the group more animated. They seem to find a pleasurable anticipation in making their own funeral arrangements. Each detail is discussed eagerly. Before they all went home, Old Moon [Mun] from the Big Hamlet, the one with a crew cut and a square, gray beard, read my palm. (Perhaps he was perplexed by my obvious lack of interest in their topic, and the fortune telling was a way to get me involved again with the group.) Moon proclaimed his interpretation to me in a loud voice: "You died as a child and were subsequently reborn; your present wife is your third true love; you will never be rich, and you will work until you die." There was a lot more, but that's all I can remember. Somehow the flickering light, the grizzled audience, the deep shadows, and my state of exhaustion all added weight to the divination, and I fell asleep trying to sort out the first two loves.

One of the regular *sarangbang* members was a nearby neighbor, Teacher Yi's father's first cousin. I could see his house about one hundred and fifty yards away from my veranda. A tough, stingy, self-assertive, old landowner, I nicknamed him "Pirate," partly on account of his character but also because of his appearance. His skin was very dark, and he had a large hooked nose, rare in Korea. I fantasized that one of his ancestors had been a Portuguese sailor shipwrecked on the Yellow Sea coast in the sixteenth century. In Korean kinship nomenclature a first cousin is separated from oneself by four genealogical intervals. A difference of one generation adds another interval. He was therefore Teacher Yi's fifth-interval uncle, and since I had assimilated Teacher Yis kinship "rank" among the Yis, mine as well. Pirate was not too bad a name for fifth-interval uncle, who in his mid-sixties was an irascible, intolerant bully. Adult male conversation in rural Korea almost always sounds pretty vehement, with all sorts of short, strong expletives and harsh, drawn-out consonants that fill the air with a fine— and sometimes not so fine—mist. But Pirate was in a class by himself. In the *sarangbang* he sat quietly smoking for a while and then barked out his views in a tone that seemed to me to require either complete agreement or a fight to the death. Since he was often the oldest and richest person present, most of his colleagues would hear him out with resigned tolerance, if not respect. He pontificated on everything—the weather, the superiority of the Yi lineage, the folly of changing time-honored agricultural practices, and the importance of geomantic principles in regulating daily life. There was nearly always someone near his own age, though, who eventually objected to a particularly outrageous opinion, and then the conversational intensity reached what to me seemed explosive levels. But it was just the way people talked.

One night in the *sarangbang* Pirate and one of his colleagues challenged Teacher Yi and me by boldly stating that the world was flat, and the sun revolved around it. We, of course, reacted strongly in defense of scientific knowledge. I had brought a tennis ball from Seoul as a toy for Teacher Yi's children, and I used that to demonstrate, moving it in orbit around the candle, while rotating it at the same time around its own axis.

This failed to convince anyone, although it had seemed absolutely compelling to me when performed by my general science teacher in grade school. Pirate then grabbed one of my books, put it on top of his fist and rotated it in the same plane while a collaborator moved the candle in a large circle around the book from the floor to the ceiling and back. There were shouts of delighted approval from the rest of the audience.

Part of our problem was that the word for scientific, *kwahakchŏk*, encompasses a rather broad area of meaning in Korean, including various traditional systems of thought that have nothing to do with proving hypotheses by objective experimentation. Truth is what ancient authority says it is, and ancient authority is just as "scientific" as anything else.

Teacher Yi did not seem to be able to hurdle this semantic obstacle any better than I, and we lost the debate, to say nothing of our equanimity. That evening was the only time I ever saw Teacher Yi show open disrespect for his fifth-interval uncle. He confided to me at breakfast the next day that there were many people in the village, even some in their twenties, who preferred the old men's explanation. Pirate was determined from the moment I moved into Teacher Yi's house next door that, if there was anything to be gotten out of me in the way of entertainment, useful instruction, or material benefits, he would get there first and get more than his share. He must have been quickly disillusioned with regard to entertainment and instruction, so he began to focus on my more tangible possessions. He got in the habit of stopping by at least once during the day for the pipe tobacco, cookies, and other precious American items that I felt compelled to offer. I knew how important it was to provide hospitality to a visitor in Sŏkp'o because I was the recipient of so much of it, although not from Pirate.

Diary Entry May 17, 1966

The night before last Pirate came in to "my" room and saw me sipping whiskey with Teacher Lee [Yi] and one of his cousins. He claims he doesn't drink, and, in fact, he always refused before. But this time he complained of neuralgic pains and was looking for a cure. I poured him the same amount I had been giving the rest of us, but he looked at me with a pained expression and said, "That's not enough; give me more." I did, and he tossed off the equivalent of a triple shot in one gulp without any apparent reaction. Before going home, he drank another triple as if it was water. Last night he was back for more, saying that the whiskey was wonderful medicine. He even forced a one hundred wŏn note on me (the equivalent of about twenty cents) and commissioned me to bring him a bottle from Seoul.

At first I wasn't really interested in Pirate's interminable monologues about the selection of a tomb site or about how his son's inheritance would pay for appropriate rituals to keep Pirate's soul content after death. Also, it bothered me when he ranted on about the inferiority of the other lineages in Sŏkp'o because this didn't fit in with what I was hearing elsewhere about communal harmony.

Fifth-interval uncle was not concerned with insim (human heartedness) or with any other aspect of village ethics that might interfere with his single-minded efforts to have his own way. He seemed to know that he was not well liked and preferred instead to be feared. He was as demanding and difficult with the members of his own family as he was with everyone else. He seemed even proud of the fact that he kept his son in line with constant scolding and the threat of withholding his inheritance. For Pirate, morality consisted of preserving class distinctions and the formal aspects of Confucian ritual. He had also preserved all the authoritarian arrogance of the old yangban without any of the concern for good manners, self-restraint, and benevolence that did so much to humanize the traditional system. The other villagers often criticized him (not to his face) for his lack of insim.

To my dismay our "intimacy" deepened after Pirate learned that I was looking for a house of my own. For some reason he was convinced that through sheer determination he could sell me an isolated house he had just built on the other side of a high pass, a forty-minute walk to the west. I tried to explain that I wanted to live in the Big Hamlet because that was the most populated part of the village, as well as being the geographic center. About forty households of Kims, Muns, Kangs, and Songs were located in the Big Hamlet, just north and east of the sandspit. The Big Hamlet was the site of the harbor, the school, the store, and several makkŏlli shops. It was not only the largest but also the most diverse hamlet in terms of the mixture of lineages and of rich and poor. One definition of a rich person in Sŏkp'o was "someone who eats rice all year long."

I pointed out to Pirate that I was interested in fishing and wanted to be near the harbor. He forcefully announced that I was wrong, and that I should stay away from the Kims, because "everyone knows they lie and steal and don't carry out the proper ceremonies for their ancestors." He was outraged by the idea that I might give serious attention to the low-status occupation of fishing. If I had to study something, it should be the gentlemanly art of growing rice. I tried to get Teacher Yi to convince him that I really did not want to become a hermit in a distant mountain valley. Teacher Yi was in a difficult bind, however. He disapproved of Pirate in general and was embarrassed by the way he pestered me, but as a fifth-interval nephew (and therefore a member of Pirate's son's generation) he could not even offer the old man advice, let alone contradict him. Filial piety is a strict and unforgiving code, and Teacher Yi, as the schoolteacher, was expected to observe the rules of propriety more faithfully than anyone else.

So Pirate would drag me after him on long, slow hikes over the steep hills, during which he checked up on his scattered fields and tenants. He carried an irrigating shovel with him that was the badge of land ownership. Well-to-do farmers in this part of South Korea carried the shovel behind their backs, or tucked comfortably into their crossed arms, almost as if it were a child, and that gave them a special bearing that meant, "I am in charge here."

Diary Entry May 19, 1966

The people we met working in the fields all greeted Pirate respectfully. Pirate responded with a short grunt or not at all. Occasionally he would stop and unblock or fill in one of the narrow channels to reroute water into one of his fields. Once, another farmer approached and complained that Pirate was taking more than his share of the water. As far as I could tell, Pirate simply used his age, influence, and bad temper to browbeat the farmer into grumbling acquiescence. In a system where most people tend to show self-restraint, cooperation, tolerance, and concern for the good opinion of others, I suppose Pirate usually gets his way. Yesterday he showed me the house on the other side of the mountain. After a long climb we stopped to rest at the top of the high pass, where thick grass and wild flowers bent under the wind. The village, the bay, the coastline, and scattered islands to the north stretched out before us, and I blurted out, "How beautiful it all is!" He corrected me, "You mean auspicious, not beautiful. But you are right; that will make a good place for my tomb." We were both looking in the same direction, but his attention was focused directly below us where the ridge flattened out for a few yards before dropping steeply again towards the village. "That is my tomb site, and it is the best in the whole village. I have bought that part of the mountain, and the chigwan (geomancer) has verified its auspicious properties." Then he pointed out a couple of old tombs visible far below—domes of grass covered earth flanked by carved stone pillars that had been set into the steep mountainside. The grass was trimmed, and gnarled old pines formed a protective ring around the graves. "Those are really yangban (aristocratic) tombs. My ancestors are buried there, and that is why we are living well (eating rice) today. Their tombs are in the right place, and we take care of them. Their spirits will thrive for five hundred years." He continued to squat on his heels, smoking several pipefuls of my tobacco and looking steadily out over the landscape. While he smoked, I was thinking in a patronizing way that his superstitious preoccupation with the grave sites made him completely oblivious to the magnificent view. But he surprised me. "You are right to admire the mountains and the ocean. It is all one village under heaven. China, Korea, America: we are all one. I do not believe in a religion. There is only this unity and the ancestors."

As Pirate led the way down the steep back side of the mountain through scrub red pine, I followed, now with a certain amount of grudging respect. The house he wanted to show me stood all by itself at the base of the slope, where the land flattened out enough for terraced rice fields to climb up the narrow valley. The hillside had been dug away for the back of the building, so as not to use precious agricultural land. Although the paper and wood door was open, the place seemed deserted. Blocked off from the sea wind and the view, the valley was hot, still, and oppressive. It seemed to me to be a terrible place to live. As we got closer, I could hear a faint intermittent wailing from inside. Abruptly Pirate put his hand on my shoulder and pushed me down into a crouch, making a sign for me to stay where I was and keep quiet. Then he minced his way along the path in a sort of exaggerated dance of stealth until he reached the open door. He paused there listening for a minute or so before plunging inside with a shout. There was some harsh, muffled language that I did not understand, and he came back out into the sunlight, dragging behind him a young man who was still buttoning up his pants. A minute or so later a rumpled woman appeared, blinking and patting her hair and blouse in a hopeless effort to tidy up. Pirate shouted, scolding the couple and pointing in various directions with extravagant gestures. He even seized the arm of the submissive youth and shook him. But a few minutes later, as Pirate showed me around the house, praising its construction and livability, I could see that he was actually in a rare good mood. On the way back to the village, we stopped again to rest at the top of the pass, and he explained. "They are just married but have no land. I let them live in the house, provided they take care of it and work in the fields. Right now they are supposed to be bringing good soil from the riverbed to build a vegetable garden. When I saw no one at work just now, I thought they would be inside playing. I was right and caught them at it." With a chuckle he got up, cradled the shovel behind his back and started down the other side. Pirate never was much good as an informant, nearly always finding a way to avoid giving any useful information about landownership, local economics, or village politics. Either his answers turned out to be dead wrong, or they were so noncommittal as to be meaningless. There was, in fact, an explanation for this kind of evasive behavior, particularly in the case of landowners. His generation, having suffered from the extractions of corrupt police and tax collectors under the Japanese during Colonial Rule (1910–45), the American Military Government (1945–48), and subsequent authoritarian South Korean regimes, had learned to be instinctively secretive and devious. Still, Pirate was an exaggerated case.

During these first months, in addition to Teacher Yi, there was another person in the village, Kim T'aemo, who answered my questions directly and frankly. T'aemo was eighteen years old and from a small and marginal branch of the Kim lineage—one of the poorest households in the Big Hamlet. His father was generally praised for his industriousness, cheerful cooperation, and blameless personal life, but without land, influence, or social standing, he just did not count. And T'aemo's close relatives were either too distant or too poor to be of any real help.

According to Teacher Yi, T'aemo was "the brightest boy who ever attended my primary school." As a young boy T'aemo had also studied at an old-style village school (sŏdang), where a handful of boys shouted out the basic Confucian primer in unison under the direction of an itinerant scholar. Conservative families who valued tradition had always sent their sons to such schools in the past, believing that true virtue and success could only be achieved by those who were able to read and write Chinese characters. By the time I lived in Sŏkp'o, the sŏdang had disappeared. Chinese characters were not taught at Teacher Yi's public primary school, which was free, obligatory, and under strict governmental direction. The South Korean primary school system had only been established in the late 1950s, and T'aemo had been able to take advantage of the relatively short period when the two educational systems overlapped. But since T'aemo's family was poor, he was not able to continue his education beyond primary school. He had attended middle school for part of one year in Inch'ŏn by living with a married sister, but the expense had been too great. Now he was back in Sŏkp'o, wandering somewhat disconsolately around the village with nothing much to do, waiting to be called up for military service. He continued to teach himself Chinese characters, however, and could read and write at the high school or even college level.

T'aemo's house was near but not part of the harbor area. The family had very little land, just a small kitchen garden and a couple of sandy plots that were only good for growing peanuts. In Sŏkp'o if a family had neither a boat nor enough land to stay busy, idleness was the result; leisure was the most conspicuous badge of poverty. Men and boys from poor families were always ready to help in cooperative projects of any kind or to assist their more prosperous relatives, friends, and neighbors during the peak agricultural seasons. All they expected at such times was to be fed. While roaming about the village, I kept running into T'aemo. As a teenager, he was expected to stay quietly in the background if I was with other adults. But he managed to intercept me in out-of-the-way areas between hamlets or along the shore. I thought at first that he must want something from me—possibly to practice his English the way high school boys did all over the rest of the country. I was wrong. T'aemo had not studied English. He just longed for mental stimulation. He wanted to make contact with someone from the world beyond Sŏkp'o. Unlike nearly everyone else in the village, he took the trouble to speak slowly and distinctly, so I could understand his Korean fairly easily, and he seemed to have no trouble with mine.

T'aemo was more than an excellent informant. He designed and built an earth oven for me so I could bake bread. He provided seeds for my vegetable garden and helped me patch up an ancient junk-rigged fishing boat that I bought from the local shaman. For T'aemo the problem of too much leisure was exaggerated by the fact that he got seasick and was therefore unable to work on the boats. But once we got my leaky junk repaired enough to sail around in sheltered water, he often came fishing with me, and his knowledge of where to find fish and what kinds of bait to use made a big difference at mealtime, both at his house and at mine. Sometimes at dusk we would go out with the ebb tide and anchor in the strong current at the edge of the entrance to the bay. After nightfall we could hear waves breaking on the rocks fifteen or twenty yards away, but all we could see was the dark mass of the steep hills against the sky. One or two lonely, dim lights were visible way across the water to the east. The old boat seemed terribly vulnerable as it surged back and forth in the dark against the flow of the current. If the anchor rope parted, we knew we would have to scull quickly to shore with the single, long sweep at the stern in order to keep from being swept out to sea. But once the fish started biting, the sense of danger disappeared in our excitement. Only when the tide slacked off could we row back, keeping close to the rocks out of the current.

I was lucky. In a remote village of one hundred and seven households, where everyone shared the same customs, beliefs, and experiences, I had met two good informants who saw the world in very different ways. Both Teacher Yi and T'aemo were strongly Confucian in outlook. They believed in tradition—proper behavior and correct relationships. Education for both was a kind of supreme good. And yet their opinions on many aspects of village life and what should be done to improve it varied sharply. Teacher Yi's life was embedded in a network of well-to-do and powerful relatives. Both his personal reputation and his status as teacher were high. He nearly always tended to present an idealized picture of harmony, cooperation, and "proper behavior" when he described village life. He was never particularly helpful if I asked about fights, theft, or adultery. He generally approved of the way things in Sŏkp'o were organized. T'aemo, however, felt deeply that the system was unfair, with discrimination against the poor and landless. Unlike Teacher Yi, he was perfectly willing to discuss scandal, answering all my questions about individuals and why things happened the way they did. He understood, perhaps even better than Teacher Yi, that I was like a child who hadn't yet learned the rules and customs that everyone else took for granted. He also seemed to like the idea of contributing to a description of the village that would be read in America. Once he found out I was interested, he began volunteering information on landownership and the popular reputations of influential men. He also recounted particularly dramatic incidents from the recent past, such as cases of adultery or theft or murder that helped explain current tensions. He knew all the local gossip and was willing to talk about it.

Of course, both Teacher Yi and T'aemo heavily favored their own kinsmen. For example, in naming the most influential and respected men of the village, the lists they gave me were quite different. It all had very little to do with personal likes and dislikes, abstract moral judgment, or actual performance. Blood relatives were just a different kind of human being from the rest of mankind. If you were born in Sŏkp'o, not only would you know your exact genealogical relationship to every other kinsman or kinswoman, but you would also know the exact degree of warmth, obligation, deference, and potential benefit inherent in that relationship. If you wanted to remain on good terms with all these people, you had to behave appropriately. In a precarious world where there was so little economic opportunity, and where property, education, and special skills were so hard to come by, people were dependent on relatives. And, of course, successful or wealthy men had to spend a good portion of their income helping less fortunate kin.

Teacher Yi was usually able to find something to approve of in describing people and events, while T'aemo nearly always was critical. It was a useful antiphony, and I began to get in the habit of checking out a lot of what one told me against the views of the other. It was more a matter of making minor corrections than of distinguishing between a right and a wrong version. In this way I was able to recognize a good deal of the distortion that inevitably accompanies village gossip. Even the distortions were helpful, providing a sort of guide, not just to kinship loyalties, but also to old personal animosities, neighborhood ties, and the remains of traditional class prejudice. The case of Yi

Pyŏngho can serve as an example of what I mean. He was the only member of the Yi lineage who lived in the Big Hamlet, apart from the other twenty-three Yi households clustered together in splendid, upper-class solidarity a half mile or so away. Yi Pyŏngho was a big, good-looking man with a gregarious manner and an authoritative air, and his isolation among the Kims and the Muns across the sandspit puzzled me. According to T'aemo, Yi Pyŏngho, as Sŏkp'o's most notorious and successful womanizer, was in a kind of exile. After a number of incidents, some of which had reinforced and some of which had seriously undermined the good reputation of Yi lineage women, he had been ejected by his relatives from their neighborhood; at present he was reportedly carrying on a liaison with the young wife of a less prosperous Kim neighbor. Teacher Yi's explanation was quite different. He told me that Yi Pyŏngho's position as head of the local fishery cooperative made it necessary for him to live near the harbor area and among the fishermen.

Even after I had moved out of Teacher Yi's house, I continued to see him fairly often. As the weather got warmer, the ocean became more inviting, and I began swimming off the sandspit that connected the two halves of the village. Finally, after a good deal of persuasion, Teacher Yi joined me. Attitudes in Sŏkp'o regarding swimming were in a state of confused transition as a result of the development of a major, nationally known swimming beach about six miles down the coast to the south. People from the city cooled off there in July and August, and there was even a special boat that brought vacationers by the hundreds from Inch'ŏn and Seoul. Most adults in the village thought that women's bathing suits were highly improper. Just the idea of men and women swimming together on the same beach was regarded by the older generation as fundamentally indecent. On the other hand, young men from the village made a regular project of walking up and down the crowded beach to check on the latest fashions.

Teacher Yi's initial reluctance to swim had nothing to do with Confucian prudery, however. The real problem was that in Sŏkp'o no one went in the water at all except small children. Swimming was regarded as a childish and completely frivolous activity, and Teacher Yi was naturally concerned about the loss of personal dignity. But it was his obligation as a kind of adoptive brother to watch over me. So we swam and enjoyed ourselves. We also took fishing rods and a little something to eat and drink with us on these weekend excursions. Later on we tried places further out on the headland away from the village, where big rocks offered better platforms from which to cast for eel, corvina, pollock, and urŏk (sea bass).

When we first began swimming in early June, the water was still pretty brisk. After drying off, the sun was wonderfully warm on our bodies as we sat out of the wind on the rocks above the sea. We would fish and then stop to drink makkŏlli and nibble at crisp chunks of rice—the scrapings from the bottom of the big breakfast cooking pot that are usually reserved for children. The talk here was more personal than in the sarangbang and included such topics as our wives, growing up, hopes for our children, and our own goals and discontents. Here by the waves we confided in each other and became friends.

NOTES

1. In 1966 the pattern of rural hole-in-the-wall stores (kumŏng kage) was pretty much the same throughout the region: a small ramshackle thatched-roof building completely open on one side to the path or road, with two or three rooms in back as living quarters for the store keeper. There might be a small maru or place to sit and drink, while the remaining space was taken up by the various items for sale that were not produced locally. Some households made their own makkŏlli, but mostly it was brought in from Taean, the nearest town. The homemade product was generally considered to be superior. As economic development began to trickle down in South Korea from the mid-1960s, kumŏng kage were being steadily upgraded, with whitewashed walls, tiled roofs and a much larger inventory of items for sale, including even hot noodles.

3

Patriotic Journey

If you are not born and raised in Korea, making the transition to rice as the steady staple, day after day, three times a day, takes time—possibly more time than the average American adult has left. Having already spent four years in Japan, I was certainly used to rice. And with my Korean wife in charge of our kitchen at home in the United States, I usually ate rice four or five times a week. But in Sŏkp'o, confronting an enormous, heaping bowl of rice and very little else at every meal was becoming more and more of a challenge.

South Koreans in 1966, especially rural South Koreans, still obtained most of their nutrition from rice or other grains, and they had to eat an awful lot to make up for the lack of other foods, particularly those rich in protein. Except for special occasions, eggs and any fish larger than a few inches were regarded in most households as too valuable to consume at home and were sold in the market towns nearby. The villagers ate pork, beef, or chicken only rarely a few times a year at the feasts accompanying weddings, funerals, and ancestor worship ceremonies, or at New Year's and Chu'sŏk (the harvest festival). Even tubu (tofu), which has a lot of protein, was a luxury that turned up only occasionally on the meal trays of well-off households. Although Koreans believe that a bit of plumpness is physically attractive for both men and women, there was not one single person in the entire village population of about nine hundred who was at all overweight. In a very literal sense Sŏkp'o had a subsistence economy.

Most families couldn't afford pure rice at every meal. In accordance with personal taste and the degree of a family's poverty, their bowls usually contained a mixture of rice and either millet, sorghum, peas, beans, or barley. Really poor families ate mostly barley, and in the spring there was never enough even of that. I found these mixtures much tastier than pure white rice, but I was unable to obtain them except in token quantities while I was living at Teacher Yi's house. Nearly everything is ranked in South Korea in terms of status, and pure rice is by far the most prestigious food. Hospitality is a sacred obligation, and the best of whatever is available must be offered to guests. Since the Yis were fairly well off and conformed rather strictly to traditional customs and standards of conduct, I was invariably served vast quantities of pure white rice at every meal. Etiquette required that I empty the rice bowl, which I was increasingly unable to do. I was not getting fat; I just couldn't eat that much rice. But getting Teacher Yi's wife to give me smaller portions turned out to be beyond my powers of persuasion. Part of the trouble was that good health and eating a lot are closely related in Korean popular attitudes. The less I ate, the more my worried hostess tried to fill me up.

To try and work off the rice and regain my appetite, I began climbing the small mountain directly behind Teacher Yi's house early every morning before breakfast. The round trip, if I ran part of the way, took only about forty-five minutes, including calisthenics on top. I could slip directly off my veranda without waking anyone and swing up into the woods along the edge of the threshing ground. The path led through a small bamboo grove, up past some barley fields on a ridge overlooking the sea, and then more steeply up into the big pines that surrounded the Yi clan's ancestral tombs. Here, monumental stone statues of ancient sages presided over the well-tended grassy grave mounds. The statues were covered with lichen and worn almost smooth by time and the weather. Early sunlight slanted through the trees, dappling the grass. A gap in the trees opened up a view of the rest of the village, the sea beyond, and endless islands to the north.

After running up the lower slopes, I usually paused for a minute or two to catch my breath. The pines thinned out further up, and the path gradually traversed along the shoulder of the mountain, until suddenly there was only the ocean, filling the entire landscape and extending westward all the way to China. On this high, exposed slope it was always cool and the grass and wildflowers bent and flowed with the wind. Someone had once tried to plant barley way up here, but the field had been abandoned, presumably after a dry year. Higher still, the trees had all been cut, shortly after Korea's liberation from the Japanese in 1945. Now there were shoulder-high saplings everywhere planted a few years before by school children as part of a national reforestation campaign.

The final scramble to the top was over jagged rocks and gigantic flat stone slabs. Sŏkp'o was there below, serene and lovely in the distance, the coastline stretching away both north and south into misty infinity. My separation from the village felt almost complete. For a few minutes each day I could stop trying to be part of the community, stop trying to understand what was going on, and stop trying to pretend to myself that lack of privacy didn't matter.

At the summit I did every exercise I could remember, going back through time from the highly disciplined movements we performed in Japan as part of the collective tyranny associated with membership in a Japanese ski club, through the much sloppier physical training required by the infantry in World War II, to my distant recollections of warming up for football practice in high school. Soon I was in superb physical condition, and it was possible to eat the breakfast rice. But I still had to cope with the other two meals.

My next countermeasure was to be away from the house at lunchtime. This worked as long as I hid out down by the ocean; otherwise I was likely to run up against the villagers' compulsion to share their food with anyone who happened to be around at mealtime. If I wouldn't eat, they insisted that I drink. All sorts of special foods went with the makkŏlli, but fortunately steamed rice wasn't one of them. I discovered with some satisfaction that by sticking to alcoholic drinks I could keep the rice bowl at bay. Thus my days, in addition to some anthropological research, consisted mainly of frantic exercise, a good deal of drinking, and a certain amount of skulking around alone by the seashore.

One day in late spring I put on my knapsack and hiking boots, summoned the ferryman who sculled me across the bay, and struck out briskly for the mountains of the interior. It was lovely weather for hiking, breezy and cool, with a bright sun that exaggerated the contrasts of light and shade. After a half hour or so I could no longer pick up the glint of the sea behind me. There were no roads, and the path that linked the villages threaded its way through a maze of mountains. Out of each valley there would be a climb to a high, windy pass among the pines, where swallows swooped and darted just past my head. From such heights I could sometimes get another glimpse of the western sea before starting down to where terraced rice fields marked the contours below.

Everywhere teams of farmers were transplanting rice into shining fields of water. Here and there some men plowed through the mud with oxen, while others gathered seedlings and brought them to the paddy fields. Most of the men and women were strung out in long lines, advancing together through the calf-deep water as they jabbed rice sprouts into the mud. The work was accompanied by a lot of noisy, outrageous banter, but the women and girls were too busy, too splattered with mud, or perhaps too used to crude village jokes to blush.

I was a strange enough apparition in this isolated countryside that if the field being planted was anywhere near my path, work would stop, and everyone would straighten up and stare. Someone invariably shouted a rough but friendly greeting, and if it was time for a break, the farmers invited me to share their makkŏlli and food. When I answered in Korean, people crowded around, gratefully accepting cigarettes and asking questions about Miguk (beautiful country), the Korean word for America.

After several hours of hiking and several stops to drink and eat with groups of farmers, I was tired and euphorically drunk, not just on the makkŏlli but on the scenery, the sunlight, and the special goodwill that always seems to accompany collective labor in Korea. Later in the day a solitary farmer on the path—in return for the cigarette I offered— urged me to come home with him and spend the night. But, visualizing the heaping bowls of rice that would accompany his hospitality, I pressed on.

"Where is the Miguk mi-sa-il base?" I kept asking, and the farmers would point vaguely eastward, adding encouragingly, "It is only about isimni." Now isimni or 20 ri is a very flexible, all-purpose unit of distance in the Korean countryside. If you are walking, it seems to apply to any objective, whether it is just out of sight over the next hill or half a day's journey away. One never hears of 4 ri or 17 ri or 26 ri. It is always isimni (20 ri). The words are easy to say and have a nice ring to them. Thanks to my early morning physical training in Sŏkp'o, I had maintained a fast pace up and down the mountain paths, and even though the villagers along my route kept telling me all afternoon that the American missile base was still (or only) 20 ri further on, I was not dissuaded from my objective.

Perhaps my expedition could best be compared to the voyage of a salmon returning up some wilderness stream to spawn. Enduring great hardship against terrible odds, the fish follows a supremely powerful internal drive without any clear idea of what is going on. In my case I had suddenly become motivated by a peculiarly irresistible urge to visit an isolated American missile base, deep in the mountains to the eastward. What I really wanted was to eat fresh bread.

Some six hours after leaving Sŏkp'o, I emerged from the hills onto a paved road and started walking north towards a distant group of buildings that had the obvious regularity of an army installation. As I got closer, I noticed that opposite the American base a peculiar cluster of shacks was strung out along the road for a couple of hundred yards, looking more like a Hollywood set for Dodge City than a Korean village. The ramshackle buildings were garishly decorated with such signs as "Honeysuckle Rose," "New York Saloon," "Cafe Dancing," and "American Bar." Heavily made-up young women with fantastic hairdos and brightly colored, American mail-order catalog clothes lounged in the doorways or on the verandas. At the door of a beauty shop one of them smiled and called out, "Hello, where you go?" Older women of conventional rural appearance washed clothes or prepared food outdoors, and a few men painted or hammered away at the haphazard buildings.

Across the road everything was spit and polish. High, barbed wire fences enclosed the compound, and large signs decorated with gilt and red paint announced the name of the military unit. Jeeps and trucks were, like the buildings, lined up in orderly rows. All the cement and stonework was newly whitewashed, and the boots of the American sentry on duty at the front gate shone almost as brilliantly as his brass belt buckle. In 1966, at the height of the Cold War, there were more than 60,000 US troops in South Korea. In addition to major army and air force installations, small isolated missile bases such as this one dotted the country. Hot, tired, and bedraggled, I trudged up to the small gatehouse where the sentry stared at me blankly, his mouth open and his eyes blinking.

"Who the hell are you?" he said, not with hostility but in pure astonishment. "Take me to your leader," I answered, the whole strange scene reminding me of some intergalactic episode from science fiction. It was my first encounter with Americans in a couple of months. It was also the first time soldiers at the missile base had ever seen anyone other than Koreans on foot at their front gate.

The sentry's face lit up. My cliché seemed to have struck the right note. He called in to headquarters to report the visitor from outer space, and a sergeant soon appeared. He too liked the phrase and repeated it with laughter, as he ushered me into the captain's office. After explaining that I was conducting anthropological field study and pointing out where Sŏkp'o was on the map, I confessed with some embarrassment to having made the pilgrimage to the

missile base mainly in the hope of procuring a change of diet. More specifically, I wanted to learn how to bake bread.

I felt I had failed badly in not being able to stick it out and adapt completely to village eating patterns. But to these men the idea of a lone American
trying to live in the manner of a Korean peasant was outlandish, and they
sympathized completely with my longing for bread. The captain said, "We
heard there was an old French priest out there somewhere who had been in
Korea for thirty years, but we never expected to see anyone like you. We figure
this [Korea] is the asshole of the universe. I don't see how you can eat that
Korean stuff for one day, let alone all the time." His statement made me a
little uneasy, since I personally thought most Korean food was delicious, and
I was beginning to admire a lot of things about peasant society. But I didn't
argue. I went ahead and explained my plan and why I needed the Army's help.

There was plenty of American flour in the South Korean countryside during the 1960s. The country was economically prostrate after the Korean War
and almost completely dependent on the United States. As part of American
aid, the US Food for Peace program furnished surplus flour in order to pay
the labor costs of rural development projects. An example was the dike in
Sŏkp'o where workers were paid in flour. But, unless they were starving,
Korean farmers had about as much use for flour as I had for rice. Much of it
was sold on the black market and found its way back to the cities. The rest
was consumed in the villages in the form either of noodles or makkŏlli. This
mild, fermented drink had always been made out of rice, but farmers discovered they could make it even more easily and much more cheaply out of US
surplus flour. I told the captain that I wanted to learn bread-making, get hold
of some yeast, and then bake my own bread in the village using the surplus
flour that was available locally.

He assured me that his unit would give me all the assistance I wanted and
told the sergeant to make certain in the meantime that all my personal needs
were taken care of. I had arrived during "happy hour," and soon found myself
celebrating along with the sergeant, who asked me to call him Mike, and a
young lieutenant, Pete Stevens. We drank Wild Turkey at a lavish, highly polished bar that had obviously been the focus of much loving craftsmanship by
homesick members of the unit. Other officers joined us. With just one company of about 250 men manning the base, the officers' and NCO clubs had
been combined. There were pinball, slot machines, pool, Ping-Pong, and

television. Adjoining the bar and a small dining area was a larger room with a dance floor and bandstand. Mike pointed it out proudly. "We have a dance party for the whole company once a week. The outfit has its own band."

An hour or so later the captain presided at the officers' dinner table, where I was served a thick steak, peas, and baked potatoes, accompanied by a really good Bordeaux red in addition to delicious bread and butter. We finished the meal with pie, ice cream, coffee, and brandy. My love of country has never been greater.

As we got up from the table, Pete looked me over with a critical eye and asked, "Would you like to clean up a little before we go over to the ville?" It had been some two months since I'd had a real shower, although I had been swimming several times in the ocean. The endless supply of hot water at the base was a wonderful luxury. Aside from the purely sensual pleasure, I was eager to get rid of the lice that had taken refuge in various parts of my body. Emerging pink, fresh, and steaming, I found that my filthy clothes had been whisked away and replaced by a small pile of clean army garments without insignia or marks of rank.

All this care and luxury had a kind of make-believe, dreamlike quality, as if I'd been rescued after years on a desert island. In fact, that apparently was the attitude of my hosts, whose thoughtfulness and hospitality seemed limitless. Someone who had been lost had been brought back into the fold, and the entire resources of the United States military were ready to carry out his rehabilitation. The captain and the sergeant major had work to do, so Mike, the staff sergeant, and Pete, the lieutenant, were my guides for the evening.

It turned out that "ville" was the standard US military term (standard in South Korea at least) for the cluster of bars, dance halls, and bordellos outside every base. Across the road lights had been turned on, and music from several loud speakers competed discordantly at high volume. Some places had bulbs that blinked, and there were even a couple of neon signs, although half the letters were missing. Occasionally a flash of brighter light accompanied blasts of louder music, as groups of soldiers entered or left one of the buildings. The lights, the noise, and the shadowy tangled structures stretched for one hundred yards or so along the road in both directions, then ended abruptly in the absolute still emptiness of a summer night in the mountains.

At the ville, bars, nightclubs, and "coffee shops," all crudely decorated in imitation of Seoul establishments, were liberally staffed with flamboyantly decorated young ladies. We wandered in and out of a series of bars and dance halls, spending only a half hour or so at each one. Inside there was familiarity and camaraderie, a feeling of having joined old friends for an evening on the town. My guides greeted the women everywhere by name, and they joined us with easy informality. In one bar where another group of Americans was already ensconced, only one girl was available, but in a few minutes two more, hastily summoned from next door, came in to pour the makkŏlli, pressing close against us on the narrow, rustic benches.

It was obvious, given the isolation of the place, but I asked anyway, "This whole town is here just for one company of Americans?" "Sure, every base has a ville," the lieutenant said. "We let indigenous personnel use the coffee shops and restaurants during the day, but at night everything is off-limits to Koreans. Some of them can't hold their liquor, and we don't want any fights."

What was most surprising to me, in addition to the size of the entertainment operation, was the crazy air of normalcy about it all. It was evident that unless someone was on duty, worn out, suffering from religious fanaticism, or sick, a visit to the ville was part of the day's routine.

In the mid-1960s South Korea was still very poor, hardly better off than Bangladesh or Paraguay. The driving energy that would transform it in fifteen to twenty years into a prosperous, rapidly industrializing nation was only just beginning to be apparent. South Koreans were eager for change, but in spite of their desire to work, there was no capital and no economic opportunity for the vast majority of the population. During this period the United States was regarded as the land of milk and honey, but the only direct access for ordinary people to its cornucopia of material wealth was either through American servicemen or by obtaining missionary handouts from the church. The ville as an institution was one example of how well South Korean entrepreneurs were rising to the challenge. It enabled substantial numbers of South Koreans to tap directly into the flow of American money and goods overseas.

The women who flocked to the villes had different objectives and used different strategies. Some were determined to marry Americans and emigrate. Others were mainly interested in obtaining PX goods. At the PX you could buy cameras, radios, cosmetics, clothes, cigarettes, and liquor—just about anything that wasn't available on the Korean market. Many saved every cent that was not spent on dresses and hairdos, and funneled profits back to their families to pay for a brother's education, to buy land, or to start small businesses. Some, dazzled by the hedonism of American pop culture, carelessly broke all ties with their own families and tradition to become permanent hangers-on in the foreigners' world. The heedless or easygoing or stupid ones often drank too much, had too many abortions, and spent their money on clothes or other personal extravagance, allowing themselves to be exploited by both American and South Korean masters. But most of the women played a hard, shrewd game in this economic arena and made out extremely well. That night, it seemed to me, an ethnographic study of the financial and personal arrangements between the young women, their American clients, and the South Korean entrepreneurs who employed them would make a rewarding research project, and I thought seriously of redirecting the focus of my dissertation. Surely the Department of Defense would be delighted to have a thorough, scientific study of the temptations that our boys in service overseas were being subjected to!

I made a tentative start. Certainly the informants were friendly and willing to talk. It turned out that the 250 Americans were complemented by 170 young women in the ville. There were quite a few devoted couples, who paired off exclusively during a soldier's entire tour of duty, but most of the women had to be content with multiple, temporary relationships. My drinking companions, who as officers felt a strong responsibility to prevent marriages, said approvingly that most of the servicemen found the chase to be as satisfying as the consummation.

It turned out that different establishments in the ville were associated with different ranks at the base, and my guides did not take me to the really boisterous places where ordinary enlisted men let off steam. There was no shortage of fresh faces anywhere. Most of the women worked on a rotation system so that the men could meet almost all of them within a few weeks of random visits. Some of them were "fixed assets," attached permanently to certain clubs or bars through special ties to the owners, but most were free to circulate, spending a month or so in one place and then moving on. There was also a good deal of turnover throughout the country among different villes. Women who were restless or who had gotten into some sort of trouble, either with a soldier or a proprietor, could always leave for a ville somewhere else. And, of course, bar owners and the women themselves were constantly recruiting new talent from the countryside.

In addition to the working women, the ville supported a couple of hundred additional Koreans engaged in administration, cooking, washing, dressmaking, hairstyling, construction, money changing, and the disposal of PX items. I was told that even though the real owners of the bars and cabarets were mostly former hostesses, these women invariably hired men to run their establishments.

Still, I thought it was a little incredible. The infantry in Italy during World War II and even the US Army in South Korea after the Armistice had never had services available like this. I asked, "But what about the commanding generals in Seoul, or touring senators, or chaplains, wives, mothers, and sweethearts? Aren't there people at home who will raise a fuss when they realize that a woman is immediately available across the street for every single American soldier who has even the slightest inclination?"

But my guides insisted that the women were not prostitutes. "It's more like a large, well-organized dating bureau," Pete explained, as he was pulled onto the dance floor by a lovely woman undulating in a tight black sheath. Mike continued, "Of course, some of them will take on just about anyone for a one-night stand, but there's a lot of competition for the girls who are really popular. They get to be very choosy, even about who they drink and dance with."

I asked if the Americans tried to restrict ville development in any way. He answered, "We don't care how big or how small the ville gets. The South Koreans and the law of supply and demand take care of that. But we can exert some control over what goes on, as long as it's all right here in our front yard. The way things are now, it's nice and manageable. The girls are inspected regularly [for both STDs and stolen goods], we do our best to keep the number of marriages as low as possible, and we don't have men chasing around after tail all over the boondocks, getting poisoned on bad liquor, and causing trouble."

Pete and another lieutenant, now back from the dance floor, further developed the theme of the beneficial effects of the ville system on the local economy. "Many of these girls are putting their brothers through college or supporting parents who lost everything during the Korean War. My girlfriend is lending money to her cousin who has a garage in Sŏsan. They are all exposed to American living standards and ways of doing things, and this is going to have a good effect all around. God knows, they [the women] need someone to tell them what to do." In one sense he was right. This segment of the South Korean provincial society that was untouched by American economic aid to the South Korean government was receiving a steady infusion of capital, most of which was being rechanneled into productive use.

But there was a less positive side to the story. The overwhelming majority of South Koreans regarded the villes as shameful and demeaning and pretended as much as possible that they did not exist. They were taboo in the South Korean press. Women who worked there became non-persons in South Korean society and were looked down on even by the relatives that they helped support. And no villes existed outside Korean Army bases. There also seems to have been something of a taboo regarding the villes among the American military authorities. Their existence was never acknowledged in *The Stars and Stripes* or on The Armed Forces Korea Network (US Military Television broadcasts) or in announcements from Washington. Those crusading senators and chaplains existed only in my imagination.

We finally settled in for the evening at the California Cabaret. By then Myong Sook had been assigned to me. At the beginning of the evening when we changed bars, the girls mostly stayed behind, but at some point in our wanderings, she had simply joined the party, without, as far as I could tell, any invitation. She was attractive, danced well, and didn't make a fuss about talking Korean with me, so I was content.

After a while the sergeant major, who was older (in his forties, like me) came over from the base and joined us "to make sure that the kids are treating you right. We come here to the ville to try and forget that we have to spend eighteen months in this godforsaken hellhole."

It startled me to hear the constant denunciation of South Korea and everything Korean as a normal part of conversation, even though the women were sitting at the table with us. There didn't seem to be a serious problem of communication between the Americans and the Koreans, although the hostesses' English was limited. There was a lot of joking, with the girls faking it all fairly successfully when they didn't know exactly what was going on. But they obviously understood a good deal, and I protested, "It seems kind of mean to keep insulting Korea right in front of them." Pete laughed, "They're used to it. Besides they agree with us. Don't you honey?"

The woman that had been dancing earlier in the skintight black sheath, Yong Hee, snuggled up to him and smiled, "Korea no damn good." The sergeant major shifted to a more positive note. "There are some real nice girls here, a lot of them just as faithful and honest, if you give them a chance, as the girls back home . . . maybe more so. The ones that go steady won't look at another guy as long as their boyfriends are here in Korea."

But Pete wanted to go on explaining what was wrong with South Korea. "Look at the way they live. There's no culture or civilization. You know how filthy the toilets are. Nobody takes a bath. The kids run around naked with snot running down their faces and flies crawling in their eyes. People sit on their haunches in the dirt to wait for a bus. The houses are dark and dirty and falling apart, and the farmers just sit around drinking most of the day and let the women do all the work." He was wound up now, and Yong Hee was no longer snuggling. "They're all lazy and dishonest; everybody's begging or stealing or trying to con us out of anything worth having. And the smell of that kimch'i they eat, no wonder so many people are sick and so many kids die young. Why don't they clean themselves up and get to work and make something out of this place?"

"But it's a poor country," I said. "They're just trying to survive. They've had a tough war, and there are too many people. There aren't any choices. If a man has enough—land to keep himself busy or a decent job—he'll work his head off. Only the ones who don't have enough to do hang around. What about the South Korean employees at the base? Are they all lazy and dishonest?"

"Oh, they're different!" The sergeant major was emphatic. "We couldn't get along without them." The others joined in, all talking at once, telling me how good the South Korean employees were as carpenters, drivers, mechanics, plumbers, and maintenance workers. It was Pete who came up with an explanation for the anomaly. "But they've all been working for the US for a long time. They're the cream of the crop. My driver, for example, is one of the finest guys you'd ever want to meet. I'm going to get him a job in the states when I go home."

It was puzzling. On the one hand, my new friends thought of the Koreans with whom they had little or no direct contact as almost beneath contempt. Military folklore, handed down since 1945 and exacerbated by the Korean War, decreed that South Koreans (specifically South Korean men) were lazy and dishonest. But the Koreans they knew well and worked (or played) with on a daily basis were somehow different, transformed by their close connection with Americans. Unfortunately, there were always enough thieves, con men, and greedy women in the ville to give some substance to the stereotypes. That and the almost perfect isolation of the soldiers from local society had kept the myths intact. The Americans knew nothing about South Korea, except what they learned from the ville or witnessed when they traveled through the countryside in speeding trucks. I did not tell them what most South Koreans thought of the ville and the ville women.

At the same time there was also plenty of goodwill. The company as a whole was continually engaged in local good work, and its members were proud of these efforts. I heard about the annex they had built for a local orphanage, and how American bulldozers had moved in to clean things up after a flood. And how everyone contributed to provide medicine, clothes, and food to the local authorities for the distribution to the poor. When I asked Myong Sook in Korean how she felt about the Americans' constant denunciation of Korea, she started to pour out all her indignation, resentment, and unhappiness. The other women quickly joined in, and I became the focus of a general outburst. It came out in a jumble of exclamations: "They [the Americans] don't know anything about us." "They don't understand how we feel." "I can never express my real feelings." "They don't care what we are really like." "They never treat us right." "They insist that everything American is always best." "We are always the ones who have to change." "Why don't they respect anything in Korea?" "Why can't they appreciate our feelings and treat us like real human beings?" "They have no insim [they did not possess the fundamental decency in the context of Confucian ethics]." There was that word again; the one thing the villagers in Sŏkp'o possessed, even if they were poor and uneducated. At least the folks in Sŏkp'o knew how to treat each other.

The Americans wanted to know what all the excitement was about, and I asked the women if I should interpret what they had been telling me. Myung Sook shrugged. "What's the use?" she said. "It will only cause bad feeling. We can't change anything." I told my hosts something to the effect that the Korean women were frustrated by the language barrier and wanted to be able to exchange more complicated thoughts. Mike said, "All they really want is more pearls and more perfume and more dresses and more money." There was general laughter as we got up and headed back across the road to the base. Pete stayed behind with Yong Hee.

I never found out whether there was reveille and early morning physical training at the missile base. If there was, I slept through it. After breakfast the mess sergeant, Joe Calicchio, taught me how to bake bread. He was a second-generation Italian American who loved his job and he insisted that I work right along with him, mimicking all the operations on a very small scale, while he prepared enormous quantities of dough for the entire company. At the end of the lesson he offered me two nesting bread pans, a supply of yeast, and a large sack of flour. Since I had to carry everything back to Sŏkp'o in my rucksack, I turned down the flour but managed to get it replaced with bacon, coffee, butter, and condensed milk.

When I left in the early afternoon, my new friends gave me a heartwarming send-off, providing assorted presents from the PX and a jeep ride to where the footpath headed up into the mountains. The sergeant major himself helped me put on my pack. His last words were, "If you need any help, just send us word." I wasn't sure how I was supposed to send word, but it was comforting to know that I had such important and powerful allies in the same county.

At first I welcomed the day's cool, cloudy weather as I began climbing the steep trail. But after an hour or so it started to rain. With slippery footing and the added weight in my pack, the hiking was much tougher than the day before. The hills seemed endless and steeper than I remembered. Although a few farmers were out working in the rain, their greetings this time were perfunctory, and by about five o'clock the steeply terraced hillsides were deserted.

It was dark by the time I finally reached the strip of sand backed by reeds and long grass that served as a ferry landing opposite Sŏkp'o. A half mile across the water I could just make out the shapes of the Big Hamlet in the dusk, but no one answered my hail. I had a vivid mental picture of Teacher Yi and his family snug and warm around their evening meal while I stood hollering in the rain. Wet, tired, and chilled, I cursed myself for not having negotiated a night's lodging earlier along the way. Loaded down as I was with newly acquired cigarettes, pipe tobacco, and candy bars, I knew I would make a desirable houseguest anywhere in the South Korean countryside. Now the only alternative to spending a night out in the rain was to retrace my route a mile or so to the last village, where I knew no one, and pound on doors until someone gave me shelter. But I wasn't at all sure I could find the village again at night, since there were all sorts of branching paths that petered out in rice fields or up in the pine woods. As it turned out, I took a wrong turn somewhere and never found the village I'd turned back for. But after another hour of muddy slogging, I saw a dim light higher up and off to my right. There didn't seem to be any path heading in that direction, so I simply turned right and walked precariously along the tops of paddy field dikes, slipping occasionally down into the mud. It didn't matter where I walked; I couldn't have gotten any wetter. After a final short climb up a rocky slope, I could just make out the dark rounded forms of farmhouses against the hillside. The familiar smell of a night soil pit exclaimed, "There are humans here."

A persistent cough and the crying of a child came from the house with the light, explaining why precious kerosene was being burned so late. Worried that the last thing people with a sick child want is an unknown late visitor, I nevertheless pounded on the courtyard gate until someone opened an inner door and muttered something to the effect that there was a lot of noise at the gate. I called out, "I have lost my way. I am an American. I need a place to sleep." There was no answer. The door slammed shut, and I stood wondering what to do next. My accent should have made it obvious that I was not a North Korean commando—the only thing, I figured, besides a ghost that would frighten anyone. Finally I heard noises from inside the courtyard, and the gate creaked open far enough for the farmer to get a look at me.

"It really is an American. Where have you come from? You must have had a terrible time getting to this far-off place. Have you eaten?" Shutting the gate behind him, and without waiting for any answers from me, the farmer added, "Come with me." He led me to the only house in the hamlet that had a tiled roof. "Tae Young, wake up! You have a guest."

It is considered an auspicious event when guests arrive in Korea. The host has a chance to demonstrate both his wealth and his generosity. Ordinarily the household is full of a pleasant hustle and bustle at such times, as an elaborate welcome is prepared. On that particular dark, wet evening at about 11:00 p.m., there may have been some question as to how auspicious my arrival seemed to Kim Tae Young and his wife, but they certainly rose to the occasion. As the richest man in the hamlet, there was no doubt that it was Mr. Kim's responsibility to take care of the unknown foreigner. Lamps were lit, a fire was started in the kitchen, and dry clothes were brought out. Children woke up and peered wide-eyed at the stranger. I took off my wet clothes and put on ankle-length, white cotton bloomers, and a long-sleeved undershirt provided by my host. He also poured out *soju* for us. From the kitchen came the agreeable sounds of a knife on a chopping board and the clinking of bowls and pans. At that moment the idea of hot, steamed rice was not at all unpleasant.

The heavy oiled paper that covered the hot floor had turned a deep rich brown with years of use. In the dim light it had a dull gloss. Where the heat was greatest the color deepened almost to black, and it was here that Mr. Kim urged me to sit. Gradually the heat of the freshly kindled kitchen fire seeped up through the stones, dried mud, and paper of the floor into my legs and body. Above my head the rough-hewn pine poles that served as rafters disappeared into dark shadows. It was all familiar; one Korean farmhouse is very much like another. The base and its ville seemed far off, and the stress of culture conflict was gone. Here custom and propriety prevailed; creating order, harmony, and a kind of beauty. These philosophical musings may have been fueled somewhat by *soju* on an empty stomach; but I knew that somehow the excursion to the missile base had satisfied deeper discontents than just the longing for bread. It was good to be immersed again in Korean country life. Now I could get back to work.

Kim Tae Young's wife brought in a tray of oysters in hot bean paste sauce to go with the *soju*. The combination of cool, slippery freshness and thick pungency seemed more wonderfully refined than all my memories of snails, à l'Alsacienne , and caviar in Europe or the steak and *makkŏlli* from the night before.

Mr. Kim's father, a still-agile man in his eighties, joined us. The rest of the family—a bent and wizened grandmother, my host's younger brother, and four or five children—peered from a discreet distance out of the shadows. The children scuffled a little as they tried to get a better look at the strange spectacle. The brother's young wife helped Mrs. Kim in the huge, dark, semi-subterranean kitchen.

It wasn't long before three more men came in out of the rain, so that now we had a representative from each of the five houses in the hamlet. The kitchen began filling up with women. More *soju* and various kinds of appetizers appeared. Thoroughly warmed both inside and out and being the center of attention, I forgot all about the earlier misery of wandering around lost in the mud and rain and tried as best I could to keep up with a steady stream of questions.

Our little drinking group was on center stage, lit by an extravagant candle, while the audience silently watched every move and listened to every word from the dark corners of the room. The spectators' absorption in what was going on was not necessarily related to my ability as an entertainer. Nevertheless, as a foreigner, I was entertainment for the villagers, and somehow I felt compelled to put on an adequate show. How old are you? Where are you from? Are you a soldier? Why are you here? Why don't you have a jeep like other foreigners? If you are a scholar as you say, why don't you wear a decent suit and a tie? How much money do you make? How many children do you have? Do you have a Korean wife?

The idea that someone would come from across the ocean to study village life in a poor and out-of-the-way part of the coast did not inspire any more confidence in my truthfulness here than it had in Sŏkp'o. I divided my annual income by about five, and they still thought I was bragging. Translated into Korean *wŏn*, an ordinary American academic salary in 1966 would have seemed utterly fantastic to these subsistence peasants—probably as morally obscene as the earnings of professional athletes, automobile company executives, or rock stars seem to us today.

The old man, upon finding out that I was only forty-two years old, commented, "You look much older. Have you been very sick? Of course, America probably does not have a healthful climate such as ours." Since I prided myself on my youthful vigor, this kind of remark, which I was not hearing for the first time, always came as a slight jolt. Rural Koreans associated blond hair with the white of old age, and this, combined with the fairly deep lines in my face, made them overestimate my age by fifteen to twenty years. And since age is intimately related to social status in the Confucian scheme of things, Korean farmers constantly placed me on an undeservedly exalted level. No one has ever shown me as much respect since. Today, when pushy Boston women force their way in front of me in department stores or at checkout counters, or I am served last in ice cream parlors after eager teenagers, I remember with a certain nostalgia the dignity of my premature old age in the Korean countryside. The women's questions about a Korean wife were tougher to handle.

"Yes, my wife is Korean; she is in Seoul."

"Where is your American wife?" "My Korean wife is my American wife."

"That is nonsense. Why do you answer like that? Are you angry for some reason? We know that all foreigners except missionaries take Korean wives when they are here."

"I have only one wife. She is Korean, and now she is in Seoul."

"But what about your American wife?"

I tried to explain:

"My wife was born in Korea as a Korean. She went to America to study. Now she is with her family in Seoul."

At this point the grandmother announced with authority from a shadowy corner,

"He is trying to say that he also has a concubine. But I can't tell from his poor speaking ability whether the concubine is Korean or American."

She encouraged me to come clean.

"Don't be ashamed. We have concubines here too, even though the authorities in Seoul now say that it is immoral. It's all right as long as everyone is treated properly."

In addition to the direct questions and conversation of my immediate male drinking group in the center of the room, this external commentary from the spectators continued, along with cries and murmurs of wonder or disapproval at each new fantastic revelation about life in America.

The grandfather wanted to know how long people lived in the United States. He was obviously satisfied when I said that Americans regarded eighty as quite old, and only rarely did anyone live to be ninety. But the idea that when someone in America died we only performed one ceremony, a funeral at the time of death, was utterly incomprehensible to my companions. They returned to the subject again and again, convinced that I was misunderstanding their questions. Continuing rituals honoring the death days of parents and grandparents were such an integral part of custom and propriety and the rhythm of life that orderly ethical social existence without them seemed impossible. My questioners also found the idea that our young people of marriageable age go off on their own, hunting for mates on the basis of mutual physical attraction to be repugnant. As their shock and obvious disapproval increased, I began to have an uneasy feeling of having sold out my country's reputation as a civilized nation to pay for the night's lodging.

As the novelty wore off and my "poor speaking ability" further degenerated from fatigue, the children went back to sleep, and some of the neighbors returned home. Even though I was anxious to call it a night and get some rest, I hated to see them go, realizing how a nightclub entertainer with a lousy act must feel.

Mr. Kim's house also had a *sarangbang* or guest room, and he deserted his wife in order to sleep with me there. It would not have been polite to let a guest suffer the terrors of an empty room all by himself. Our small mats were placed close together with a disturbingly conjugal sort of intimacy, and I would have much preferred to be alone. But experience in Sŏkp'o had taught me that our Western ideas about privacy were almost completely incomprehensible to villagers, and in any case I was much too tired to protest and risk offending my host.

The fire had evidently been well stoked in my honor; the hot floor was really hot. The thin mat under me provided little insulation, and for a while I turned restlessly, thinking of the inquisition. But the Korean hot floor has been perfected over thousands of years, ever since neolithic times, and when I woke up the next morning my hips were not singed; in fact, I had the same easy, loose feeling as in Teacher Yi's *sarangbang*—as if someone had given me a massage during the night.

Explaining that I had eaten a great deal very late for supper the night before, I begged Mr. Kim's wife to give me only a small portion of rice for breakfast, and she complied. Her husband was horrified when the meal tray came in and scolded her fiercely, but I managed to divert his attention by bringing out some of the PX supplies acquired the day before as presents: candy for the children, pipe tobacco for the old man, and cigarettes for Mr. Kim and his brother.

Nearly everyone in the hamlet gathered to send me off, and there was some further depletion of my supply of chocolate bars, since word had gotten around to the children of other households. Someone helped me with my pack, and a teenager was delegated to show me the right path. Everyone bowed. I tried to reciprocate; it must have been grotesque with that heavy load.

The path was muddy, and every leaf and blade of grass was still wet. But the sun was out, and a soft glowing mist hung over the landscape. Young rice plants shimmered restlessly everywhere against the bright water. There were no more high passes to cross to the westward, and if I couldn't quite see the ocean yet, at least I could smell it on the light breeze that came up the valley. The pack felt good on my back as I headed for Sŏkp'o, elated by the simple pleasures of rustic hospitality. I felt like the hero of some medieval tale out to seek adventure on a spring morning.

4

Settling In II

In spite of the advantages of being Teacher Yi's guest, I had thought about finding a place of my own right from the start. It seemed obvious that I should live in the Big Hamlet, a half mile or so to the north across the sandspit with the school, the store, the harbor, and the *sulchip*. The Big Hamlet was the core area for two of Sŏkp'o's four lineages and contained almost twice as many households as the Yi neighborhood. And I realized that if I wanted to look at the village as a whole, I would have to get away from my cozy relationship with the predominantly agricultural Yi gentry.

But most of all I needed more space so that my two older children could come and join me. My wife, who is Korean, was living in Seoul with her parents, two sisters, a brother, and our three children. The youngest was only eight months old, and my wife was not at all eager to leave the relative luxury and security of the city for an isolated village where there was no electricity, running water, or access to a doctor. But I had some sort of vague idea that the people of Sŏkp'o would find me more appealing as a family man, and besides, I missed the children. We decided that my wife's next younger sister, who had just finished college, would come down with my four-year-old daughter, Kim, and two-year-old son, Richie, as soon as accommodations were available.

The trouble was that we would need at least two rooms, and no household in the Big Hamlet had that much space to spare. The solution, which at first seemed outrageously extravagant, turned out to be simple. I would just build a new house. The idea had first come up during my third week in the village, when, after helping all afternoon with the roof on the house being built next door, I asked Teacher Yi about construction costs. His estimate was startling. Everything, including materials, the wages of a carpenter and his helper, the plasterer, and all the food, liquor, and tobacco for volunteer labor would come to no more than four hundred dollars. Since my house would be smaller, he thought three hundred would be enough. (At that time a small house in Seoul cost the equivalent of nearly ten thousand dollars, while three hundred was only a fraction of what we had to pay for the privilege of renting one.) It seemed too good to be true, but, as Teacher Yi explained further, building a house made sense. Posts, beams, rafters, and the roof ridgepole were all made of local red pine. The cutting of large trees was strictly controlled by the government. But ways could always be found to get around the local authorities. And besides, a Korean farmhouse doesn't require really big timbers. The wattle and daub construction of the walls and partitions required only mud and sticks, while the roof was thatched with locally produced rice straw. Flat stones set in mud formed the hot flue system under the floors that keeps Korean farmhouses warm. Since country houses had no electricity, plumbing, or glass, nothing was needed from outside the village except a few nails, translucent paper for the doors, a couple of bags of cement, and the thick oiled paper that would cover the floors. Most of the cost of a house was labor, and in Sŏkp'o labor was almost free.

I had already found a favorite spot on a sunny southern slope overlooking the Big Hamlet where I would stop occasionally to write notes, sketch, or just enjoy the landscape. There was a clump of four pine trees framing the view along the coast to the south and a small barley field where the slope leveled out for twenty yards or so. The place seemed ideal for a house. When I asked Teacher Yi about it he said, "The owner of that field is my cousin by marriage, and I know he needs the money. I will ask him about it." A few days later Teacher Yi took me over to the Big Hamlet to meet the cousin, Kim Ŭigon, who was waiting for us on his veranda. Kim Ŭigon was in his forties, and like all the fishermen, his face was very dark and deeply lined. His close-cropped, bristly hair and terrible teeth gave him a distinctive, raffish look,

Kim Ŭigon's house leaned away from the wind and in places was streaked with soot where the chimney and the hot floor system needed repair. The thatch was old and gray and rotting; trash littered the courtyard. His wife seemed tired and sullen, as if overwhelmed by all the children and the squalor. But the makkŏlli was good and the roasted eel that came with it excellent and plentiful. Dirty children squabbled around us until Kim Ŭigon shouted at them with practiced fury. Apparently the seven-year-old girl was tired of carrying her small brother around on her back, but he would start to wail each time she tried to put him down. A swarm of flies left the fish heads on the ground and attacked our eel and kimch'i. I had never seen a courtyard like this in the Yi neighborhood. Among the Yis, even the houses of the poor were well kept. In fact, they were likely to be particularly neat, because the people who lived in them had so few possessions.

The demands of hospitality having been satisfied, we strolled up the hill and squatted at the edge of the small barley field as we talked about the shortage of land in Sŏkp'o and how there was never enough grain to go around. Kim Ŭigon was successfully reinforcing my growing guilt at the idea of taking his barley field out of cultivation. He insisted that my prospective house site had the highest barley yields in this part of the village. Also, he was particularly fond of it because it was close to his house. Feeling that I was being set up to pay an outrageous amount, I was relieved finally to hear that this pearl of barley fields would only cost the equivalent of about forty dollars. It was, in fact, a very high price by local standards, but I didn't find that out until much later.

After the land price was settled, Kim Ŭigon began to develop his next objective. "I will take care of everything for Your Honor. I will buy the logs for the posts and beams, although they are very hard to get just now. I will personally select the stones for your hot floor and supervise the installation. I will see to it that only the finest new straw is used for thatch, and I will go to town to get the cement. Just leave everything to me. I will hire the carpenter and the plasterer. It will all go smoothly. I am on good terms with everybody."

I was surprised when Kim Ŭigon pulled a stub of pencil and a grimy, torn piece of paper out of his pocket and began writing down a list of materials and estimated prices. He belonged to the generation of villagers who were almost completely illiterate. It turned out that he had attended the local Confucian school for two or three years as a small boy. Also, he had gone to Japan as a laborer during the Second World War and claimed to have been a construction foreman. In any case, his gnarled and skin-cracked hand produced coherent writing.

My impressions of Kim Ŭigon were all bad. He was obsequious and at the same time insistent—overwhelmingly insistent. When he talked, he came too close, and his voice was too loud. He used excessively honorific language. He smelled of rotting teeth and years of heavy drinking. He treated his wife and children with crude and practiced contempt. But Teacher Yi seemed to approve of the arrangement, and if there was one thing that I was sure I could count on, it was Teacher Yi's goodwill and advice. I still had more to learn about the force of Korean kinship loyalty.

Another problem was that I wanted to handle the house building arrangements myself. The anthropologist is usually prying into things that people do not particularly want to reveal to a stranger. The house seemed like a good opportunity for me to deal with individuals and groups in the village on a more normal basis. Although I tried to fend off Kim Ŭigon's insistence that he take complete charge of the house construction, he and Teacher Yi gradually wore me down. "Exalted Teacher," he said, "this is the slack season for fishing, and I can devote myself full time to Your Worship's house. You will never be able to get everyone to come and help the way I can." This was complete nonsense, but at the time I worried that he might be right. Then Teacher Yi chimed, "Mr. Kim has good connections and knows how to get things done. He could be a great help to you." I finally gave in.

As it turned out, everything cost more than it should have, and Kim Ŭigon managed to make money for himself on nearly every transaction connected with the building. Discussions turned into long, drawn-out drinking sessions, at which he gained stature by treating everyone ostentatiously with my money. The money was never enough. "To find the best stones, we have to go across the bay and that means hiring a boat. If the Honorable Teacher will just give me 20,000 *wŏn* more, everything can go ahead on schedule." Kim Ŭigon was resilient and irrepressible, winning most of the time. If one scheme was thwarted, he quickly came up with another.

I had my victories, too. I made an ally of the carpenter, and as long as we planned and worked together, we were able to block Kim Ŭigon's most outrageous ploys. Carpenter Mun was a quiet teetotaler who had little respect for Kim Ŭigon and refused to let him interrupt the work. He had his own secret sources and was able to get the pine logs for a good deal less than Kim Ŭigon's estimate.

Most satisfying of all was the affair of the glass door. This was one innovation that I insisted on from the start and that the villagers regarded as an outrageous luxury. I wanted a sliding glass door for the largest of our three rooms, all of which opened to the south onto the veranda. In a conventional farmhouse with paper-covered doors instead of windows, the inside is always dark, and I was determined to have at least one bright room. In rural South

Korea at that time only stores had glass windows or doors. The door would have to be made in town and this gave Kim Ŭigon a particularly attractive opportunity. There would be one trip to order it and another to pick it up. He would have to spend the night in town, since negotiating payment and arranging for transportation would take a long time. The cost was going up and up, and I had no idea how to keep things under control without a fight. In the middle of these difficult negotiations, Carpenter Mun came to me with the wonderful news that he had already ordered the door from a relative of his who was a woodworker in town. Kim Ŭigon accepted the setback with equanimity and moved right on to his next opportunity.

I can now see that I let him make a successful minor career out of my affairs. Throughout my stay in Sŏkp'o, Kim Ŭigon was constantly promoting deals, trying to find a way to inject himself into the middle of any situation where money changed hands or makkŏlli was flowing. As the eldest son of a well-to-do family he had inherited a good deal of land, but nearly everything had been consumed by drink and a series of disastrous fishing ventures. As Teacher Yi put it, "He has had an awful lot of bad luck." Known to be a drunkard and untrustworthy in financial matters, Kim Ŭigon could no longer work his guile on his fellow villagers. Still, he had a certain popularity and influence by sheer force of character, persistence, and the fact that he was always at the center of things. Articulate, clever, and manipulative, he was constantly on the move, looking for the right situation to exploit. He seemed to create excitement and trouble, and as long as the trouble was someone else's, people were tolerant.

What puzzled me a good deal was that even when I was really angry, the local system of social organization did not allow me to be on bad terms with Kim Ŭigon, or anyone else. There was no room for a permanent grudge. The villagers must often have been as bewildered by my behavior as I was by theirs. They knew when I was upset, but they usually didn't know why. My first instinct when things went wrong was to look for someone to blame. It had to be somebody's fault. In Sŏkp'o, however, the first reaction was to make allowances for human failure. Almost any misdeed could be explained by circumstances. The important thing was to smooth over the differences and get people to agree to do better in the future.

Kim Ŭigon even managed to convince the other villagers that he was my favorite—a constant, valued guide and the chosen instrument for carrying out my plans. I tried to avoid him, but he always turned up, certain I was glad to see him and confident that I was delighted to have him look after my affairs. Finally, because there was no other alternative, I just decided that if everyone else could put up with him, I could too. And somehow we did manage to stay on good terms, superficially at least, not only during the time I lived in Sŏkp'o, but also through the years, whenever I returned for a visit.

Once construction got started, it went quickly. By early June my house was nearly complete. The pine posts were really just small tree trunks with the bark removed. They were so bent and twisted that Carpenter Mun only squared them off in the places where horizontal beams were attached. It was a tricky job for him to get everything lined up and plumb, since he was dealing with curved pieces of wood. The completed frame was beautiful—a piece of folk sculpture, in which the rectangular house shape existed as an abstraction in and around the actual structure.

There was so much underemployment and curiosity in the village that more people usually turned out whenever there was a call for volunteers than were needed for work on the house. So we were also able to do some fancy landscaping—building up a hard-packed courtyard in front and hacking a place for the toilet shed out of the hillside in the rear. Kim Ŭigon did not stint on the food and drink, and when the momentum of collective goodwill started building up, I felt like a host at a highly successful lawn party.

Teacher Yi had said that everyone had the necessary skills to build a house. But I certainly didn't. The only time I excelled was in throwing balls of mud up to the gang at work on the roof. On the other jobs I only got in the way. Korean farmers have a distinctive wooden pack frame called a chige, that can be adapted to carrying different kinds of loads. I had seen them in use everywhere around the village for the transport of firewood, fertilizer, rice seedlings, fish catches, stones, manure, bags of grain, or any other heavy object. But I had no idea of the actual weight of the loads. Eager to "participate," I insisted on helping carry the dirt for the courtyard. A crowd gathered to watch. There was a loaded chige on the ground, propped up by a stick that forms a tripod with the two main pieces of the frame. The carrier has to squat down, remove the stick, put his arms through the straps, wriggle a little to get the balance right and then get up. I went through all these motions except the last. There was absolutely no way in the world that I could lift that load of dirt. I couldn't even get any upward motion started.

Figure 4.1 Roof ceremony. Learning to enjoy ceremonial drinking. (1966)

Figure 4.2 My first ethnological experience of village-wide cooperation—house building. (1966)

Since I was taller and huskier than the villagers and thought I was in good shape, it was a humiliating moment. But there was cheering and applause. Everyone was pleased that I had tried and delighted that I had failed. In a world where everything was always stacked against peasants, they could still take pride in their ancient skills.

With the aid of a tipsy local shaman, we all assisted at an impressive and exuberant two-stage ritual when the main roof beam was put in place. This was the only straight piece of wood in the whole house, and it was planed on all four sides. I had already been a part of the ceremonies when Yi T'aryŏng was building his new house near Teacher Yi 's *sarangbang*. It seemed strange to be in charge now, when I had been a gawking neophyte just a few weeks before.

To begin the ritual I placed a piece of paper between the beam and its support at the "head" end of the house where the kitchen is located. The Chinese characters for turtle and dragon were written on the paper for long life and good luck. Then I poured *makkŏlli* over the wood while murmuring an incantation to the effect that I wanted the house to be solid and durable.

Kim Ŭigon told me that I should also ask the pardon of any local spirits who might have been disturbed during the construction process. Then he added that I should try to placate the geomantic forces of "wind and water" in case any of the principles of proper site location had been violated. This last instruction seemed terribly abstract, and I wasn't altogether satisfied with the way I expressed my appeal. But since I did all this ten feet up in the air in a low voice in English, there was no way for the assembled crowd to judge my performance. Teacher Yi, Carpenter Mun, Kim Ŭigon, and I had another ceremony on the ground under the roof tree, and this time we poured *makkŏlli* for ourselves as well as for the house. More *makkŏlli* was brought, and the ceremony flowed outward to include all those present.

The second stage of the ceremony, which began after an hour or so of drinking and feasting was slightly more professional and much noisier. The shaman thumped a drum, chanted, cried out, and threw things. In the beginning I asked a lot of questions. But the analytic approach didn't seem to fit the rambunctious mood of the occasion, so I just drank along with everyone else and had a good time. The shaman placated powerful gods with offerings and supplications. Then his manner changed as he angrily expelled minor evil spirits; the villagers drank and danced, shouting insults and encouragement to the shaman and the spirits.[1] It was a good party—money well spent

Figure 4.3 My $300 house. A neighbor is harvesting soybeans. My thin straw roof is an indication of the newness of the house. (1966)

Figure 4.4 Looking northwest, threshing rice on an unirrigated rice field. (1966)

to get my house off to a good start and to create so much excitement, laughter, and goodwill.

I still felt a little guilty about displacing one very small barley field in a village that was short of grain, but neither Kim Ŭigon nor anyone else ever mentioned it. And there was explicit and grateful recognition that I had injected almost 150,000 wŏn (about $400) into the local economy. People did wonder about the house site, though. In the several hundred years that the place had been settled, no one had ever built a house up on the hill overlooking the Big Hamlet. Water would have to be carried up a couple of hundred yards from the nearest well, and there were ominous predictions about the ruinous effect of southwest storms on the exposed mud walls. This did, in fact, turn out to be a problem when high winds drove the rain in horizontally under the eaves. It was easily solved, however, by hanging rolled up reed mats from the ends of the rafters and then lowering them to keep out the storm-driven rain.

Shortly after the house was finished, my choice of site was vindicated. A well-known geomancer had come all the way from the county seat to pick out a gravesite for his kinsman in the northernmost hamlet of the village. Having taken the path that led by my house, he insisted on stopping to greet me. After bowing and warmly shaking my hand in both of his, he said, "No one in this backward place has enough learning to choose a site like this. I am delighted that you Americans also know the principles of wind and water." The new house was officially designated as auspicious.

The house had been built too late in the year for swallows to nest under the deep eaves, as they did everywhere else in the village. I was always startled and a little envious at other people's houses when the birds swooped in for a landing inches from my head. But I took great pride in my new house, even though it still had a raw quality, with lingering smells of newly sawn wood and fresh rice straw thatch from the last harvest. It lacked the patina of age and use, and in the dry weather of early summer a few cracks appeared in the plaster. But the whitewashed mud walls contrasted smartly with the wooden beams and rafters, and everything gleamed in the sunlight.

The branches of my pine trees framed a view of the ocean to the southwest, and their slim, crooked trunks served as end braces for stacking our fuel supply. The villagers hauled wood for household fires down from the mountains in huge bundles lashed to pack frames. Carrying as much as their own weight, they staggered along, dwarfed by the size of these loads. Since the cutting of trees was strictly controlled, they only burned the lower branches and twigs gleaned from the ground—kindling by my standards. But it worked fine. The twigs and pine needles made a hot fire in the kitchen that lasted just long enough to cook the rice and boil soup.

My kitchen had been dug down into the hillside at one end of the house so that its dirt floor was about four feet below the level of the veranda and living quarters. In this way the cooking fire could also be used to heat the flues under our rooms. Next to the kitchen was our main room (with the glass doors), where I slept with the children, and where we spent most of our time in bad weather. Alongside that was a smaller room for my sister-in-law and our household helper. These rooms had no furniture. At the other end of the house, farthest from the kitchen, I had a tiny study with a ramshackle, homemade table and chair. A few yards behind the house there was an outhouse, where the "plumbing" consisted of a board laid over a cement pit. The construction here was of rough poles, with thatch used for the roof, walls, and door.

In good weather during the day the veranda (toemaru) was the center of family life. Raised about two feet above the packed dirt courtyard, it was made of wide boards that gradually darkened in color and took on a dun shine with daily use and cleaning. The veranda extended along the southern side of the house forming an outdoor sheltered area under the eaves about twelve feet long and four feet wide. At one end there was a small square opening to the kitchen through which trays of food could be passed. We left our shoes below in the dirt to keep the veranda as clean as the interior. At the end of a summer day, in the rich light of the setting sun, the breezy toemaru was a fine place to eat supper, play with the children, or write up the day's activities.

Kim and Richie, accompanied by their aunt, Hi Young, and a maid, Kyung Sook, together with piles of baggage, had made a sensational arrival in mid-June. I had gone up to Seoul, planning to bring everyone back with me by train, bus, and on foot. But during my stay in the city I met the same Korean friend who introduced me to "rustic pleasures" on the trip to Mohang some months before, and it turned out that his brother owned a forty-foot motor launch. It was all decided with one impulsive phone call. We would travel the sixty-five sea miles from Inch'ŏn (the seaport for Seoul) to Sŏkp'o by yacht, thus sparing the children the rigors of the long and tiring trip by land.

Since neither my friend's brother nor his launch captain had ever been out of the Inch'ŏn harbor area, I was afraid that finding Sŏkp'o after cruising along the deeply and erratically indented coast for five or six hours was going to be a problem. Fortunately, I had my sketch book with me, containing drawings of the coast that I had made from fishing boats off shore. It all worked out perfectly. The distinctive, jagged land forms of Sŏkp'o were easily recognizable, and we had no trouble finding the harbor entrance.

Even though we were not expected, a good sized crowd had gathered on the jetty by the time the launch was tied up. Someone out on the point by the harbor entrance had spotted us coming in and alerted the community. The villagers were truly astonished, and the rumor circulated that my wife must be a relative of the prime minister. The idea that there could exist a boat that size with an engine for purely recreational use was beyond their powers of imagination.

In rural South Korea, moving into a new house is another occasion when the machinery of community cooperation swings into gear, and we were not allowed to carry anything from the boat up the hill. Well-meaning neighbors even tried to carry Kim and Richie, but this first cross-cultural encounter with my family was not a success. The children fought and screamed until they were back on their own feet, and after that the astonished villagers tended to leave them alone except for visits by women and girls—more out of curiosity than anything else.

NOTES

1. He was not really a professional shaman. Self-taught and usually drunk, he was openly derided by villagers. Nevertheless, he performed from time to time.

5

Getting Involved

Administering my little household, sailing my boat, fishing, roaming the hills along the coast, and sampling the food and drink of generous neighbors sometimes threatened to fill up all my time. My small family quickly settled into a fairly normal routine. The children loved the ocean and played endlessly in the clean sand of empty beaches. Their favorite place, facing west towards China, was an inaccessible indentation in the cliffs at high tide. But as the water ebbed, white sand emerged, and we could get to it by scrambling over wet rocks. Here the beach sloped so gradually that the children could wade out more than 150 yards and still keep their heads above water.

Kyung Sook made friends with girls her own age at the well below our house while washing clothes and gossiping. My sister-in-law, Hi Young, had a little more trouble fitting in because of her anomalous status. As an unmarried young woman from outside the village her prestige was low, but as a university graduate and close relative of an illustrious foreigner, Hi Young had a unique, even glamorous aura that was completely outside the villagers' normal system of rank. One well-to-do family in the Big Hamlet startled us by proposing that she marry their eldest son.

Each morning, while eating breakfast on my sunlit, breezy veranda, I had the renewed feeling of having somehow stepped into a scroll of a Ming landscape. There I was, a tiny figure sitting cross-legged, looking impassively out across the water to the misty mountains in the distance. Peasants with straw hats toiled in rice fields below, while junks moved with immense deliberation across the bay beyond. Probably the only truly appropriate activity in this setting would have been to get drunk and write poetry, but it was too early in the day.

The big difference between my life and the abstract, two-dimensional world of Chinese landscapes was that I was required at some point to get down off my veranda and become involved with those people in the distance who worked in the fields and on the boats. There was a stack of empty notebooks in my "study" waiting to be filled with analytical observations concerning village behavior patterns and social organization. Even though I had numerous encounters every day with all sorts of people and wrote everything up in detail in my field notes, it was becoming impossible to pretend that this easygoing existence had much to do with systematic ethnographic investigation. I had to get to work.

Anthropologists, particularly English social anthropologists with extensive colonial experience in Africa and Oceania, have written elaborate guides to help the beginner get started with fieldwork. I had read some of these in graduate school, admiring the experienced ethnologist's perseverance and resourcefulness under trying circumstances. I remembered their useful instructions for mapping a village, systematically recording the grammatical structure of a previously unstudied, never-written language, uncovering the murky secrets of kinship structure, avoiding malaria, and developing strategems for politely refusing nasty native delicacies.

But these guides were not much help. I had an excellent US Army topographic map derived from aerial photographs taken during the Korean War that indicated every house, as well as paths, rice fields, forest land, but also ten-foot contour lines. Korean grammar and phonemics had already been scientifically analyzed by superbly talented linguists when England was just emerging from the Dark Ages. Lineage and family organization were of such obsessive interest to nearly all elderly males in Sŏkp'o that it was hard to get them to talk about anything else. And the one time I got really sick, the cause was not mosquitoes but ghosts.

As far as native delicacies were concerned, aside from the surfeit of rice, getting enough to eat was our biggest challenge during the first few weeks in my new house. When I had lived by myself in Teacher Yi's guest room, food had never been a problem. On the contrary, I was fed too well. Now we were trying, not very successfully, to keep house on our own. Knowing that Sŏkp'o was very poor, we brought our own rice with us when we all came down on the boat together from Inch'ŏn. We had counted, however, on being able to buy all sorts of local products, especially greens, eggs, and seafood. After all, I had plenty of money, while the villagers had almost none.

Fish, oysters, octopus, clams, vegetables, and eggs from Sŏkp'o were all sold in modest amounts in the nearest small town on market days, but they were not available at the village store. There, you could buy shoelaces, pencils, kerosene, matches, candles, soap, school notebooks, dried squid, *makkŏlli*, *soju*, candy, and rubber shoes. And that was all. People ate their own fish and vegetables themselves, sold their goods in the market town, or exchanged goods on a customary basis with neighbors and close kin. The children complained about their diet of rice, powdered milk, roast squid, and cheap candy. Hi Young, who had always lived in the city, came back in tears from unsuccessful buying expeditions to the Big Hamlet, convinced that the villagers were hostile and trying to drive us out. In desperation we organized day-long trips to the market town. Kyung Sook joined a group of girls and gathered oysters on the rocks at low tide. After T'aemo helped me build an outdoor oven, I was able to make missile base bread. I also spent more time fishing, first from the rocks, and later out in the bay in my own boat. With the addition of fresh oysters and an irregular supply of fish and bread, our diet was much healthier and more varied, but there were still times when I thought we would have to become farmers and fishermen to survive.

Finally Kyung Sook found out from her oystering companions about the money taboo. Except for very large transactions such as the sale of land or a boat, there was strong prejudice against the use of money within the village. The idea seemed to be (although it was never stated explicitly) that all exchanges of goods among members of the community should take place on the basis of mutual help, cooperation, or the paying back of obligations. Something similar evidently also existed in Kyung Sook's native village in more vestigial form. All she could say was, "With certain people it's not right to use money; here, that includes everyone." Food was to be shared with neighbors and relatives, not sold to them. The only significant exceptions to the money taboo, in addition to the store, were the *sulchip*, where men flamboyantly treated each other by flinging very small bills and coins around with abandon as symbols of their generosity and disdain for petty material concerns.

The people of Sŏkp'o may have been reluctant to use money, but they were extremely conscious of obligations and indebtedness. In their daily lives the villagers were constantly involved with members of other households, and much of this involvement had to do with lending, borrowing, giving, taking, helping each other out, and joining forces to accomplish heavy work. Everything had to be repaid sooner or later. Everyone was so enmeshed with nearly everyone else in so many ways that the network of remembered

obligations and claims was complex, and no two people were likely to calcu-
late the continuing balance between them in exactly the same terms.

I was able to start tapping into this system of more or less balanced obligations thanks to my supply of medicine and powdered coffee and milk. The
footpath that passed by my gate came from the Big Hamlet below and continued on over the hill behind my house, leading eventually to two other small
hamlets and some scattered houses at the extreme northern end of the peninsula. Because it angled steeply past the house, there was one point along
the path where a passerby could look over the flimsy, makeshift hedge and
under the pine branches directly into our courtyard. As a rule, all but the
poorest Korean farmhouses have a substantial hedge or wall for privacy, and
a couple of my neighbors had already suggested that I would probably want
to put up a higher and sturdier barrier. But since this would have meant cutting off both the view and the breeze, I preferred exposure.

Not that many people walked by anyway. Children were too small to see
over the hedge, although they would sometimes jump up to get a quick look
on their way to and from school. Adults for the most part discreetly kept
their heads straight ahead as they passed by. Gradually a special custom
developed, however, among some of the middle-aged and older men, as it
became known that I regularly served coffee and even, on certain occasions,
whiskey, to visitors. If someone wanted to stop and, as the Koreans say,
"play" at my house, he would pause in the path just at the place of maximum
visibility until he caught my eye and then give a hearty greeting that I could
not ignore. This was the signal for me to invite him in for coffee. Once one
person had stopped by, others were likely to join us, so I could count on
attracting small groups of neighbors two or three times a week for the coffee
hour. Several men from other hamlets who had no ostensible reason for
crossing over the hill at that particular time of day also turned up, but none
of them became regulars.

Most villagers did not really like the taste of coffee, at least at first, and
they told me so quite plainly; it was the sugar they craved. There were two
coffee shops at the nearest town, a place with a population of about 2,500,
that Sŏkp'o villagers might visit once a month or so to buy or sell goods at
the market and to meet relatives or friends from other parts of the region.
These coffee shops represented the cutting edge of cultural modernization in
rural life. Cattle brokers, the police chief, the head of the farmers'

cooperative, local officials, and other notables used them as regular meeting places. The waitresses flirted with customers during the day and could be persuaded by money, charm, or both to accommodate them at the inn at night. Very few Sŏkp'o residents had either the money or the sophistication to go to such places, so my veranda provided a free and convenient substitute for the town's more glamorous pleasures.

Hi Young and Kyung Sook were not always pleased at having guests just as they were trying to get supper ready for the children, but for me these sessions were ideal. I could listen to the latest news and gossip and ask whatever questions were left over from the day's informal investigations. More than this, though, it gave me a profoundly satisfying sense of being part of the local scene. The villagers evidently enjoyed themselves, and I certainly had no objection to bribing them with coffee and whiskey. It was a great deal easier than hunting them down and pestering them with questions at their own houses. I had stumbled on a new form of "sympathetic, participant observation"—a Westernized *sarangbang* of my own.

My visitors were more circumspect, though, than the regulars had been at Teacher Yi 's *sarangbang*. If I showed an interest in rumors of scandal or anything else that my guests thought reflected badly on Sŏkp'o's reputation for upright human heartedness, their first reaction was to deny that any such event had taken place or that a particularly shameful situation even existed. For example, Kyung Sook would come back from the well with a story about a drunken brawl involving a man and his second cousin once removed. Then, if I asked the coffee drinkers for details, they would pretend to be shocked, insisting that nothing like that could possibly occur between such close relatives. I had come up against a core Confucian value: among family members there must always be harmony.

There was also something more basic at stake—the cohesion of the community—that went beyond imported Chinese kinship codes. No matter what situation was under review, my guests were careful to avoid assigning blame or making accusations against any particular individual. This defense of the village's reputation for communal tranquility may have preserved their sense of collective virtue, but it caused me all sorts of anxiety. I wondered if my hard-won progress in Korean was evaporating, and at one point I even accused Kyung Sook of making up slanderous gossip. But, of course, Kyung Sook was not making anything up. There was plenty of personal conflict in

Figure 5.1 Mun lineage women returning from the well. Adolescent girl wears Western-style clothes. (1966)

Sŏkp'o, and a good deal of it existed among close relatives. It was a relief to discover that, in fact, there was a conspiracy of sorts to uphold the good name of the village and its inhabitants. Word had come all the way down from officials at the county seat that only good impressions should be given to the prying outsider, and the village chief had even held meetings with some of the more influential household heads to instruct them accordingly.

Front porch ethnography had other limitations as well. I asked questions constantly about everything I saw or heard. Sometimes the answers made sense to me; often they did not. The villagers had trouble understanding what it was that I wanted to know because it was all too obvious to them—rules of behavior, customs, relationships, obligations, and motives that they had taken for granted since childhood. I began to realize there was just no way to make up for the fact that I had not grown up in the village.

Three months had already gone by. At the end of the year, on returning home, I would have a book-length dissertation to write and a committee of demanding professors to face. Perhaps a more rigorous, quantitative method was necessary. My notebooks were gradually filling up with descriptions of congenial, hospitable individuals and halcyon communalism, but I seemed to be gathering very few firm facts. So I drew up elaborate outlines and prepared a long questionnaire that would, I hoped, elicit "hard data."

By now it was early summer, between the barley harvest and the first major weeding of the rice fields, when farmers enjoyed a couple of weeks of relative leisure. This seemed to be an ideal time to begin surveying the entire village with no-nonsense interviews on other people's verandas. I had 110 copies (the number of households in Sŏkp'o) of a questionnaire printed up in Seoul, and in the course of the next three months Hi Young and I visited nearly every family, asking more or less the same questions and writing down the answers on our forms. The statistical tables based on this data would, I thought, look impressive in the text or as appendices at the end of my dissertation, giving my work the kind of rigorous "scientific" underpinning that it needed.

Hi Young, a recent graduate in home economics of South Korea's largest and most prestigious women's university, was my research assistant. She was very shy and had to be dragged out to work nearly each day. I, too, wasn't at all happy about barging uninvited into strangers' courtyards, with no more excuse than that I wanted to ask prying questions. So we set out hesitantly, armed with excessively polite excuses and apologies; all were phrased in a high-flown Seoul dialect that was never used in the village. In addition I presented the lady of each household with a bar of laundry soap, on the advice of a Seoul University sociologist who frequently conducted survey research in the city. This, at least, made a favorable impression, since the soap was of higher quality than that available at the village store.

In spite of our timid approach, we stuck with the survey and spent long hours in the courtyards and on the verandas of our native informants. It wasn't until much later that I found out how much dismay and outrage we caused by asking for detailed information on income, property, debt, infant mortality, inheritance, second marriages, concubines, adoptions, and other personal matters. Only then did I understand how much tolerance and good manners had been shown to us, even though we were flagrantly violating local custom.

Many of the answers surprised me, and a little cross-checking afterwards revealed that most of the quantitative data on property, income, and debt was completely false. Word had quickly gotten around, so that after the first few interviews people knew what we were going to ask and fended us off with whatever answers they felt like making up on the spur of the moment. Watching me laboriously write down complete nonsense in the blank spaces of the questionnaire turned out to be a source of entertainment that helped compensate for the inconvenience of our visits. I didn't fully realize what was going on until some months later, when after an impromptu party had reached a fairly boisterous stage, two of the younger men engaged in a little skit in which they parodied my interview process, complete with probing questions and outlandish answers. It was a wild success.

At first I was puzzled and upset by the obvious discrepancies and evasiveness. As usual, it was Teacher Yi who explained. From ancient times, bitter experiences had taught the villagers to be close-mouthed with strangers, particularly regarding financial and political matters. Oppressed and exploited by tax collectors, the police, and other official parasites for thousands of years, Korean peasants had adopted secrecy as a survival tactic and learned to lie low and fend off outsiders as much as possible. In 1966, when a South Korean was asked something outlandish by a foreigner, the first reaction was likely to be in terms of observing proper etiquette. The thought, "What does this person want to hear?" was of far greater importance than "What do I really think about the issue?" The next concern would probably be, "Is there some way this conversation is likely to get me into trouble?" And then, of course, there were the brokers and manipulators, who would be thinking, "How should I answer this in order to make a good impression and turn the situation to my advantage?"

Among all these perspectives, objective truth had a relatively low priority. Teacher Yi also tactfully hinted at another problem. I had not considered the fact that since nearly everyone in the village talked more or less constantly about everyone else, no one wanted to reveal personal information that might provide ammunition for malicious gossip.

If getting accurate figures on land ownership and income was difficult, prying loose the villagers' innermost thoughts on more abstract topics proved to be nearly impossible, at least by a formal survey method. In addition to compiling statistics, I also wanted to use the survey to gather information about values and attitudes associated with work, savings, and the desire to get ahead. In other words, were Sŏkp'o villagers motivated to be innovative and achieve progress? What were the prospects for future development in Korea? It seems strange today, but in 1966 no one realized that a South Korean industrial "miracle" was already underway, or that the one thing that was not in short supply on the Korean peninsula was an almost universal and obsessive drive to succeed combined with the willingness to work hard. Korean bureaucrats in Seoul, American Embassy officials, and World Bank economists all clung to the conventional wisdom that Korean peasants were hopelessly conservative and would have to be somehow jolted out of their stagnant, traditional ways. It turned out to be very difficult to ask about such things in a way that made sense to the villagers or that provided me with useful answers. These question-and-answer sessions kept degenerating into the obvious, or I found myself telegraphing the reply I was looking for. A typical interview might go something like this:

Anthropologist. What kind of future do you hope for?

Villager. I want to buy more land [or a bigger, engine-powered boat], work hard, save money, and send my children to college.

Anthropologist. Would you like to try new and better ways to grow crops (or catch fish)?

Villager. Of course; please teach me some. Will you pay the cost of these new methods?

Anthropologist. Do you think some people here stubbornly cling to old-fashioned customs and ways of doing things?

Villager. Anything new and different costs money. I don't have any extra money, so I do everything the cheapest way I know how.

Anthropologist. Would you be willing to work harder, drink less, and save more if you were convinced that this would make you prosperous?

Villager. I work as hard as I know how. If I had more land I would work still harder. When the work is done, I have a bowl of makkŏlli. What is the point of living if you don't have a bowl of makkŏlli after hard work?

Anthropologist. Do you think people here spend too much time and money on ceremonies for their ancestors and on weddings and funerals? If they spent less, wouldn't they have more money for fertilizer or fish nets?

Villager. When people are poor like us they spend most of their money on food to stay alive. After that, they have to pay for seeds and fertilizer. The poor get their well-off relatives or neighbors to help pay for the weddings and other ceremonies.

Anthropologist. They told me at the County Administrative Office (Myon samusŏ) that even if the Nonghyop [the national agricultural cooperative] lends farmers money, most of them spend it on food and drink instead of investing it in more productive ways.

Villager. If we are hungry we spend it on food. If my son needs it for middle school, we eat less and spend it on school fees.

Anthropologist. But the loan is supposed to help increase agricultural production.

Villager. Only the rich can improve agricultural production.

Anthropologist. What would you do if you had two million wŏn [an astronomically large sum for a Sŏkp'o resident; equivalent in 1966 to about $6,000]?

Villager. That is more than I need, even to buy land and send my children to college. Can you get me a loan from America?

All this was good language practice, and it was certainly a startling conversational change of pace for the villagers. I still have all those questionnaires that we laboriously filled out, although the ink has faded, and the cheap paper is moldy and torn. I made little use of them. At the time, the fact that the villagers' answers seemed to be at cross purposes with the assumptions behind the questions I asked bothered me a good deal. It took a while before I realized that the problem was inherent in the survey method itself. The whole idea of asking subsistence farmers and fishermen a standard set of questions based on the hypothetical musings of middle-class intellectuals in cities ten thousand miles away made little sense. Basically, there were three things that governed the fortunes of an ordinary individual in Sŏkp'o in 1966. First, because of the shortage of land and capital and the village's geographical isolation, there were no economic opportunities available other than subsistence farming and fishing. Second, no one except the "rich" could afford to take any risks. Any kind of failure meant slipping below the subsistence level and falling into debt, which inevitably led to the sale of land. Third, the rural population was squeezed inexorably by a national system that paid low prices for agricultural products while charging high prices for fertilizer, pesticides, engines, nets, and all the other manufactured items that farmers and fishermen had to buy. In this context the issue of whether farmers were motivated to change their behavior and undertake innovative practices was irrelevant.

Even though our standardized questions elicited few accurate answers, nevertheless at some point people would always begin talking about the things that really interested them. And then, if we listened carefully and cross-checked what we heard in other households, we might learn something significant. For example, I eventually found out that the stereotype of the conservative peasant clinging to tradition was largely inaccurate. Farmers and fishermen were well aware of their backward technology, and most were desperately eager to learn new and better ways of doing things. They welcomed innovation, provided that they could afford it and that it worked. I was also surprised to discover that a high proportion of the population was blessed (or cursed) with a bold entrepreneurial spirit. On the basis of very little experience or knowledge, some people were ready to sell everything they owned and gamble on the latest get-rich-quick schemes. As a result, con men from the city had easy pickings, and investment disasters far outnumbered successes.

In the very long run, the answers of Sŏkp'o's farmers and fishermen to my strange questions taught me a great deal, and I wish now that I had studied those questionnaires more carefully and tried harder in my dissertation to describe the economic outlook of Sŏkp'o villagers. To simplify things, the villagers were right, and the vast majority of community development theorists throughout the world were wrong.

When ecological and economic conditions are sufficiently adverse, there is little that a really poor farmer or fisherman can do other than hang on and hope for a miracle. No amount of hard work, saving, or cooperation is likely to make a significant difference. Only an extraordinary stroke of luck or a wild gamble will pay off in this kind of situation. The kind of fundamental changes that allow subsistence farmers to earn more and save more have to come from outside, and only the rich and the powerful can initiate them.

Although the answers to my questions turned out to be almost useless, asking them gave us an excuse to sit for a while in the inner courtyard of each house and watch family life unfold around us. Children were fed, scolded, petted, and assigned small tasks. Daughters-in-law were reprimanded by the mistress of the house or shown social favor by her husband. Most of the time the home was full of cheerful good humor, but sometimes tensions developed and were resolved. Neighbors stopped by and joined in the interview discussions. News and gossip were exchanged, and there was laughter at earthy jokes. I learned to put my preconceptions and self-consciousness aside and concentrate on becoming a pure observer. As the weeks went by, I developed closer personal ties with my neighbors, and my involvement in the village system of reciprocity finally helped me solve my two most pressing problems: obtaining food and information.

Perhaps my "medical practice" was of even greater importance than free coffee on my veranda or visits to villagers' houses in developing closer relations with the people of Sŏkp'o. I know it was decisive in improving our food supply. During my last term at the university before leaving the United States, I had attended the Traveler's Course given by doctors from the School of Public Health for those of us who would be doing research overseas out of reach of medical care. My medical kit was full of fancy prescription drugs, among which an ointment called Vioform (hydrocortisone cream) was miraculously effective in getting rid of a nasty, thick crust that covered the scalps of several small boys in the neighborhood. After this treatment their mothers were convinced that I could cure anything, and people began dropping by with bad cuts, sick babies, and occasional burns. I was not at all happy about these new responsibilities and told anyone whose problem seemed at all serious to go to town and see a doctor. But Sŏkp'o residents never did that unless they had a good deal of money (ruling out all but five or six of the 110 households) or were close to death. Those who finally did seek medical help at a town clinic or the provincial hospital in Sŏsan were usually so far gone that little could be done to help them. The patient was brought home to die, and family members then complained bitterly about the needless expense and incompetence of Western medical practitioners.

A couple of years before I went to Sŏkp'o, pharmaceutical plants in South Korea had begun producing antibiotics, and these, as well as other drugs, were just starting to be sold in the countryside by peddlers. Traditional herbal remedies, referred to as Chinese medicine (hanyak), were still the most widely used treatment for illness. When hanyak did not work, the people of Sŏkp'o turned to peddlers, shamans, their own resident anthropologist, and doctors—in approximately that order—depending on individual beliefs, resources, and current fashion.

Whatever the reasons, some of my regular coffee drinkers and patients began showing up alone at odd hours with quite different versions of incidents that had been brushed aside as of no importance during interviews or in conversations on my veranda. No one ever could figure out why in the world I wanted to learn about such unpleasant and sordid things as family quarrels, theft, and adultery. Nevertheless I made it clear that I did want to know, and quite a few people were beginning to be indebted to me, both because of the medicine and because they drank my coffee. Bit by bit, I began to acquire a much more complicated map of village relationships, "official" values, informal codes of conduct, and actual behavior. Whispered accounts of family quarrels and village scandals may have often been biased and distorted, but they certainly made me more sensitive to points of tension in village life. Equipped with this new perspective, I could go to other villagers, knowing enough to ask questions that could no longer be ignored.

The survey did a lot to quiet my conscience with regard to the problem of obtaining "hard data" and undertaking a "rigorous investigation." I was relieved when it was finished. It had become obvious to me that the more I tried to be "scientific," pushing the villagers to provide specific information in accordance with a preconceived, external paradigm, the less real progress I made. I took considerable satisfaction in the discovery that I could carry out my work better by just living tranquilly in Sŏkp'o in accordance with the villagers' expectations of "proper behavior," than by ardently following the demands of "social science."

To my delight, we also began receiving unexpected presents (usually delivered by a child with no message) of a few eggs, a fish, potatoes, or bunches of fresh greens. So part of the time we lived very well, while on other days we went back to rice, pickled cabbage, dried squid, and the children's complaints.

6

Getting There

It wasn't so far in distance from Seoul, perhaps only 150 kilometers, but in every other way going to Sŏkp'o was like falling over the edge of the farthest horizon. Every couple of months or so I would go up to Seoul from the village to see my wife and youngest child, eat steaks, take hot showers, and get rid of lice. After a few days of extravagant pampering and luxury I would then load up my rucksack with whiskey, batteries for my radio and tape recorder, and presents for the villagers and go back down (in Korean any time you leave Seoul to go anywhere, it is always "down") to the village. In 1966 there were four distinct stages to getting there, with the entire trip taking about ten hours. (Today it takes about three hours.) A subtle shift took place at each stage, transporting me (in a science fiction sense) farther and farther from the modern city. Every dimension, even time, was different. Gradually different rules applied, voices and dialect changed, clothes became more ragged, and the smell of unwashed bodies more pungent. All hurry eventually disappeared, money counted for less, manners improved, and ancient rules of respect for the aged took precedence over nearly everything else.

The first four hours of the trip were by way of a slow, ordinary train—crowded, dirty, noisy, and full of the camaraderie of travel. This stage served as a sort of cultural bridge between the metropolis and provincial towns. Most people who boarded the train were well provisioned with both food and drink. Travel was an adventurous break in the ordinary austere routine of life, and it was just as well to make the best of it.

Once we got moving, there was a certain enforced intimacy right from the start, because our knees and hips were all pressed tightly together on the hard, third-class benches. Most of my traveling companions took obvious pleasure in showing off the good things they had brought and sharing them

Figure 6.1 A member of the Yi lineage singing (chanting) sijo into the tape recorder. (1966)

with the foreigner. In return for the hard-boiled eggs, the dried squid, the pickled oysters in hot sauce, and the rice wrapped in seaweed that were continually thrust at me, I supplied *soju*, which was sold in small bottles at every station. The train jounced slowly along, making lots of stops, and it was easy to replenish the supply. After an hour or so of travel, the *soju* really loosened things up.

Everyone seemed to feel sorry for me. The idea of a foreigner traveling alone in a strange land seemed tragic to Koreans, who live in a world where nearly every aspect of life is determined by intricate networks of relatives, friends, and neighbors. They grieved for my presumed loneliness, and many of them were determined to do something about it. There were times when their attention and generosity became overwhelming, and I longed for the tranquil anonymity of the solitary traveler. But the only way to get that on the Seoul–Hongsŏng line was to travel second class (there was no first class), and the social anthropologist's creed of sympathetic participation usually (but not always) kept me from that.

On the train I discovered, or rather experienced, a close, although inverse, correlation between social class or status and *insim*. Passengers who wore coats and ties were townsmen. They were usually pale and plump, and either ate and drank by themselves or whooped it up on the train with colleagues. They left me alone. My companions on the third-class benches, however, were entirely different. They were always thin and burned dark by the sun. The skin on their hands was hard and deeply cracked. In South Korea in the 1960s most farmers were subsistence peasants, "subsistence" meaning that there were barely enough calories available in the village diet to sustain them during their long hours of hard work. But they could not ignore the socially deprived creature who sat among them. They shared their food. This kind of experience, multiplied over the years on South Korean trains, buses, inter-island boats, and footpaths in the mountains, has given me a sort of radical-populist outlook on South Korean society; I'm still a little prejudiced against the provincial middle class.

After four hours or so of *soju* and togetherness, I would usually be slightly light-headed when we reached Hongsŏng, a sleepy town made famous by being the site of a sixteenth-century battle against Japanese invaders. Dilapidated buses lined up in front of the railroad station, and the bus girls accosted each descending passenger as he or she got off the train. This was the beginning of travel stage two. As soon as I called out, "Sŏsan," the name of the county seat, I would be forcibly seized and marched off to a Sŏsan bus. There were always several Sŏsan buses competing for passengers, and the powerful country girls who worked on them depended on brute force. I never really understood the reason for all the competitive hustling, because as far as I could tell, every bus was always crammed full by the time it left the sta-tion. It all seemed to be just a matter of style. Shouting, physical jostling, and the continuous sense of activities nearing explosive crises were integral parts of bus travel anywhere in South Korea.

The roads were terrible, the equipment ancient, and the drivers men of reck-less daring. The almost inevitable result was that a major mechanical disaster would take place at some point during the trip. It wasn't just that tires went flat, or that the engine coughed and stopped, although that happened, too. What was more typical, as we careened along the roads of South Ch'ungch'ŏng Province, was the breaking of axles or the snapping of drive shafts. Then, after all the passengers had uncomplainingly gotten out of the bus and made them-selves comfortable along the roadside, the driver and his teenaged assistant would proceed to jack up the bus and fix it. With a little more foresight I might have predicted the outburst of industrial dynamism in South Korea that was about to startle the world, just from watching eighteen-year-olds with a primary school education replace drive shafts on remote country roads.

Getting up and running again was not always so easy. During the hour or two that was required for repairs, several of the adult male passengers would have dispersed among the nearby farm hamlets, looking for *soju* or *makkŏlli*. The general rule seemed to have been that they should stay within range of the bus's horn, a fixture that never broke down and that the driver leaned on long and hard when we were finally ready to leave. But the rule was not always strictly observed, and in any case, the sense of hearing of some of these passengers, along with most of their other senses, might have become somewhat dulled in the meantime. If the missing men had women or children traveling with them, they would be sent out to scour the countryside. Otherwise, it was the miracle-working young mechanic who had to hunt them down. Usually, when the missing passengers finally returned to the bus and got aboard, it was with the dignified air of having been somewhat rudely and unnecessarily interrupted while carrying out important affairs.

As a result of these interruptions we usually arrived in Sŏsan too late to catch the last bus for the coast, so I would have to spend the night at an inn. Sŏsan, the county seat with a population of about 20,000, had five or six inns and about the same number of coffee shops. In addition, there were a few restaurants and innumerable sulchip. A restaurant in a South Korean provincial town in 1966 was not just a place to go for food. It also supplied young female companions, who poured makkŏlli, joked and flirted with the patrons, and performed songs and dances. The inns also served food, but it was simpler, much less expensive, and often tastier than at the restaurants. The sulchip, although they did not provide a regular meal with soup and rice, had all sorts of good things to eat.

All these small establishments together offered a rich nightlife that was easily accessible to someone whose research grant was in US dollars. I conducted informal investigations into folk and classical music, I even learned how to do some of the dances, and I got to know several very attractive young women, all thanks to the fact that the Sŏsan bus kept breaking down and arriving an hour or two late.

A traditional South Korean inn is usually U- or L-shaped—a long, low, tiled-roof building surrounding a large central courtyard. A four-foot-wide wooden veranda, sheltered by the deep eaves of the roof, runs all the way around the building. And the rooms, which are small and square, open directly onto it. This creates a friendly, almost communal arrangement. Guests sit out on the veranda in their pajamas and read the paper, smoke, drink, or chat. The doors of individual rooms are only closed at night for sleeping. Otherwise, guests are all together, spaced at intervals in a large, connected, semi-outdoor space. Consequently it is easy, almost inevitable, in fact, to make some sort of contact with the person in the next room. Even today in the big, international hotels in Seoul, Koreans who have come up from the provinces usually tend to leave their hotel room doors open when they are there during the day. It's a nice custom. They don't want to be shut up in boxes, isolated from the rest of the world.

After the other patrons heard me talking Korean to the inn waitresses, one or two of them would almost always come over and sit on my portion of the common veranda, in order to keep me from "being lonely" (*honja kasiuu*, literally "are you alone"). In this way I learned quite a bit about the local Sŏsan cattle markets, the difficulty farmers had in getting enough fertilizer, the booming market for fish, and (more rarely and in very guarded terms) hostility towards the government in Seoul. Sometimes my new acquaintances asked me to join them on joint expeditions into town after supper in search of entertainment.

In the morning at the inn we washed and brushed our teeth together in the courtyard, where there was a well, a couple of hollowed-out gourds for dipping out water, and a half dozen large basins. If I asked for hot water to shave, the inn girls would cheerfully supply it, but it was never available as a matter of course. The courtyard before breakfast was crowded, noisy, and sopping wet. Koreans living in small towns usually only wash their hands, head, and feet on a daily basis, but they do that with enormous gusto. Unfortunately most of the men had the habit of leaving the basins full of dirty rinse water from their feet. If I wasn't an early enough riser to get a clean basin, the basins would be covered with a brown-gray scum that was very hard to remove. I always felt foolish scrubbing my basin each morning before I used it. No one else bothered to do that, and the girls laughed at me, saying that I was trying to steal their jobs.

There was also the long, drawn-out throat clearing that everyone indulged in each morning. As a result, the courtyard was heavily spotted with gobs of phlegm that had been dredged up with enormous, cacophonous effort. It was all a little like being in the army again—everyone together in close quarters washing and brushing teeth and spitting on the ground. At such times Koreans ignored each other, thereby constructing a kind of fictive privacy that was almost as good as the real thing.

Then came breakfast, and that was always a pleasure. Steaming meat soups, roasted fish, rice, and kimch'i were at the heart of those wonderful meals. In addition each breakfast tray was covered with ten or twelve small dishes filled with various vegetables and dried, salted, or boiled fish and shellfish. Nothing has ever tasted better. American breakfasts, especially those advertised as "hearty," are just heavy, greasy, and routine by comparison.

The third stage of travel to Sŏkp'o comprised two half-hour bus rides, the first from Sŏsan to T'aean, and the second from T'aean to Mohang—a fishing village on the coast that was the end of the line. If the Hongsŏng–Sŏsan buses had been dilapidated, these were totally decrepit, continuing to function only because cheap labor was available in unlimited quantity to make endless stop-gap repairs. Windows were stuck, either open or shut; pathetic curtains, nearly black with age, bounced with the vehicle's violent motion; and the seats steadily exposed more and more of their inner organs to public view.

On one trip, thanks to an introduction by a mutual friend in Seoul, I was entertained in Sŏsan by the president of the local bus line. At some point in the evening I tried to find out why the quality of bus service should deteriorate so radically as one proceeded farther into the countryside. Under the circumstances my question was rude, but the bus company entrepreneur turned it aside easily, saying that rural people were poor and couldn't afford to pay much for transportation, forcing him to use old equipment. But I figured it all out later and determined to my satisfaction that the actual principle under which he operated was quite different: rural people have no power and don't complain; therefore, the bus company can get away with anything. In terms of money per kilometer, poor farmers paid just as much as more affluent customers on the major intercity routes.

There was no space for baggage on these rural buses, but many of the passengers had enormous loads. Chickens, small pigs, bags of grain, irrigation pumps, pails of raw oysters, fish nets, an occasional black goat, plus mounds of other, indeterminate belongings, clogged the aisle. At the frequent stops, the young and agile could enter and leave by an open window, but most passengers had to struggle over the mass of boxes, livestock, and bundles, urged on by the furious impatience of the driver.

In addition to an engineer-mechanic, there was often a bus girl on board who called out the destinations in a nasal sing-song voice and collected the fares. Her job was also to help passengers on and off the bus. In practice, however, this usually amounted to a frenzied pulling and prodding in an effort to hurry people up and contain the driver's rage. The drivers, aristocrats of the road who had authority and prestige at least as great as that of a 747 captain, were unable to control the chaos that occurred at each stop, and this seemed to be a source of endless and deep frustration. It puzzled me a little that the same scenario unfolded each time I rode the bus. Didn't the driver know that the peasants would have a lot of baggage and that the bus would be overloaded with everything dumped in the aisle? Why did he always get so upset about it? Didn't the bus girl know that old people were likely to resent being handled by a teenager as if they were pieces of firewood? The same kinds of wild arguments always seemed to break out as the helpless passengers were put through the obstacle course that ran down the center of the bus.

It took me a long time to discover that, as a rule, no one was really all that angry, and the excitement was just typical, appropriate behavior—the way things were on country buses. There were some real fights, though, usually between old people and the bus girl. The issue nearly always had to do with her lack of properly respectful language in trying to collect fares. An old man might have spent all his money in town (possibly most of it on makkŏlli) with nothing left for the bus. But he would get on anyway, counting on the deference that tradition demanded for his age. Or a grandmother might be furious at what she regarded as the rude and peremptory manner of the bus girl and refuse to pay on the grounds that propriety had been violated. The bus girl in turn would become upset, and her language and manners would become even more disrespectful. At some point the other passengers would join in, almost always in support of the old people. I have seen bus girls cry in frustration, caught between their allegiance to the traditional values of respect for the elderly and their desire to do a good job by enforcing the bus company's regulations. It is possible too, that the missing fares came out of their meager salaries.

Children and goats pissed on the floor, and we were frequently airborne, as the driver desperately tried to make up lost time. Usually I had a seat, because I didn't wait until the very last minute to come running for the bus just as it started, the way most of the other passengers did. If I was standing, however, there was likely to be at least one man of refinement on board who, while not getting up himself, would point out to one of the women that she should give the American "guest" her seat. The crowding was so great that it was always a relief when the drive shaft snapped, or we had to stop at a military checkpoint. Sometimes all of us had to get out and hike a few hundred yards so that the tired bus could get up a steep hill. Now, of course, the roads are paved, and the buses hardly ever break down. The arrogance and daring of the drivers has not changed, though, so that when there is an accident, the much higher speeds usually result in fatalities.

Our next stop, T'aean, was a place of special interest. There was a big dirt square in the middle of town where the buses maneuvered, and overlooking the square were three second-story coffee shops. Patrons could sit up there and talk over coffee or tea, while observing the panorama of small-town activity below them. Travelers could watch the bus crews getting ready and then board at the last moment. Since coffee was not served at the inns, I was always eager for a cup by the time I had survived the Sŏsan–T'aean section of the bus trip. It was usually instant Maxwell House, obtained from the nearest US military installation through various informal transactions.

Activity inside the coffee shops was extraordinary. These places functioned as social and recreational centers for the influential men in town. The girls who worked and lived there were often part-time prostitutes at night, and during the day their job was not only to serve coffee but to sit and talk with the male customers. Actually, "sit and talk" was a euphemism for the combination of free-for-all wrestling and foreplay that went on a good deal of the time. Men reached inside the women's dresses or up under their skirts almost casually, as if adding sugar to their coffee. This was usually countered by a squealing and writhing protest that only attracted more attention. While extremely crude and direct, there was at least a sexual rationale for such behavior. But occasionally the sport changed inexplicably into a kind of indoor football practice. A woman might playfully hit one of the men after an excessively funny remark, and he would respond by slamming her into the wall. It seemed like a punishing way for the women to drum up trade. Coffee shops operated under more or less the same system in most provincial towns, but for sheer gratuitous violence against women, T'aean seemed to be in a class by itself.

From T'aean to the coast the buses were even older and more worn out. On the other hand, they weren't driven as hard, partly because the road was much worse, but also because nearly all the frantic haste of the scheduled runs between towns had disappeared. There was no real urgency in rural villages in South Korea in 1966. It didn't matter when the bus left or arrived, and there was no reason for the driver to pretend that it did. Would-be passengers waited by the roadside for as long as it took the bus to get there. None of them had watches or clocks anyway. If someone missed the bus, he could always go to a kinsman's house nearby to pass a few hours before the next one came along (there were two a day), or he could go home and try again the next day.

In addition to the lack of urgency, two other factors distinguished the T'aean–Mohang bus. It smelled strongly of fish and shellfish, and there would always be people on it whom I knew. Their greetings had a special warmth, giving me a nice feeling of being part of the local scene. I think I had some sort of fantasy that we brave souls from Sŏkp'o, who lived together in impoverished isolation at the very tip of the peninsula, shared a special bond. On the other buses and even to some extent on the train, there was always a certain sense of "what are you doing here?" I was a curiosity, well off the beaten track followed by most foreigners. But now I was returning, if not "home," at least to the place where I lived and worked, and it was deeply satisfying to be hailed as someone who belonged.

All this travel by a lone foreigner on country buses did not escape the attention of the local authorities. I was not a tourist visiting Buddhist temples, and my travels had nothing to do with American military bases. Missionaries, who were the only non-Koreans likely to be living in rural areas, were all well-known and had their own Jeeps and converts to accompany them. Any other foreigner, who had a legitimate reason for being in the remote countryside would have had official status—meaning that they would not only have a Jeep but also a driver, an interpreter, and at least one accompanying local official. The Republic of Korea in the 1960s may not have been a totalitarian police state, but it was nevertheless a very tightly run operation, often referred to informally by foreign critics as a thinly disguised military dictatorship. The Democratic People's Republic of Korea in the North was still sending suicide commando forces South on raiding expeditions, and spy rings were being uncovered and the members executed every few months. The military authorities in the South regarded internal security as a life-and-death issue, a matter of national survival. Combat police detachments were everywhere, more powerful and much more ruthless in governing and supervising rural South Korea than the civilian administration.

Buses had to stop from time to time at regular check points, where beautifully groomed young policemen jumped aboard to check everyone's ID papers. It was always done with snap and polish and included polite but crisp, formal greetings and farewells. The policemen would usually treat my passport as a precious object, but it was obvious that they could not read English, and none of them ever checked to see if the visa was valid. Probably most had never seen a passport before. They must have dutifully reported my presence to their superiors, however, because it was not unusual for a man in a blue suit to board the bus a few stops further on down the line and find a seat either next to me or nearby. If he hadn't been able to get the seat beside me, he would at some point whisper a few words to my neighbor and take his place. I learned by heart the standard list of questions that suspicious foreigners are asked and could answer one step ahead of my interrogators. The only embarrassing thing about these encounters was the level of English displayed by the plainclothes agents. On the one hand I didn't want to humiliate them in public by not being able to understand their questions, but on the other I was thoroughly annoyed at being singled out for what I regarded as harassment.

These interrogations never occurred between T'aean and the coast, a stretch where I was well known and that was, in any case, more lightly policed. But on the way from Hongsŏng to Sŏsan, or if I was traveling all the way to Seoul by bus, I could usually count on at least one blue suit every other trip. On one occasion I was sitting next to a congenial, talkative farm wife who was explaining at length how farmers were cheated and mistreated by merchants and officials in small provincial towns. I was fascinated and began taking notes. A blue suit, who had been sitting across the aisle and one row in front, abruptly got up and told the woman to keep her mouth shut. Then he ordered her to get up and sat down in her place. By then someone else had taken his seat, so she had to stand.

I was furious. When the agent started with question number one, "What are you doing in this part of Korea?" I answered in Korean, "I am a North Korean spy." Then I pushed up the corners of my eyes to make them into slits and asked, "Can't you tell?" There was complete quiet on the bus. No one in his right mind ever joked or challenged the authorities on political matters in 1966, particularly with regard to North Korea. The other passengers must have been appalled. I think I had hoped for supporting laughter, but this kind of American irony doesn't translate into Korean as humor. There was only silence. The blue suit looked at me contemplatively for a long time before saying sadly, "You are angry."

The final stage of the trip to Sŏkp'o was on foot, at a pace slow enough so that I could savor the gradual turning back of time. There were two possible routes: a two-hour hike north along the coast from Mohang (where the bus line ended) and the somewhat shorter but much more hilly inland path.

The route along the coast from Mohang to Sŏkp'o led, at first, up a long, gradual slope through a grove of well-spaced pines and past the long, low, wooden Mohang middle school. Usually a few oxen and goats were tethered here under the trees. If I ran across groups of students going to school or on their way home, most of them would stop, bow stiffly, and shout out honorific greetings in a shrill and formal style. The girls were much shyer, but they too would bow, only from farther away, and their polite phrases were softly mixed with giggles. Obviously the teachers had given special instruction on how to cope with the foreigner. But there were also always a few who ducked into the trees when they saw me in order to avoid the encounter. At first I wondered if this represented some sort of personal hostility or anti-American feeling. Then one day I realized that if I had been a Mohang schoolboy, I would have been one of those who slunk away into the woods rather than demonstrate my good manners in public.

A couple of hundred yards beyond the school the trail forked, with the branch on the left leading up over the top of a hill and down a steep slope to the harbor. My path, which was less traveled, continued north among the sandy hills and scrub trees. Small, terraced rice fields were fitted into the hollows, wherever irrigation was possible. On my left there were expansive sand dunes covered with grass, and whenever the path climbed up over high ground, I could see over the dunes to the ocean and feel the wind.

After about fifteen or twenty minutes, the path joined a sandy Jeep track that crossed over the dunes. Cement cubes about ten feet high and twelve feet square began to dot the landscape, suggesting a system of fortifications designed to protect the magnificent beach against amphibious attack. What looked like gun emplacements were strung out behind the beach in irregular rows for nearly a mile, forming a broad band several hundred yards wide. On my first trip it took some time for reality to sink in. There were no glass windows or wooden doors, just rectangular openings in the concrete cubes. There was neither electricity nor people. The only clue to the frivolous nature of all this grim architecture was the fact that the cubes were painted in every conceivable color. The place is called Mallip'o, and in spite of the beauty of the natural setting, it would be an understatement to assert that in 1966 the Mallip'o beach resort lacked architectural charm. Closer to the water, the villas disguised as pill boxes gave way to inns, restaurants, bars, coffee shops, and places to buy souvenirs, all in square concrete. When I first saw this resort in December of the previous year, it was deserted, with everything boarded up for the winter. But every day for six or seven weeks in midsummer, thousands of bathers would arrive by boat, bus, and Jeep from Seoul. Then, loudspeakers blared, neon lights flashed, hawkers called out to passersby, and a certain amount of urban affluence trickled down into provincial and rural pockets.

For the next half hour or so I walked on the hard, damp sand of an immensely long, gradually sloping beach that was several hundred yards wide at low tide. When the tide came in, there was just a narrow strip left in front of the grassy bluffs. A mile or so farther north, a rocky headland jutting far out to sea finally broke the long curve of the beach, and beyond that, the landscape returned to the familiar clusters of thatched-roof farmhouses and well-tended fields. This was Chollip'o, the last village before Sŏkp'o.

The beach at Chollip'o is only a couple of hundred yards long, and at its northern end there is a small harbor with a seawall. Fishermen mending nets, repairing boats, or boiling anchovies on the beach might ask me to join them for *makkŏlli* and *anju*. They wanted to hear the latest news from Seoul. If they didn't call out an invitation, all I had to do was stop and chat for a while, and at some point there would be an inevitable but imperceptible (to me) signal, and we would all move to the *sulchip* over behind the breakwater. So many appetizers of seafood and pickled vegetables accompanied the drinking that it could go on almost indefinitely without any serious effects. I learned that although my companions acted outraged at first and would refuse three times to let me pay, even stuffing the money back in my pocket, on the fourth try they would reluctantly give in, and everyone would be content.

At Chollip'o the villagers spoke patronizingly about the people of Sŏkp'o, and they often tried to persuade me to settle in and study them instead. Perhaps they thought I was a potential benefactor for their community. "Why do you walk so far to reach such a poor place?" they would ask. "Trucks and Jeeps and taxis come here, but they don't go to Sŏkp'o." It was true; at low tide vehicles could drive on the hard wet sand from the Mallip'o beach resort. "We have engines for our boats, and we catch lots of fish. Here, we live like people in town." In at least one respect, this too was true. The beachfront and harbor at Chollip'o was typical of any small port, with its corrugated iron roofs and all the cast-off tin cans, rusty machinery, card-board, bottles, plastic containers, and oil drums that were strewn about the waterfront. On one occasion, after a few drinks the villagers were especially insistent. "There, you can have that house up on the hill. Why not live here instead?" I didn't know how to answer gracefully and finally mumbled something about it being cheaper in Sŏkp'o. This finally seemed to satisfy them, and they stopped pestering me, perhaps now a little doubtful whether I would be such a generous neighbor after all.

There was no way I could have explained to these men why I preferred Sŏkp'o to their village. For the villagers, any connection with the modern industrial world was glamorously positive, and they looked with contempt on symbols of the past such as sailboats and thatched roofs. In this more prosperous community, class differences were much more obvious than in Sŏkp'o. In Chollip'o I always seemed to end up drinking with the same group of boat owners and well-off farmers, the storekeeper, and a fish broker or co-op official, while ordinary fishermen and laborers stood outside or on the fringes gaping at the spectacle. One group had clean clothes and sometimes even wrist-watches, while the other wore dirty rags. In Sŏkp'o, things were more egalitarian—and more traditional. No one was excluded from the drinking groups, and everyone wore old, patched clothes. Only some of the elderly, carefully tended by devoted daughters-in-law, roamed about idly in clean clothes.

Moving on from Chollip'o, the coast was steep and rocky. The road to Sŏkp'o climbed and twisted, up and down and in and out among the contours and folds of the hillsides, in most places more than one hundred feet above the ocean. During the previous three years, the village of Sŏkp'o had mobilized all its labor in a burst of strenuous cooperative effort to carve out a track wide enough for a Jeep or a small truck. The villagers had been convinced that if a road existed, they would somehow be able to share in the same delights of modern civilization that Chollip'o enjoyed. It had been an extraordinary undertaking—three and a half miles of mountain road hacked out with only picks and shovels by men, women, and children. But after it was finished, no Jeeps or trucks came. Or rather, they came very rarely and then only at great expense. The road rapidly deteriorated, and by the time I arrived local drivers were unwilling to risk plunging into the sea. The road did, however, allow several people to walk side by side, and this made the trip much more sociable than in the days when everyone had had to follow along a narrow footpath in single file. Although people complained a lot about the long trip on foot, the groups that I usually encountered—often women and children all dressed up for a trip to town or to see relatives in another village—seemed invariably to be in high spirits.

"*Odi katta oshiouuu?*" they would ask. They knew I was coming back from Seoul, but "Where have you gone and come back from?" was the standard greeting on the paths. Sometimes it varied to "*Odi kashiouuu?*" (Where are you going?). They knew the answer to that, too, but I had to say it anyway, "*Uri chip e kayo*" (Back to my [our] house).

In addition to its shorter length, the inland route had a special attraction, particularly if my rucksack was heavy. Young people from Sŏkp'o always went this way, and there would usually be at least one youth who had no load to carry. Without saying a word and certainly without any suggestion on my part, he would simply take the pack off my shoulders and go on ahead, leaving it at my house in the village. Confucian propriety can be comforting for those over forty.

To walk home by the inland path, I had to get off the bus halfway to Mohang in the middle of nowhere (here there was only a small shop by the side of the road) and take the unmarked path to Sindongni. Sindongni was a cluster of three houses and a wine shop at the top of a long gradual hill about a fourth of the way to Sŏkp'o. It was a good place to stop and rest. Often there were other Sŏkp'o travelers returning home from the market town, and we could share something to eat and drink.

But this route had other advantages as well. There were several wealthy farms just beyond Sindongni, on the long fertile slope that eventually ended at the bay. Each holding had three or four times as much land as the largest farm in Sŏkp'o. Although the extent of land ownership was usually a fairly well-guarded secret, I learned after considerable asking that such farms, which included irrigated rice fields, orchards, and unirrigated cash-crop land, might comprise as much as twenty acres. On several occasions I was stopped on the path, either by one of the farmers himself or by a child who had been sent out to intercept me. This always meant makkŏlli, a big meal, and if I chose, a night's lodging. The houses were much grander than I was used to, with imposing tile roofs and interiors that were cluttered with things like inlaid mother-of-pearl wardrobes, full-length mirrors, big wall clocks, radios, and even in one case, a piano. These farmers subscribed to newspapers and sent some of their children to college. They had full-time, live-in agricultural laborers as second-class household members. It was an entirely different level of rural existence from that of my Sŏkp'o neighbors.

In return for the hospitality, I found that I was expected to examine the English proficiency of the middle or high school youngsters of these households, reassuring the parents that all was well at school. But things were really terrible at school, and there was nothing I could do about it. The students' English pronunciation was so badly distorted, exactly like that of their teachers (who in rural South Korea at that time had no access to genuine, spoken English) that I often couldn't make out what the children were trying to say. On these occasions everyone seemed puzzled and a little resentful at my inability to understand English. The only solution was to have the students get out their textbooks. Then, by actually looking at the sentences they were trying to pronounce, I could make the connection and carry on some sort of dialogue. Unfortunately, the better and more conscientious the student was, the more hopelessly ingrained was the appalling accent.

The last climb before reaching Sŏkp'o was over the same pass I had crossed with Pirate, when I was living at Teacher Yi's house. The young couple was still there, still working Pirate's land without much enthusiasm. From the top of the pass, the path led steeply down into the eastern end of the Yi lineage neighborhood. From there, if the tide was out, I could cross the mudflats directly to the Big Hamlet. If the tide was in, I would have to traverse the entire Yi Hamlet and join the coastal path just before the sandspit.

Whichever route I took, as I got closer to "my" village, the feeling of being pulled back into the community was reinforced by every encounter. Sometimes, as I reached one of the first few outlying houses of Sŏkp'o, there would be a peremptory summons from the courtyard to "come up" (olla osiuu) and share a bowl of makkŏlli. Recognizing that these blunt commands were really expressions of hospitality and goodwill, I usually obeyed, meekly leaving the road, taking off my shoes, and climbing up on the veranda to join the group. It was only then, with the sour fermented taste of makkŏlli in my mouth, that I knew I had come home. The bright red oysters in hot sauce tasted better here than they did in Seoul, and I could look out through the pines and see the glint of the afternoon sun on the Western ocean.

Then, back on the path with the water still on my left, it took only a few more minutes to walk down through the trees past Teacher Yi 's house, across the sandspit, past the salt pans, through the lanes of the Big Hamlet, and up the hill to my house. Sometimes there were further stops for salutations and additional refreshment. If the weather was good, I would arrive home in a euphoric daze. If there was rain, it would help to sober me up and wash off the dust of the long journey.

7

Fathers and Sons

Diary Entry August 17, 1966

I know that Kim and Richie are both spoiled—badly spoiled by village standards. I'm not a bit strict, and sometimes I wonder if I shouldn't follow the Korean way of bringing up children. But Kim's occasional crying spells and angry outbursts can always be cured by heavy doses of attention and hugging. She has periods when some little thing will infuriate her. Then she can be really balky, glaring at people, Korean style, out of the corners of her eyes with a ludicrously ferocious look. But most of the time she is delightful, sometimes joining me in my study to conduct *yŏn'gu* (research) with all sorts of invented gossip, inspired by what she hears on the *toemaru* about village affairs.

This morning Kim was really annoyed because the ferry boat ride across the bay didn't last long enough. Richie got jostled by someone with a big load getting into the boat and nearly went in the water. He wailed a little at first, but soon began to enjoy the ride. His pleasure at being with me, his blissful smile, and the way he says "Daddy," as if I were the only thing in the world that matters, are all so wonderful. How can I resist? With the children I have moments of the same kind of exaltation that I suppose makes people write "God is love" all over the highways at home. They ask constantly for affection and attention, and I'm delighted to provide it. We are all thriving here together.

As Richie got used to his new world, he was also becoming much more active and adventurous. This bothered my sister-in-law, who wanted to keep him close to the house and in sight at all times. Still, there were really no

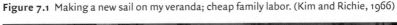

Figure 7.1 Making a new sail on my veranda; cheap family labor. (Kim and Richie, 1966)

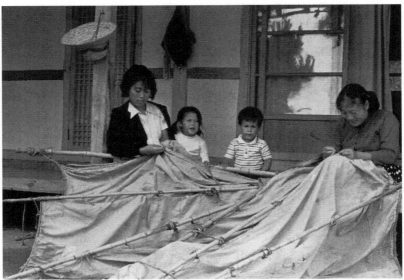

dangers that I could imagine—unless he tried to swim to China—and I told her to let him roam about pretty much as he pleased.

When Richie finally did get into serious trouble, it was right in our own backyard. His entomological investigations that day happened to focus on the maggots that covered the foul mess under the boards of our toilet shed. As in most other Sŏkp'o outhouses the boards were loose, making it easier to wash them off (which we did every day) and to empty the pit (usually after several months). Richie moved the boards, opening the slot up a little too wide. Then, when he put his weight in the wrong place, a board flipped up and dropped him into the pit. It was only a little more than waist deep, but he was screaming so hard that he had trouble getting out. Luckily, Kyung Sook was nearby and rescued him.

The Sŏkp'o solution to babysitting was simple. Once small children were weaned and off their mothers' backs, they were usually in the care of an older sister or cousin. In many families girls from six to ten years old would carry infant brothers or sisters around on their backs most of the day, especially if the mother had a new baby, or when all hands were needed for farm work. But my daughter, Kim, absolutely rejected these Confucian obligations. She would sometimes tease or desert her brother, leaving him in tears and horrifying the other girls.

To make up for the trauma of the toilet pit, to get him away from his sister, and because he was the apple of my eye, I began taking Richie with me for part of the day when I wandered around the village. He would run happily in front of me on the paths, and then when he was tired, ride on my shoulders. He always wanted to climb the high hills or head for the rocks and beaches by the sea. If I spent too long talking with farmers or fishermen, or if some-one invited me to have a bowl of makkŏlli and settle in on the veranda for a longer visit, Richie would sometimes get impatient and insist on leaving.

I was a typical, fond American father and catered to his whims. Proud of my son and eager to show him off, I was surprised and a little annoyed when word got back to me (through more than one channel) that there was a good deal of critical talk about my behavior as a father. The villagers were both puzzled and outraged. Why would a grown man take his infant son around with him, fuss over him, and act like a doddering old grandmother without dignity or pride? Infants belonged at home with the women. The village men wondered how I could bear to lose face publicly, allowing a child to interrupt serious conversations with other adults and to order me around.

Kyung Sook picked up a lot of gossip from other young women while washing clothes at the well, and she brought back one explanation for my strange behavior that was being circulated at the time. The rumor was that my wife must be from a wealthy, yangban lineage, while I was a low-born commoner without property of my own. This was the only way the villagers could explain why my wife stayed in Seoul with her own family, while I was sent off to the remote countryside to take care of the children.

Finally, as an anthropologist determined to play by the rules and avoid doing anything that might jeopardize the field work, I reluctantly conformed to village custom and decided to leave Richie at home. But I did not really understand until later that the way I had behaved with my son—or rather, how I allowed and encouraged him to behave towards me—was a direct chal-lenge to the central core of village ethics. Father-son relations were supposed to be stiff and distant—weighty with virtue and obligation. The open expres-sion of an emotionally intimate, mutual, and informal relationship with my son had shocked people in Sŏkp'o more, I think, than any of the other strange things I did in their village.

Filial piety as a core value is simple enough to describe. It requires total respect and obedience on the part of a son towards his parents, particularly his father, and to a somewhat lesser degree, by extension to all other relatives of older generations. I knew this from my reading, but truly appreciating the degree to which filial piety forms the basis of traditional Confucian morality, taking priority over all other moral principles, was still a problem for me. It took quite a while before I fully recognized the astonishing (to me) fact that failure to show appropriate deference and devotion to parents was regarded a greater sin than murder, stealing, adultery, or drunken violence. In the West, with our pop-Freudian perspective, we often tend to assume that severe family conflict (or anything else that doesn't work out for that matter) is probably the fault of our parents. But in areas where the values associated with Confucian doctrine have been deeply internalized—Sŏkp'o in 1966 was certainly such a place—no one would hesitate in placing one's dedicated obedience to one's father at the top of the list of human virtues. Disrespect and disobedience towards parents were seen as an indication of the greatest possible human degradation.

The reasoning goes something like this: every good and positive thing in life—harmony, love, decency, order, and stability—depends on getting human relationships right and on being able to count on these relationships continuing to be right. Virtue and morality are not conceived of or defined primarily in terms of the individual, but rather as a way of regulating relationships among groups of people in order to achieve social harmony. The Confucian primer that used to be memorized and shouted out loud by every first-year student in the old-style schools (sŏdang) spells it out right at the beginning: So the father must love and the son must be filial; the ruler must be just and the subject loyal; the husband gentle and the wife obedient; the elder brother friendly and the younger respectful; and friends must be helpful and charitable to each other. After these things man can fitly be called human. The Confucian ideal is particularistic, not universal. It is hierarchical, not egalitarian. There is nothing about all men being brothers or about loving one's fellows as oneself. There is nothing about equality, before God or anyone else. Perhaps it is a limited, parochial view of virtue, best suited to a small, self-contained, and relatively isolated agricultural community. Ideal relationships are defined in reciprocal pairs. But reciprocity does not mean equality. A father's love is benevolent, stern, and just. He looks out for his son's best interests and firmly checks any wayward tendencies. He must take responsibility and lead, and the son must follow—respectfully and obediently. Even if the father is neither benevolent nor just, that is no excuse. There are no allowable exceptions to filial piety; the rule is absolute.

After several months in Sŏkp'o the system no longer seemed strange to me, either from the standpoint of abstract morality or as a practical way to regulate everyday life. Most villagers most of the time tried to conform to the ideal. Because it was such an important condition for respectability, every family tried to give at least the appearance of living together harmoniously. Failure to keep conflict within decent limits unfavorably affected, not just the reputation of members of the household, but also the mood, morale, and prestige of an entire neighborhood.

There was, of course, plenty of family conflict, and in a place like Sŏkp'o everyone knew about it. Privacy did not really exist, even as an ideal. Each particular household, however, had a slightly different standard with regard to maintaining "decent limits." What was remarkable to me, though, was not the fact that the rules were constantly being broken, but rather that the moral consensus was so widespread and so firm.

Teacher Yi's family was at one extreme end of the village spectrum of Confucian propriety: The entire neighborhood of "upper-class" Yi lineage households, presented an image of solid respectability. People in this part of the village tended to keep closer control over their emotions, and family life did, in fact, appear to be more tranquil. The noisy, out-in-the open shouting matches that occurred fairly frequently in the fishing neighborhoods of the Big Hamlet, were rare.

Having lived in Teacher Yi's guest room for two months, I knew a good deal about the inner workings of his family life. His father, Yi Chanok, was a vigorous, handsome man in his mid-seventies, with a long, wispy, white beard—the image of sagehood. He was not a large landowner. He did not interfere in the affairs of his neighbors or relatives, and he did not play a major role in village politics. He was illiterate and had never lived anywhere but in the village. Yet somehow he created a mood of refinement and good order at any gathering. At home he usually spoke in a low voice, but his authority was absolute. For example, his two-year-old granddaughter cried a lot during the day, but when he told her to be quiet, she stopped. Or, if his wife grew a little shrill in directing her daughter-in-law's household activities, he only had to mutter, "It's noisy," and her tone would change.

In a work group Yi Chanok was usually the oldest and stayed back from the others, performing tasks where skill and experience were more important than strength. Compared to the noisily vivacious village norm, he did not talk much, but when he offered a suggestion it was usually adopted without question. Younger men would be on their good behavior, toning down their normally boisterous language and politely turning their backs when they smoked. Because Teacher Yi's father was relaxed and good humored, no one seemed to mind the slight constraint imposed by his presence. His advanced age, devoted family, good personal reputation, and unfailing natural good manners gave him a dignity and standing in the village that no amount of education, wealth, or aggressive energy could have matched.

Teacher Yi was somewhat stiff and formal in his father's presence. He displayed the correct awkwardness, symbolizing the proper feelings of awe, gratitude, and respect that a son should feel towards his father. The old man adopted a benevolent stance towards me, since I was of his son's generation. While showing respect for my scholarly status, he was amused by my activities in Sŏkp'o and proceeded to ask me what scandals I had recently uncovered, or whether America was going to pay the village back after I had stolen all its secrets. He seemed to me to be the embodiment of Confucius' teaching that after a lifetime of struggling to acquire virtue; the superior man behaves correctly without thought or effort.

Teacher Yi's father was not so much concerned with local attempts to link the village to national economic development, a subject that was of passionate interest to the village leaders who were in their forties and fifties. But he and a few others like him were an important moral presence in the community. They stood for something fundamental and provided tangible evidence that the ethical system worked—that one man's correct behavior could have a benign influence, not just on his own family but on all those in the vicinity.

There were rewards for all this traditional virtue. Teacher Yi's father lived a simple but comfortable life. He never visited the *sulchip* but rather drank moderately with his friends and relatives in his own guest room or in theirs, where both the food and liquor were of higher quality, and where they were not bothered by coarse women. His sons were hardworking, obedient, and respectful, surrounding him in his old age with cheerful, subservient daughters-in-law and playful grandchildren.

The character and integrity of Teacher Yi and his father, as well as the quality of their relationship, was about as close to the traditional ideal as anyone got in Sŏkp'o. Quiet, restrained, and hardworking, they were models for others to respect and emulate.

At the opposite end of the respectability continuum was a fishing family named Kang, living below me in the Big Hamlet. Theirs was the poorest and most disreputable of the three Kang households in the village. I got to know Kang Yong Ju, the head of this family, who was five or six years younger than I, quite well. He lived with his father, who although now too old to fish, was still, when his alcoholism permitted, the village's most popular shaman. Even though the old shaman was nearly always drunk, his services as chŏmjaengi (diviner) were preferred to those of the other village practitioner. He not only cured illnesses but also performed the incantations and prayers over boats that brought good luck at sea. But with antibiotics invading the countryside, and the overall decline in fishing, it was no longer a rewarding occupation.

The old man, three sons, and their wives and children all lived together in the crowded, ramshackle house. Without land, the brothers worked more or less steadily on other people's boats, or at anything else, when an opportunity turned up. My friend, Kang Young Ju, had tried peddling fish and oysters door-to-door in Seoul, but he had returned to the village with nothing more tangible than stories of his amorous conquests in the city. The family owned an old twenty-one foot, two-masted junk that lay rotting on the beach, but it was too unseaworthy to be of any use.

The Kangs had not always been so poor, but with the three sons drinking as much as their father, things had steadily gone downhill. They not only had trouble with drink, but also with women. On one exciting occasion Kang Young Ju tried to set up a young woman from Seoul as his concubine in an extra room of a neighbor's house. We could hear the shrieks of quarreling women from our veranda for a couple of weeks until the new favorite had been driven back to the city by an outraged wife and her sympathetic neighbors.

A couple of weeks later an event took place that seemed natural enough to me, but that was regarded by the neighbors as even more scandalous than the affair of the concubine. The attractive and hardworking wife of Kang Young Ju's younger brother deserted the family and returned to her native village far off in a different province. Although fond of her husband, she had often complained of the constant drunkenness and lack of money. The young man, after waiting for a couple of weeks for her to come back, followed his wife all the way to her aunt's home in a fruitless effort to get her back. Village gossip had trouble determining which act was the more outrageous—the girl's flight or her husband's pursuit. Older people shook their heads over the incident for a long time, expressing their consternation with all sorts of variations on the general theme of, "What is the world coming to when a young wife can just pick up and leave for a little thing like that?"

The curious thing about the men in this family was that they were all well liked, even if their prestige was very low. They all had personal charm as well as *insim*. They were always ready to share whatever they had at the moment, to help neighbors put on a new roof, haul boats up on the beach before a coming storm, or carry the coffin at a funeral. I tried to make sense of all this as I wrote down the events in my journal. There seemed to be a basic inconsistency: if propriety and self-restraint were so important in determining a man's reputation, why were the Kangs popular and well integrated in the life of the village? Finally I decided that there must be a second, less formal, egalitarian, and more individualistic set of values at work. Instead of proper behavior, hierarchy, and pride of lineage, this unstated but deeply internalized code emphasizes generosity, expansiveness, personal charm, self-expression, and a willingness to take risks. These individual and emotional characteristics are intimately tied in with shamanism. Koreans are not just Confucianists. They also like noise, flamboyance, and vivid action.

The men of the Kang family (if not all the women) got along well with each other, as well as with their neighbors. When the old *chŏmjaengi* got sick, Kang Young Ju and his brothers devoted all their energies and resources to taking care of him. One way they raised money was by selling me the disintegrating family boat. Their filial devotion evoked surprise and admiration. The proceeds from the boat sale were used to pay for a real *mudang* (professional female shaman), who came all the way from the county seat. But she danced and banged her cymbals and drum and spoke in tongues without success. The old shaman died anyway, and a few weeks later my friend, Kang Young Ju, left the village for good.

Pirate, Teacher Yi's father's first cousin, lived next to Teacher Yi's house, about 150 yards away. Aside from the fact that Pirate had more land, other villagers spoke of his household as being much richer than Teacher Yi's, because Pirate's only son, Yi Pyŏngbu, would inherit everything. In Sŏkp'o calculations of wealth also had a dimension of continuity through time.

Even though these two Yi households were close geographically and genealogically and both were part of the village elite, the mood within the two households and the way they were evaluated by their neighbors was quite different. When I lived in Teacher Yi's *sarangbang*, I could occasionally hear angry voices (usually Pirate scolding his son or his daughter-in-law) coming from inside Pirate's courtyard. There had also been a number of noisy confrontations on the nearby path between members of Pirate's family and various people from outside the hamlet. When I asked Teacher Yi about these extended shouting matches, he was very reluctant to explain, commenting only that Pirate had "complicated business affairs."

Unlike Teacher Yi's household, neither Pirate nor his son participated in the large, joint agricultural work parties that linked most of the Yi relatives. Teacher Yi's explanation was that Pirate's fields were scattered and far away, and he preferred to use hired labor. But someone from another lineage gave me a different explanation: while Pirate complained that the other Yi's had not worked hard enough on his fields, he and his son had always skimped on the work that they did for others. So, in addition to the personal impressions I had gained from my own contacts with Pirate, I began to perceive his role in the village as that of a grasping old landowner who went his own way, leaning hard and greedily on everyone he dealt with and endearing himself to no one.

Pirate's son, Yi Pyŏngbu, was short, stocky and well-muscled—the best arm wrestler in the village. While not outstandingly gregarious or popular, he was nevertheless recognized for his industry and the fact that because of his wealth he would eventually, after Pirate's death or retirement, be one of Sŏkp'o's leading citizens. The trouble was that Pirate refused to retire. He insisted on making all the decisions in the household, even though Yi Pyŏngbu was thirty years old and had a small son of his own. Probably a lot of the squabbling that I had heard next door from Teacher Yi's *sarangbang* was the result of Yi Pyŏngbu's attempts to get out from under Pirate's tyranny. When Pirate spoke, it was only to scold or to give commands. More than once I saw him provoke his four-year-old grandson to tears, apparently just for the fun of it. If Pirate was perpetually irascible, Yi Pyŏngbu was almost always sullen and subdued.

One day in late summer, some months after I had left the Yi's neighborhood and set up housekeeping on my own, I met Yi Pyŏngbu on the bus coming back from the county seat. He insisted on carrying my rucksack in addition to his own heavy parcels, and we walked together silently up the long first hill on the inland route. At the Sindongni rest house on top I paid for a pot of makkŏlli and some dried fish. Then Yi Pyŏngbu treated me to a second pot in spite of my protests.

As we started down the long valley past terraced rice fields and an occasional outlying farmhouse, Yi Pyŏngbu blurted out, "Please find me a job in Seoul." I was astonished. "What kind of job? Why do you want to leave Sŏkp'o?" Younger sons, especially those from poor families, were beginning at that time to leave for the city, but for Pyŏngbu it made no sense.

"I am stifled here. I have no control over anything I do. I work hard, but I have no life of my own." I had never before heard anything as individualistic as this in the village; it was particularly surprising coming from a household that prided itself on maintaining conservative, upper-class traditions. Even as I was protesting, "But you will inherit a lot of land, and you can live well here," I understood Yi Pyŏngbu's problem. He had Pirate for a father.

Yi Pyŏngbu was frank. "My father is still healthy, and he will not give me any land of my own so I can set up a separate household. I want to leave this village. I can't stand it here anymore." "But what will you do in Seoul?" I asked. "There are only low-paid construction jobs, and they stop in winter."

"You know important people there. You must have a friend who owns a factory. Just speak to him and tell him that I am strong and a good worker. My wife is strong, too. She can work at his house."

In fact, I did have some influential friends in Seoul, and some of them did own factories. But I could never persuade any of them to give uneducated peasants a job on my simple recommendation. Certainly that is the way most Koreans find jobs or houses or wives or loans or anything else for that matter. But foreigners seem to be out of the loop. What was most disconcerting was Yi Pyŏngbu's complete confidence in the power of my Seoul connections. He was sure that if I wanted to, I could find him a good job.

When I tried to explain not only how little influence I had on the Seoul labor market, but also how miserable life would be in a squatter slum with a family to support on the wages of an unskilled manual laborer, Yi Pyŏngbu did not want to listen. His face darkened in anger, and he walked faster to get

Figure 7.2 One of the village's "weighty" men. (1966)

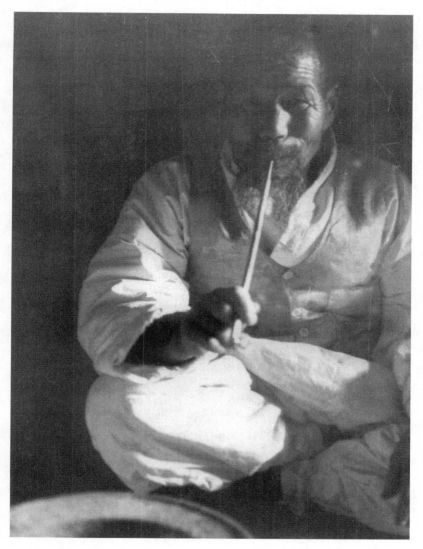

away from me. I thought I heard him mutter, "I will kill him if I don't leave." I knew I had to be mistaken—the result of my bad Korean.

Two weeks later Yi Pyŏngbu and his family were gone, and they did not come back until after I left the village. In 1966 the number of unskilled laboring jobs in Seoul and other cities was rapidly increasing, and tens of thousands of young men from villages all over the country were taking advantage of the new opportunities to leave home. Economists and demographers have developed elaborate formulas to explain this kind of massive rural-urban migration in terms of individual calculations of material gain. But I wonder if in South Korea there weren't also a great many other cases like Yi Pyŏngbu's, where individuals left for the city to escape the tensions generated by filial piety's impossible demands.

Pirate announced that Yi Pyŏngbu had moved to the city so that his son could get a good education, and he hired laborers from the next village to work his fields. But eventually Pirate gave in, and Yi Pyŏngbu returned, more or less on his own terms. Pirate died three years after that, and now Yi Pyŏngbu is one of the "weighty" (yuji) men of Sŏkp'o.

There was only one family in Sŏkp'o in which a son openly defied his father. Mun Ch'ilgap spoke out against his father without restraint and, most terrible of all from the perspective of kinsmen and neighbors, he refused to pay any kind of ritual obeisance on his father's sixtieth birthday. I heard that there had always been tension between father and son and that even as a child Mun Ch'ilgap had frequently been punished for lack of filial respect.

Mun Ch'ilgap, like every other healthy village youth, had served for three years in the army. But after getting out, Mun Ch'ilgap had no desire to come home and instead found a job on a deep-sea fishing boat based in Inch'ŏn. It was a lucky boat with a skilled captain, and Mun Ch'ilgap made a lot of money. But like nearly all young fishermen in the big ports, he spent everything he earned in the sulchip, on a motorcycle, and on women. Then he met a "decent" girl, married her, and began to save his earnings. He stopped going to sea, and the young couple started a small waterfront restaurant in Inch'ŏn. Before long there were children, sizable debts, and finally bankruptcy. Mun Ch'ilgap and his family had no choice. They came back to Sŏkp'o to farm.

Mun Ch'ilgap's father was addicted to women and soju. The old man gave Mun Ch'ilgap a house and enough to live on, but he refused to give him his share (as the eldest son) of the family property, preferring instead to sell off land whenever he needed money to placate a favorite concubine. Aside from vague, general, and unenforceable principles of virtue and benevolence, there is nothing in the Confucian code—or rather the Sŏkp'o version of it—to stop a household head from doing exactly as he pleases with the family land. The young have an absolute obligation to the old. If the old are benevolent, so much the better. If not, the young must still fulfill their obligations.

Mun Ch'ilgap was hardworking and ambitious. During his military service he had become an ardent believer in progress and economic development, both for himself and for the nation. Over coffee on my veranda he would sometimes criticize his fellow villagers for their lack of energy and vision. But most of all, Mun Ch'ilgap denounced his father for making him do most of the agricultural work while depriving him of his rightful inheritance.

Since the two households were jointly farming the same land, father and son were in constant acrimonious contact, and the sound of their quarreling carried throughout the hamlet, all the way up to my house. In malicious gossip around the well they were commonly referred to as "the fight factory" (ssaum kongjang).

There was no question in anyone else's mind as to whose fault was the greater. The other villagers understood the young man's frustration and to some extent were ready to make allowances for him, but his acts of direct rebellion were a far more serious violation of village ethics than the old man's scandalous addiction to liquor and women. Teacher Yi was unusually critical, saying that if Mun Ch'ilgap could not control his behavior, he should leave the village. Older Mun relatives visited Mun Ch'ilgap's house, sometimes scolding and sometimes begging him, for the sake of the reputation and solidarity of the lineage, to pay ritual respect to his father. It was as if the entire community was suffering from an open, infected sore. Even the old man's wife publicly denounced her son for his stubborn opposition.

Eventually Mun Ch'ilgap gave in. He took substantial presents of fish and liquor to his father's house and made ritual bows, congratulating him in formal terms on having attained a ripe old age. But the next day at my house he denounced his father as strongly as ever, sneering as well at the villagers' "useless, old-fashioned" way of thinking.

Many years later, when I revisited Sŏkp'o, I heard the rest of the story. The father died and Mun Ch'ilgap, then in his late thirties with three children, had begun slowly and arduously to gain back his lost inheritance. In time he prospered, but neighbors and kinsmen, while giving him credit for hard work, criticized him for being grasping and stingy. Eventually, dissatisfied with village life and without close ties in the community, Mun Ch'ilgap decided to sell all his land and move to the city.

Like Teacher Yi's father, Kim Pŏbyong was a handsome, energetic man in his seventies. But that is where all resemblance ended. He lived alone in a tumbledown shack near the shed where the village's cooperative funeral bier was kept. Most Sŏkp'o residents didn't even like to walk past the shed in daylight. To them the idea of sleeping nearby was grotesque. Monumental bad luck and a bitterly hostile relationship with his son, Kim Ŭigon, had condemned Kim Pŏbyong to a lonely, impoverished old age.

There was a slightly monkish look about the way he dressed, with a floppy broad-brimmed hat and baggy pants that, no matter how filthy, were always neatly wrapped tight at the ankles. Kim Pŏbyong never wore anything but traditional Korean clothes, and except for the missing top-knot he might have stepped right out of a seventeenth-century painting. He was deeply tanned and had an almost military bearing, but perhaps that was just the stiffness of old age. I referred to him as In Sun's grandfather, the way our neighbors did. My children just called him grandfather.

I first got to know Kim Pŏbyong as a regular coffee drinker who usually turned up at odd hours so that he could be sure of having our veranda all to himself. In his case there was never a greeting from the path. I would simply find him sitting quietly on the veranda with his legs hanging over the edge. Only when I asked him formally to come in, or rather "up," would he drop off his shoes and pull his legs up to sit at ease on the boards, and only then would he light his pipe. My other visitors somewhat patronizingly praised Kim Pŏbyong for his honesty, sincerity, and avoidance of strong drink—three qualities that sharply differentiated him from his son, Kim Ŭigon, the man who had "helped" me build my house. Some villagers pitied him for his misfortunes, but many others believed that Kim Pŏbyong himself was to blame. In any case pity does not engender status and respect in Sŏkp'o. Kim Pŏbyong was eccentric. He did not assert himself, and he bothered no one. Yet he seemed somehow to have renounced his claims to full membership in the community, and even in his lineage.

My children, for some reason, liked Kim Pŏbyong at once, and he was obviously content, sipping coffee or tea on our veranda. At first I had a lot of trouble understanding his thick dialect and found his visits to be hard work. But it didn't seem to matter whether I nodded and grunted at appropriate intervals or not; he went on talking steadily, and gradually by some mysterious process of exposure, I began to understand.

Kim Pŏbyong frequently brought us presents of small fish, and our appreciation, which was not great at first, increased as we learned how to eat them. They were a silvery, thin fish about six inches long, made up almost entirely of sharp bones. Without any commercial value whatsoever, they were netted only for local consumption. I never found out for certain but thought they might be a kind of miniature shad. Kim Pŏbyong demonstrated the eating technique to the children on the veranda with exaggerated facial motions. He would put a whole roasted fish in his mouth and munch slowly with a faraway look in his eyes for a minute or two. Koreans don't talk much while they eat in any case, and the flesh of this fish is really delicious— deserving slow, meditative appreciation. Finally, a discreet, whitish ball about three-sixteenths to a quarter of an inch in diameter containing the bones and other inedible parts would emerge from one corner of his mouth, fall delicately into his hand, and be deposited on a corner of the food tray. It takes a lot of practice, and today, when I can find the right kind of fish, I still like to demonstrate my expertise.

Kim Pŏbyong had begun stopping by my house in early summer on his way over the hill to check a stone fish trap that had belonged to his lineage for generations. Sixty or seventy years previously, before the Japanese colonizers had introduced their long-line fishing techniques and elaborate nets, the catch from boats had often been less important along this coast than that from the stone traps. Schools of fish, migrating close to shore—particularly herring, mullet, and shad—would strand themselves in these large, laboriously constructed stone corrals when the tide went out, and then there would be enough to eat for everyone in the village for several days. By the 1960s, however, with heavy over-fishing throughout the Yellow Sea, the fish had become scarce, and most of the traps had been dismantled by storms. But Kim Pŏbyong, alone among the local fishermen, stubbornly continued to rebuild his stone walls, and he was just barely able to live off the occasional mullet or shad that was left behind by the ebbing tide. Once or twice a year, though, when a whole school was trapped, it was like the old days, with half the village gathering in frenzied excitement to club hundreds of fish, as the water gushed out through holes between the stones.

Over the next several months Kim Pŏbyong's story came out bit by bit, with his own meandering account supplemented from time to time by the comments of other villagers. Everyone had something to say about him, even if some of the stories were contradictory. As usual, I ended up sorting things out with Teacher Yi and T'aemo. As the eldest son of a prominent branch of the Kim lineage, Kim Pŏbyong had started life in Sŏkp'o with good prospects, but things had gone badly for him and his family for as long as anyone could remember. Now in his old age, when he should have been fussed over and spoiled by a wife and daughter-in-law, and when respectful grandchildren ought to have been hanging about ready to light his pipe, listen to his stories, or run errands, he lived alone.

In normal, respectable households old people live with the eldest son, who inherits the largest portion of land and other property and who takes on the responsibility for carrying out family rituals and looking after his parents. As a man gets older he turns over more and more of his work and authority to his eldest son, receiving, in exchange, increased respect from everyone in the family, the choicest bits of food at mealtime, the warmest part of the floor, and freedom to work or not as he pleases. When he feels like it, he can put on his best clothes and join colleagues of similar age in other hamlets or nearby villages. At these frequent gatherings the old men talk, smoke, drink, and chant ancient poems. But Kim Pŏbyong, fending for himself in lonely squalor, had none of these consolations of old age. He did seem to have a stiff pride in his independence—a kind of solitary personal dignity that was rare in the village. And yet he must have craved companionship, for he found the relatively exotic atmosphere of our veranda congenial.

As a young man Kim Pŏbyong had married a village girl for love, against the wishes of his parents. There are, of course, plenty of tragic accounts in the Western world of lovers who defied tyrannical parents to their sorrow. But the extent to which such an act was rebelliously antisocial in a pre-modern Korean village is hard for us to imagine. Not only was it a direct violation of parental authority, but it challenged a number of other moral principles as well. Romantic love itself has no legitimate place in the Confucian scheme of things. It is unpredictable, irrational, and promotes disorder, interfering with proper relationships. That kind of love belongs to the disreputable world of concubines and female entertainers and can only be dangerous when injected into the weighty business of producing heirs to perpetuate the family line. In 1966 the display in public of real affection between a man and his wife was still considered rather nasty by respectable people in Seoul as well as in the countryside.

When Kim Pŏbyong was young, the ideal (and typical) marriage was one in which the bride and groom had never seen each other, all arrangements having been made by a go-between. True propriety required that mutual physical attraction be entirely eliminated from the process of marriage. If it developed afterwards, it had to be concealed from everyone, particularly the bride's parents-in-law. Marriages within the village were therefore, in principle, taboo, since it was inevitable that the two young people would have known each other growing up. Actually, taboo is too strong a word to use for the prejudice against marrying someone from within the community. When I was in Sŏkp'o, the villagers certainly talked as if there was such a prohibition, and as if it was invariably observed. But I discovered eventually that in nearly a fourth of all marriages both partners were, in fact, from the village. These marriages, however, were certainly not shining social events, since the reason why they took place was either because the families were too poor to attract a spouse from outside (and pay for the ceremony), or because the bride was already pregnant.

Kim Pŏbyong not only married his true love, but he committed an even greater affront to the community by doting on her publicly. Under such circumstances he could not live at home, and his father refused to divide the property and give him his share. It was widely believed that some kind of evil supernatural influence must have been at work to cause such outlandish behavior, and the young couple was shunned by most of the other villagers. Without land or other property, Kim Pŏbyong had to work for a bare subsistence as an agricultural laborer in the fields of his kinsmen or as a fisherman on their boats. Soon there were two small sons, and the family was often hungry.

After the birth of her second child, the young wife never recovered, and she died about a year later. Kim Pŏbyong, inconsolable and mentally unhinged, wandered around the village in rags, wailing for his lost love. Relatives eventually took in the neglected children, and Kim Pŏbyong disappeared. After existing as an "animal" for several months in the mountains, he finally stumbled onto an isolated Buddhist temple where the monks took care of him, nursing him back to physical and mental health. For the next thirty years he was an itinerant hanger-on at mountain temples throughout east central South Korea, acting as a laborer and ritual assistant when no one more qualified was around. Although illiterate, he memorized long passages from the sutras, without having any real idea of the contents. For him they were ritual incantations, all mixed up with shamanistic cosmology and practice.

Eventually Kim Pŏbyong returned to Sŏkp'o to find that his eldest son was a drunkard, a wastrel, and a wife beater, who was steadily squandering what little was left of his inheritance on *soju*, women, and wild fishing schemes. Kim Pŏbyong found an ally in his long-suffering daughter-in-law and moved back into the household. But after so many years of Buddhist life, he was appalled by his son's behavior, and they quarreled constantly. Kim Ŭigon, who when drunk was completely indifferent to village opinion, angrily shouted back at his father, accusing him of having abandoned him as an infant. The bad feeling was so great that Kim Pŏbyong finally moved out and built himself a shack on the polluted land next to the funeral bier. He had one skill that kept him marginally involved with the community. At the temples he had learned to perform a series of curing rites, combining crude Buddhist ritual with elements of shamanism. The villagers were not particularly impressed by these performances, but he was the cheapest practitioner around, and from the point of view of the poor, better than nothing.

We continued to see a good deal of Kim Pŏbyong for as long as I lived in Sŏkp'o. He became a sort of part-time member of the family, sometimes staying for lunch or supper. And if he didn't show up for a day or two, we wondered why. For Sŏkp'o it was an unusual relationship—informal, relaxed, undemanding, and without any reckoning of obligations or concern for proper etiquette. He would sit at his ease on the veranda, chatting about the eighty-four thousand supernatural beings (*sinjang*) who crowded the ether of the Korean peninsula and of how he had fasted and prayed in the mountains many years before in order to acquire one of them as his own personal familiar spirit.

At other times he would show the children how to outwit minnows in the shallows of his stone fish trap, or where to find pheasants' nests. He listened carefully when we talked of Seoul and the United States. His questions about America were different from those asked by the other villagers. Kim Pŏbyong wanted to know who the great teachers were and what their message was. He was fascinated by my accounts of American love and marriage, although very disapproving of our predilection for divorce.

It seemed to me that partly as a result of tragic circumstance and partly because of his years at the mountain temples, Kim Pŏbyong was the only genuine non-Confucian among the older men of the village. Not at all concerned with his ancestors or the prestige of his lineage, he did not discourse constantly about the relative merits of different tomb sites the way the other old men usually did. He never scolded my children or, as far as I could tell, his own grandchildren, for failure to show him proper respect. He lived very close to nature and was in more or less constant communication with a host of ghostly creatures—animistic, shamanistic, and Buddhist—in addition to his special relationship with the personal spirit who provided him with access to the otherworld.

His story does not have a happy ending. When we left the village for good in January, 1967, Kim Pŏbyong asked if he could live in my house "to keep everything in good shape for your return." We were both delighted with the arrangement. At last he would have a decent place to spend his old age, and his daughter-in-law could easily climb the hill to bring him an occasional hot meal. And, according to Teacher Yi, his status in the village would be sharply upgraded. For me it meant that my precious thatched cottage—the most beautiful place I had ever lived—would be in good hands.

But things did not work out the way we planned. A year or so later Kim Ŭigon had to sell his own house and what was left of his land to pay off debts. He, his wife, and eight children simply moved up the hill and joined his father. Two months later Kim Pŏbyong was dead. Now, when I return to Sŏkp'o, nothing is the same. Kim Ŭigon has cut down the pine trees for firewood and built a high cement wall that blocks the view. The thatch on the roof has been replaced with some sort of factory produced, corrugated composition board. The house is filthy. Kim Ŭigon invites me to dinner and tries to get me drunk by way of paying twenty years' rent.

8

Spirits: Familiar, Benign, and Malevolent

"*Sŏnsaengnim! Sŏnsaengnim!*" I woke up bleary-eyed and cross to the sound of a childish voice close to my head just an hour after settling in for a much-needed nap. "Respected teacher! Respected teacher!" When I swung open the small, paper-covered door right next to my head there was an eleven-year-old boy, out of breath and intensely serious about the importance of his mission. "*Sŏnsaengnim*, tonight at our house there is a *chesa* (ancestor commemoration ceremony). My father asks you to come." As the boy turned to leave, I had just barely the presence of mind to call out, "Which house is that?"

He stared back blankly for a moment. It was inconceivable to him that I did not know. Finally he blurted out, "The big fishnet house!" and ran off. That meant the house of Yi Pyŏngŭn, another one of Teacher Yi's cousins. Yi Pyŏngŭn was one of the most influential landowners in the village, and although still only in his late thirties, he was a leader in trying to promote economic innovation and progress. One of his recent schemes had been an enormous fishnet that was towed out from shore by a small boat in a great horseshoe curve and then pulled up the beach at both ends by manpower. About twenty men and teenaged boys were required to operate the net. At first there had been lots of spectators and volunteers eager to pull. They all chanted together to maintain the rhythm in an excited festival atmosphere. But the catches so far had been meager, and everyone knew that Yi Pyŏngŭn's big investment was not paying off. A few nights before, while visiting in Teacher Yi's guest room, I had heard Pirate say that it served Yi Pyŏngŭn right for getting involved in such a low occupation as fishing. The others present shouted Pirate down for once, insisting it was all right because Yi Pyŏngŭn did not actually ever get in the boat or pull on the net. As long as he did not endanger his life at sea (and thereby risk dying before his parents),

Figure 8.1 Women in white; death anniversary of parent. Afterwards there would be feasting and drinking and sometimes dancing. (1966)

Figure 8.2 Pirate engaged in ceremonial activity. (1966)

Figure 8.3 I was kept busy supplying formal photographs of aging couples and individuals to serve as focal points at ceremonies after their death. (1966)

Figure 8.4 "Breakfast" after midnight ancestor ceremony. Village head (drinking) and fellow Yi lineage members at an ancestor worship ceremony. (1966)

the general feeling was that Yi Pyŏngŭn could invest his money any way he liked. The last time I had been out to watch the net in operation, the chanting was still going on, since it helped coordinate the pulling. But now it had a mournful sound.

A *chesa* usually takes place in the middle of the night, but I had no idea when I was expected to show up at Yi Pyŏngŭn's house. I assumed that Teacher Yi would also be going, so I stopped by his house to find out what was expected of me. He laughed, "We can go any time. There are only three people in Sŏkp'o who have a watch, so the time doesn't matter much. All you have to do when you get there is drink when everyone else drinks and bow when everyone else bows." This was good advice, applicable for most ritual occasions. Teacher Yi explained that the ceremony was for Yi Pyŏngŭn's grandfather, who had died five years before. The *chesa* is held annually on the death date of parents and grandparents.

We wandered over to Yi Pyŏngŭn's house an hour or so after nightfall and were shown into an inner room next to the *sarangbang*. A few other Yis of Yi Pyŏngŭn's generation were already there, and we started in on the *makkŏlli* and *anju* at once. The conversation was perhaps a little quieter than usual, but the mood was by no means one of hushed religiosity. I could see the village head, Yi Pyŏnghyŏk, busy in another room arranging the offerings and instructing Yi Pyŏngŭn on proper ceremonial procedure. Yi Pyŏnghyŏk seemed to be the ritual director, and Teacher Yi was his acolyte. Yi Pyŏngŭn had the role of priest.

When three or four older men of the deceased grandfather's generation appeared, everyone else scattered, leaving them in sole possession of the *makkŏlli* and food. I was left behind too, although all I wanted to do was watch from the sidelines. Participant observation has its duties, however, and I was obliged to sit with the old gentlemen, trying to understand their dialect and answer their questions.

Pirate, who was one of the elders present, leaned over towards me and in a stage whisper said, "No other lineage in Sŏkp'o performs the *chesa* like we do. They don't ever get the offerings right or know when to bow or how to write the summons."

Since the village head was preparing this document in the next room, I went in to watch. The summons was a sort of formal letter to Yi Pyŏngŭn's grandfather, inviting him to come and eat at the feast with his descendants. Yi Pyŏnghyŏk was even more educated than Teacher Yi, because he had attended a regular, not an agricultural, high school. He used a writing brush and ink on a long scroll of good paper. He wrote slowly and carefully, paying particular attention to the calligraphy of the name of the deceased. Others made helpful comments as he went along, and there was a general sigh of approval and satisfaction when it was done.

The women of Yi Pyŏngŭn's family were all busy preparing food in the kitchen. Occasionally a daughter would come out with a fresh tray of *makkŏlli* and *anju*. It had been a long day, and I dozed off, sitting in a corner. Someone led me to an empty room where I slept heavily until Teacher Yi woke me up, "It's starting." He showed me my place among the kinsmen—in the second row at the end. There was a third row for the young men in the next generation after Yi Pyŏngŭn's. No women entered the room once the chesa began, but they clustered around the door and watched the whole performance intently.

A lot of elaborately prepared food was arranged in pyramidal shapes or on dishes on a slightly raised platform at one side of the room. Teacher Yi told me later that in addition to the regular offerings, the women had prepared the ancestor's favorite dishes. The summons scroll was prominently displayed next to the altar. Three kerosene lamps and some candles gave off more light (and heat) than was normal in a Sŏkp'o interior after dark. Chanting began in ragged unison. We did a lot of bowing, and the room was terribly hot. Every time someone opened a paper-covered window or door, the wind blew out the unshielded kerosene lamps and the candles, so finally we just endured the heat.

The ceremony, which consisted mostly of drinking, eating, and bowing in some sort of elaborate order, was accompanied by formal statements and chants as well as by quiet, casual talk. There were occasional pauses when nothing happened, after chopsticks had been thrust into bowls of rice and other food. This was to give the grandfather a chance to drink and eat, too. Yi Pyŏngŭn read the summons out loud and then reported to his ancestor in a matter-of-fact way what had happened to the family during the past year. After Yi Pyŏngŭn was finished, each of the relatives, in the order of the closeness of their blood relationship to the deceased, made an offering, bowed, drank, and bowed again.

I felt that the mood was one of formal and yet relaxed intimacy—close kinsmen discussing matters of common concern. If someone made a mistake there would be a chuckle or two followed by a word of correction from the master of ceremonies. I detected no stiffness or awe or fear. After the ceremony was over, we stayed on, eating and drinking and talking until about 1:30 a.m.

As I walked home alone in the moonlight across the sandspit I felt vaguely deprived, because in America when I got together with relatives at Thanksgiving or Christmas we never chatted informally with our ancestors. It was hard for me to gauge the extent to which elders of the Yi lineage actually believed that their ancestor's spirit was present at the ceremony. The emphasis at a chesa is on proper behavior and correct ritual. Nothing sudden, loud, or expressive of individual emotion interrupts the stately proceedings. Confucius himself and the men who have interpreted his doctrines for some two thousand five hundred years have always played down the supernatural.

Those who were highly educated in the Confucian tradition regarded the rites primarily as necessary to instill a proper sense of order, hierarchy, and decorum among living practitioners. The objective has always been to create a harmonious society here and now, not to save individual souls or to establish a utopia in the next world. As a matter of fact, Koreans do not think of their ancestor-oriented rituals or their family-centered values as religious. The chesa is simply a normal part of respectable family life, with the term "religion" being reserved entirely for Buddhism and Christianity.

Most mature men in Sŏkp'o in 1966 did believe that the chesa "consoles" the spirit of the ancestor and helps to ensure the prosperity of future generations. From my outsider's perspective these beliefs, in fact, seemed to reflect elements of folk superstition, but for older Korean males there was no overlap or ambivalence. They made a sharp distinction between ideas associated with ancestral spirits and the chesa on the one hand, and the whole shamanistic complex of healing rituals, divination, and efforts to obtain wealth through the help of supernatural spirits on the other. The chesa puts no emphasis on a separate spirit world. Rather, in the interests of kinship solidarity and continuity, it temporarily blurs the dividing line between living and dead kinsmen. Men used the derogatory term, superstition (misin), exclusively for shamanistic beliefs and practices, those rituals that appealed mainly to women.

When I arrived in Sŏkp'o, my knowledge of shamanism was entirely academic, gained from reading books in graduate school. I knew that the Korean practitioner, the mudang, was almost invariably a woman, who, by entering a trance state, was supposed to be able to get in touch with her own particular familiar spirit. This familiar spirit would then provide her with access to the otherworld, where she could find out about the supernatural causes of human illness or failure and learn how to go about placating the angry gods or ghosts who were causing the trouble. I had read that the quest for a familiar spirit was a long and difficult one, involving extreme physical trials. In many cases the prospective mudang suffered severe mental illness, wandering around the countryside and in the mountains in a pitifully deranged and filthy state for weeks or months before making spiritual contact. Such a woman had no choice. The only cure for her insanity was to become a professional mudang. It was also necessary for her to serve a long apprenticeship with an established mudang, since she had to master an elaborate mythology, chants, dances, and rituals.

Sŏkp'o was too small and too poor to support the services of a genuine, full-time *mudang* and had to make do with male amateurs. I had already watched performances by the two impoverished *chŏmjaengi* (shamanistic diviners) who lived in the village. These men were both elderly, more or less self-taught, and worked only part time. They did not claim to be real professionals, insisting always that they only performed out of a sense of duty to the community. All they received for their services was food, drink, and tobacco, but even so, business was bad. As healers they could no longer compete against the peddlers who brought fancy new medicines from the city. Still, when an illness refused to respond to herbal remedies or antibiotics, there was a run of bad fishing luck, or if personal relationships soured for no obvious reason, some people still resorted to the local *chŏmjaengi*.

One of these men, Kang Si Hae, was a convivial drunkard who, although well liked, was only rarely sober enough or well enough to perform. When in top form, however, he was in greater demand than the other *chŏmjaengi*, the eccentric old man from the previous chapter, Kim Pŏbyong. Kang Si Hae's son, Kang Yong Ju, had adapted some of Kim Pŏbyong's techniques for his own exotic approach to womanizing. Kang Yong Ju was about thirty-five years old, handsome, and strongly built. He had a good singing voice and was renowned for his amorous conquests. Most of Kang Yong Ju's clients seemed to be young women. First he hypnotized the patient, or at least persuaded her to lie still and rigid on her back. Then, while reciting incantations, he moved his hands slowly and repetitively all over her body for ten minutes or so. After the patient came to and sat up, he would administer acupuncture needles, draw blood, taste it, and then pronounce the patient cured. At least that was the procedure each time I saw it.

Kang Yong Ju's specialized form of healing was favored by the group of young unmarried women who washed clothes together at the well below our house, and Kyong Sook, who had frequent headaches, insisted on undergoing the treatment. As far as I was concerned Kang Yong Ju was a rank amateur concerned mainly with stroking young females, but Kyong Sook claimed it did her a great deal of good.

The other *chŏmjaengi* was Kim Pŏbyong (Insun's grandfather). In his youth he, like many of the professional female *mudang*, had gone through a terrible period of lonely, half-crazed suffering in the mountains before finding a degree of peace at Buddhist temples. From him I learned about the thousands of spirits (sinjang) who roamed the rocky coasts and pine forests of Sŏkp'o. It was his favorite topic, and although I usually lost track of the esoteric subject matter of these conversations, there was no question but that many of these spirits were his close associates.

Kim Pŏbyong even tried to teach me how to carry out curing ceremonies, and a couple pages of my field notes are still full of scribbled incantations. He admitted that he was not dignified or learned enough to serve the highest ranking gods, those of heaven and earth, but he was convinced that through his sincere, faithful, and ascetic devotion to a series of lesser deities, he had obtained the power both to help his fellow men in this world and to establish himself in a reasonably well-ranked position after death. His list of "lesser deities" (he used the term "vice presidents" in explaining their status to me) was impressive. It included the Okhwang Sangje (Jade Emperor of Chinese folk origin), the Ch'ilsŏng (Big Dipper), and Puch'o (Buddha). The way he explained things, a host of sinjang (ordinary spirits that he compared to policemen) did all the work, carrying out the wishes of the gods and communicating with the living.

Kim Pŏbyong himself was in close touch with several of these policeman-spirits: the white horse sinjang, the lightning sinjang, the underworld sinjang, and the Yellow Sea sinjang. When someone was sick, he would call on one of these spirits to find out what was wrong.

Sometimes the sinjang would tell him that the trouble was purely physical and that therefore penicillin or herb medicine was the appropriate treatment. In other cases he would learn that the disease was a matter of bad personal luck or fate and that there was very little anyone could do. But if the sickness was caused by a malevolent, wandering ("floating stranger") ghost, then he knew just how to proceed. It was necessary first to get the attention of the particular floating stranger who was causing the trouble and bribe it with rice and soup to gather up the illness and take it away. Also, since floating strangers had a tendency to dawdle and want more bribes, it was essential to frighten the ghost, while at the same time offering it a safe escape route.

When engaged in his professional activities, Kim Pŏbyong did a lot of shouting, jumping up and down, and throwing of large knives into the ground. On one occasion he invited my children to come and watch. They loved it, terrified and fascinated at the same time.

For many months all of us in my household had been healthy and, except for Kyong Sook, felt no need for ritual healing experts. In my case this happy situation changed abruptly in late July. The day certainly started without any ominous, otherworldly overtones. I took the children swimming early, and then afterwards as a special treat we had pancakes with maple syrup outside on the veranda. A friend at home had sent packets of concentrated maple flavoring, and that allowed us to carry out a sort of culinary rite, reaffirming our association with a dimly remembered homeland. There wasn't any butter, of course, but still it was a real event, with the children telling each other, "This is what we used to eat when we lived in Vermont."

It was midmorning when Kim Aji stopped by and joined me in a final cup of coffee at the end of the meal. Kim Aji, a vigorous, imposing man in his sixties had a reserved but direct manner and a high personal reputation for honesty and integrity. He was the "heavy" (yugi) man of the Sixth Hamlet at the extreme northern tip of the Korean peninsula.

The Sixth Hamlet was the most isolated and reclusive part of the village, where people were known for being more industrious and somewhat less well-mannered than in the other Sŏkp'o hamlets. The fifteen or so related Kim lineage families from this area cooperated well among themselves but not with the rest of the village. It took a long time and a lot of questioning before I discovered the reason for the isolation and distrust. Early in the Korean War, when the North Korean People's Army (Inmin'gun) had briefly occupied this area, it was among the Kims that they had found their collaborators in promoting class warfare. At that time the village head and some other landowners had been executed. On the other hand, after United States forces landed at Inch'ŏn and pushed back the North Koreans in September, 1950, South Korean authorities reoccupied the area and exacted ferocious reprisals. Kim Ŭigon (my nemesis) had been a hero of sorts, intervening with the Inmin'gun on behalf of other villagers. A good deal of bitterness remained because of the killings that had taken place on both sides.

Kim Aji presided over the Sixth Hamlet with quasi-feudal authority, settling disputes, keeping his kinsmen in line, and acting as their representative in dealing with the rest of the village and the outside world. Today he came with an invitation, asking me to come and "play" at his house that evening. Having learned about our interviews, he told me to bring my sister-in-law and promised to answer all our questions. He also asked me to bring my tape recorder. I had been worried about the kind of reception we would get in the Sixth Hamlet and therefore took this invitation from Kim Aji himself as a good sign.

In the late afternoon, just as Hi Young and I were getting ready to leave for Kim Aji's house, we had another visitor. Mun Yong Bae stopped by for his daily eye treatment. Mun Yong Bae was squat, ugly, and energetic. He had a dynamism that while often abrasive, caused things to happen. Since his house was just below mine in the Big Hamlet, we were constantly aware of all the noise and the comings and goings of visitors that accompanied his various money-making schemes. This year, among other ventures, he had chartered the only engine-powered fishing boat in Sŏkp'o, an ancient, leaky, but none-theless imposing vessel. As usual he was losing money.

Mun Yong Bae, teary-and red-eyed, had come to me a week or so previously for help, so I tried out my sulfathiazole eye drops on him. At first they cleared up the trouble completely, and my reputation as a wonder worker increased. We began receiving more of his fish catch than we could eat and had to dry some of it in the sun and give the rest away to neighbors. Even though Mun Yong Bae was convinced that he was completely cured, I kept insisting that he finish the full ten-day course of treatment, in accordance with the instructions given by real doctors in the states. Mun Yong Bae obviously thought all the additional medicine was just an attempt on my part to extract more fish. On this visit it seemed to me that his eye looked irritated again, but since it could have been the result of too much soju, I didn't say anything.

The path to the Sixth Hamlet and Kim Aji's house led up through the pines past the tiny, half-hidden village shrine near the crest, and then down a nar-row, steep gulley to the level rice fields on the other side. Here was the largest rice-growing area in Sŏkp'o, the basis of the prosperity of Kim Aji's lineage. His house, or rather compound, was on the far side, about a half mile away. The softly rounded thatched roofs were turning amber in the late afternoon sun. Across the bay on our right the mountains of Ch'ungch'ŏng Province formed sharp purple silhouettes, while to the left a range of hills permitted only an occasional glimpse of the sea. On the bay side a fishing junk with tattered, reddish-brown sails slowly rode the tide back to the village, with only slight help from a dying breeze. All around us was the intense green of maturing rice plants. Here and there a solitary farmer worked in the fields. Nowhere in the entire scene was there a single straight line, except for the sea's horizon. Everything was timeworn, uneven, and natural.

The cluster of houses occupied by Kim Aji, his brother, his sons, and his nephews was nestled against the shoulder of a wooded hill. The buildings were solid and well maintained. There was the clutter of stacked firewood, sacks of fertilizer, fishnets, tools, and most importantly bags of rice that indicated wealth. But no imposing, moss-covered stone figures stood guard over ancient tombs, as they did at the other end of the village where the hillsides belonged to the yangban Yis. The Kims were a commoner lineage without illustrious ancestors.

As we approached, squinting into the setting sun, it was apparent that the place was crowded and that everyone was wearing clean clothes. It had to be some sort of lineage gathering, but we had no idea yet what was going on. A young man met us at the main gate and led us around the outside of the house to where Kim Aji was waiting, sitting cross-legged on his sarangbang veranda beside the familiar tray of makkŏlli, cups, and anju. Hi Young hesitated. As a devout Presbyterian, she detested strong drink. Secondly, in a Korean farmhouse the sarangbang is reserved for mature males. Still unmarried, she had low status in the eyes of the villagers: except as my sister-in-law and assistant, ranking far below ordinary housewives who at least had children. Just a week or two before, critical comments had reached us through the message center at the well to the effect that it was considered unseemly, even bold and arrogant, for Hi Young to wear a wristwatch, which in Sŏkp'o was a symbol of power and influence. So she was reluctant to take off her shoes and join me on the porch, only giving in finally to Kim Aji's blunt command. Just as we were getting ready to start with our list of questions, the distinctive, insistently vigorous rhythm of a mudang's drum announced that a kut, or shaman's dance, was beginning in the inner courtyard. This, clearly the work of the devil, was too much. Hi Young apologized with a set face, put her shoes back on, and walked briskly out the gate, leaving me alone to face the dangers of makkŏlli and a sorceress who could communicate with the spirit world.

With my interpreter gone I could no longer expect to pick up all the fine points of the conversations and actions going on around me. Nevertheless I could communicate, and I had long ago memorized the questions we wanted to ask—as well as most of the answers. But I also felt relieved of any pretense of scholarly decorum. Now I could forget the whole tedious questionnaire routine and enjoy the party. It seemed to me that Kim Aji had cleverly forestalled my unwanted questions by asking me to conduct the interview in the midst of what turned out to be one of the largest and noisiest gatherings of the year.

Cordially he poured makkŏlli for me, asking what it was that I wanted to know. I blurted out a few questions. They seemed even more out of place than usual in the midst of what was becoming a throbbing, carnival-like atmosphere. Children and adolescents kept coming around to the guest-room porch and staring solemnly for a little while, but they were soon lured away to the inner courtyard where the real action was taking place. When I asked about the ceremony, Kim Aji said that he had only hired the mudang to please the women of his lineage. They thought a kut was necessary at least once a year to ensure the prosperity and health of everyone in the neighborhood. The women believed that neglected and jealous spirits of the dead caused sickness and misfortune, and that the fickle and unpredictable gods must be fed and entertained periodically, or they would become angry—with terrible consequences for the living. Kim Aji, of course, didn't believe in these old superstitions, but he thought it was just as well to keep everyone happy, including the gods. In the meantime he wanted me to eat and drink as much as I pleased, and he promised to try to answer all my questions.

But I was intensely curious about the kut and longed to join the crowd. In addition to the drum I heard strangely hoarse shouts, along with occasional bursts of laughter from the spectators. The kut was always a women's show, with the men looking on perhaps disdainfully, but usually keeping a dignified distance. Confucian tradition, which is supremely male-oriented, demands etiquette, order, and decorum. Here in the kut it was all emotion and wild self-expression.

Other men had by now joined our little separate drinking party, and someone began to make jokes about the folly of the women with their "mountain god" and "seven-star spirit." But an older man rebuked him, saying, "No one knows what goes on in the spirit world after death, and in any case the kut does no harm."

Someone else added, "Why not have the gods on our side?" and the criticism stopped. Finally I was able to break away and watch the show. At a kut the deepest emotions are felt and expressed without restraint, while the gaudy and frenetically animated mudang displays disturbingly superhuman strength and endurance. The gods are being appeased, and dangerous household goblins driven out or placated. It is exorcism, catharsis, and participatory theater, all combined in a brilliantly exciting form.

The kut performed by the mudang at Kim Aji's house was entirely different from anything offered by our local diviners. For one thing, it went on for two days and all through one night and was very expensive. She had come to town with two musician attendants carrying heavy bags of ritual regalia on their backs. The several Kim households in the hamlet had prepared large amounts of food for everyone, some of which was prominently displayed as part of the gaudy decorations framing the mudang's performance. For women in an isolated village, the kut was the supreme event of the year, satisfying their need for entertainment, excitement, and spiritual consolation.

At this particular ceremony the drumming, dancing, and dialogue with the supernatural went on and on, almost without stopping. Deceased relatives were summoned and spoke through the mouth of the mudang. Gods and spirits addressed the crowd in the same way. According to the various phases of the performance, the women and children present experienced sorrow, nostalgia, ribald amusement, terror, and relief. At times the mudang would enter a trance state with her eyes rolled back and her body convulsed in strange jerky motions. Then she would talk gibberish or shout ecstatically or reproduce deep male voices with an eerie authenticity. From time to time the rhythm changed and the tension eased as the mudang relaxed, entertaining the crowd with jokes and mime and extracting money payment for the gods. I had nothing with me but a five hundred wǒn note (about three dollars in 1966), which was a lot of money in the village. Other people were giving mostly ten wǒn coins. But the mudang pestered me until I gave up my money, and then she went into a special triumphant jig, to the delight of the other spectators. Before long, though, she resumed the serious business of communicating with the otherworld.

One of Kim Aji's nephews found me in the courtyard and led me back to the guest-room veranda, where I had left the tape recorder. At the far end, well away from the dignified elders, was a group of young men. It turned out that the nephew sang popular songs and wanted to hear himself on tape. Two of his friends had guitars to provide accompaniment. The contemporary love songs seemed strangely out of place, with the mudang chants and fierce drumming going on in the background. All the young men gathered around, beating time and encouraging the singer with shouts of applause. Many had never seen a tape recorder in action before, and their delighted surprise when they first heard the playback gave me an unwanted competitive edge for a while over the kut. Kim Aji presided over these clashing harmonies with relaxed and affable goodwill, although he and the other elders made fun of the young men's music. It was a long time before I could get back to the courtyard.

That night I watched the shaman's show for several hours, with periodic visits to Kim Aji's sarangbang for refreshment. Children slept and watched and slept again. Babies cried, were fed, and went back to sleep on their mothers' backs. Old women danced with tears streaming down their faces, as long-dead relatives returned to speak again to the living. Barriers between this world and the one of the spirits seemed to be breaking down. The mood was contagious. I was no longer looking on at a primitive ritual with objective, skeptical curiosity. Rather, I seemed to be vibrating with a sort of restless, apprehensive impatience. Somewhere deep inside I was responding to the mudang's magical skill. In that crowded, noisy, lamp-lit courtyard, a century or two away from the scientific present, it was easy to suspend disbelief.

I left well after midnight, but the mudang was still going strong. Possessed by the Sea Dragon spirit (Yongwan nim), the shaman was sobbing and wailing in an extraordinary voice. Most of the spectators stayed where they were, occasionally taking catnaps. Kim Aji insisted on giving me a final cup of makkŏlli before I left, and then walked me courteously to his gate. The harsh clash of cymbals along with the constant drumming followed me in the dark most of the way home, where I slept uneasily, disturbed by threatening dreams.

The next morning I felt terrible. Was it the result of too much makkŏlli or too close an association with unfamiliar spirits? I had no energy for a climb up the mountain or a swim, and it was hard work forcing myself to write up the previous day's encounters and impressions. The medical kit offered no appropriate remedies, so I struggled through the morning with a headache and slight nausea.

By afternoon I felt a little better and wandered over to the other side of the ridge. On the exposed high ground the sound of drumming carried from the Sixth Hamlet by the north wind could still be heard. It made me restless and anxious to see more of the kut. This time I took the camera instead of the tape recorder, making sure I had fifty wŏn notes in my pocket. Pretty soon I was taking pictures of the tireless mudang, first as she danced on sword blades and then as she vigorously swung a sacrificial chicken around by the neck.

An hour or so later the mudang was in the midst of shifting spirit roles, a process that also involved a change of costume, when a boy came running in through the main gate and started whispering noisily and breathlessly to one of the women of the household. A wave of excited chatter passed through the crowd, and several people hurried outside. A young woman nearby started to wail. As usual, I was bewildered and asked the boy what was going on. He pulled my sleeve, led me outside, and pointed to the edge of the rice fields several hundred yards away. There, a small group of men was carrying something on a makeshift stretcher. "It is Mun Yong Bae's mother," he said. "She died in the rice field all by herself way over near the ocean." From inside the house the dead woman's niece continued to wail.

Some minutes later the drum began again. The *mudang* summoned all her fire to invoke the spirits, and through sheer intensity of effort she compelled the momentarily distracted audience to lose themselves again in her visions of prosperity, health, and long life. Finally the gods were satisfied and the demons expelled. The *kut* was over. As the crowd emerged from the courtyard and dispersed, the small and dismal procession was still visible, climbing the ridge in the distance. The excitement and good feeling, generated by the *kut*, evaporated quickly. People looked anxious, and there was little conversation.

Other deaths had occurred in the village during my stay, but none had ever provoked such frightened gloom. The funerals had been expansive parties, with the children of the deceased so busy demonstrating their filial piety through lavish displays of hospitality, and the neighbors so busy consuming the display, that there was little place for public sorrow. Grief was not the chief emotion this time either; rather, it was terror.

I asked Kim Aji what was wrong, and he answered simply, "She did not die at home," as though that explained everything. When I said, "She was not so far away," he looked at me as if I was half-witted and tried again to explain, "But she was perfectly healthy, and besides, no one was nearby to help her." The next day Teacher Yi explained, "They are afraid of her angry ghost. She should not have been working all alone, but she was angry at Mun Yong Bae and wanted to stay as far away from the house as she could get. And what's more, she drowned. Even though there were only a few centimeters of water in the field, that is how she died! In a fishing village like this everyone fears the ghosts of those who drown. They think her ghost is angry and will do harm."

To my surprise Teacher Yi then proceeded to pass a warning on to me, "There is already talk about the failure of your eye drops because of the ghost's interference, and people think Mun Yong Bae will probably go blind in that eye. They say you should leave Mun Yong Bae alone and not get mixed up in such a dangerous business."

I then asked what the fight between mother and son was about. Teacher Yi said, "It is about property. Any such discord is a terrible thing, and we should not gossip about it." Teacher Yi's wife was not so reticent. "Just the kind of greedy behavior you might expect from Mun Yong Bae. Now he will have to do something to satisfy her ghost."

When I got home that same evening, Mun Yong Bae was waiting for me, wearing a filthy eye patch. His eye was red and painful, and he asked me anxiously if anything was wrong with my medicine. I gave him more drops, but it was obvious that he had lost faith in the sulfathiazole.

The next day Kim Pŏbyong, my chŏmjaengi friend, told me more about the dispute between mother and son. Mun Yong Bae's father had died a couple of years before, and as the eldest son Mun Yong Bae would normally receive a larger portion than his younger brothers. But because he was domineering and selfish and needed money for his various investments, he had taken control of all the property, selling land without consulting the rest of the family. He was unwilling to share anything at all, claiming that when he was rich there would be enough for everyone.

His grandfather and mother had become allies in trying to obtain a decent portion for the second son, who wanted to marry and set up his own separate household. Everyone knew that Mun Yong Bae and his mother did not get along and that she favored the second son. Up on the hill at my house we had known for some time that there were serious family troubles, because we could hear the angry shouting down below. But we were too far away to understand what all the arguing was actually about.

It was Kyong Sook, our delegate to the nearby message center at the well, who supplied us with further information. One of her friends at the well had passed by Sok Hee's mother's house and overheard her crying out that the pain in her stomach was worse than childbirth and that she was dying. The expression "I'm dying" is commonly used in Korean for any difficult or unpleasant situation, but the group of young women at the well decided that in this case she really meant it, and that the pain must be the work of Mun Yong Bae's mother's ghost. Kyong Sook also reported the clothes washers' consensus that the ghost would probably strike someone else. Further questioning revealed that while malevolent ghosts are particularly dangerous to close kin against whom there is a grievance, they can also be indiscriminate in causing illness and disaster to anyone in the vicinity.

Later that same afternoon when Kyong Sook went down to the beach to get some promised fish from an incoming boat, she heard that another woman in the neighborhood had been stricken with the same terrible pain. She too claimed that it was worse than childbirth, and she too expected to die. Then, just before dark I noticed from my vantage point up on the hill that a small crowd had gathered at Mun Yong Bae's house. I wandered down as unobtrusively as possible, but everyone there was far too excited to pay any attention to me. Since the entire community was endangered by his mother's angry ghost, there was a feeling that Yong Bae should immediately turn over an appropriate amount of land to his brother and hold a kut to appease the dangerous spirit.

Mun Yong Bae, with his ragged eye bandage bobbing up and down, angrily shouted back that modern people didn't believe in such superstitious nonsense anymore. He made sarcastic fun of the men who had been "persuaded by old women's beliefs." This turned out to be a major tactical error, because the oldest man present then began to recite in detail and in a loud voice (by then the entire hamlet had gathered to watch the spectacle) an account of Mun Yong Bae's "improper behavior." He went on and on, publicly accusing Mun Yong Bae of three of the most dishonorable crimes in terms of traditional morality: failure to be a filial son, failure to be a benevolent elder brother, and stinginess. Finally, an old woman shouted, "Look at you! You're going blind. The American medicine doesn't work. Don't you know that it's your mother's ghost?" Publicly humiliated, Mun Yong Bae was angrier than ever, shouting back, "It is no longer possible for a man of any culture to live in such a backward place!" He went inside, closing the gate.

I woke up in the middle of the night with a dull ache low down in my abdomen. It seemed to come from deep inside my body, and I couldn't remember ever feeling such a pain before. It was vaguely reminiscent of acute appendicitis, but that doesn't happen a second time. A long visit to the outhouse did not help. By dawn I was doubled over and moaning. It got worse throughout the day. The pain seemed to spread from inside me to encompass the whole universe. I couldn't (or thought I couldn't) get up to walk, and I wouldn't eat or drink.

By evening Hi Young was frantically worried and went down to ask the village head if I could get medical help. There was talk of sending someone to the nearest American missile base (a five-or six-hour walk) to ask for a helicopter. The idea that something serious might happen to the illustrious foreign visitor was regarded as a potential calamity—a source of shame for the entire village. At one point I remember thinking I'd be happy to be whisked off somewhere by helicopter, but soon I didn't really care that much anymore or believe it was possible. I had really given up and just lay in a fetal position, trying to find ways to ease the pain. In any case it was getting dark, too late to get help from outside the village. Hi Young decided she would go to the provincial hospital in Sŏsan the next morning and come back with a doctor.

At some point during the night Kim Pŏbyong showed up and without a word of greeting or explanation proceeded to carry out his own form of exorcism. Hi Young started to protest, but I asked her to let him go ahead. Perhaps I didn't want to pass up any bets. I like to think, too, that in spite of the pain I still had some anthropological curiosity. Kim Pŏbyong planted a staff festooned with folded paper streamers in the ground and began to chant, accompanying himself with a drum. In front of him on the ground was a bowl of soup and rice, a large knife, and a gourd dipper, half full of water. For a long time he sat cross-legged, his body swaying with staccato rhythm in the candlelight. He would suddenly stiffen and tremble violently, his eyes rolled far back in his skull. Leaping to his feet, he cried out and flourished the knife, bounding about with the agility of a much younger man. The upright staff shook furiously. Finally, he overturned the gourd and plunged the knife into the ground with another hoarse cry. Then, clearly exhausted, he left.

When the ache finally dulled and went away completely a few hours later, I began to cry. I had been injured and in severe pain several times before without ever having gone through this phase of uncontrollable, almost joyful sobbing. In the days that followed, I thought back over the experience a great deal. What seemed strangest, in retrospect, was my passive abandonment of any effort to control my own fate. What had happened to my normal, rational, problem-solving activism? When my sister-in-law and the villagers had been trying to decide what to do, I had felt like a disinterested spectator, conscious of what was going on, but separate, not deeply involved.

When Kim Pŏbyong had come to do battle with the malevolent spirit, it had all seemed completely appropriate, a little melodramatic perhaps, but comforting. After it was all over and the pain was gone, I felt lighthearted, invulnerable, and confident, as if, indeed, a noxious influence had been lifted. It was like a rebirth into a bright new world. I wandered out into what was now a shining landscape and walked along the edge of the high barley fields above the ocean in a daze, still crying. This post-pain "high" lasted for several days, with its exhilaration and sense of power. Two more women in the neighborhood came down with the same ailment. I began to feel rather proud at having undergone the equivalent of labor with no more serious aftereffects than a crying jag.

Everyone got well eventually, the floating stranger having been pacified rather economically. Mun Yong Bae attracted considerable ridicule and a certain amount of grudging, amused admiration, because instead of hiring an expensive *mudang*, he had gotten by with the services of the village's old, alcoholic *chŏmjaengi*. Fueled by large amounts of *soju*, Kang Si Hae had put on an excellent show, I was told, although at one point he had fallen in the fire and slightly burned one foot. According to reports from the well, the villagers believed that Mun Yong Bae's division of the estate had been more important in giving solace to his mother's ghost than the cut-rate, local brand of shamanism. In any case, his mother's funeral was a splendid one, and Mun Yong Bae's eye gradually improved without any further treatment by me.

9

Fishing I

Along the beach where the boats were moored, poor fishermen lived in a row of ramshackle hovels. Each one had a small plot for kitchen greens, but the soil was too sandy for successful gardening. On the lopsided roofs the thatch was old and moldering, because the owners had no paddy fields to provide them with rice straw. The beach in front of these homes was often a lively, cheerful place, a kind of social center for the Big Hamlet. It was protected from the wind and close to the sulchip—an ideal place to mend nets, work on boats, talk, and drink.

One of the places that sold makkŏlli was run by a particularly attractive woman in her early thirties whose husband, Kim Ch'angdok, was often away fishing in the offshore islands. Not only did Ok Hi's mother, as she was usually called, share a glass with her customers now and then, but she also joked, argued, and flirted, while using extremely earthy language. This kind of behavior was so distressing to the good wives of the Yi households across the mudflats that they either pretended she didn't exist or gossiped about her in hushed voices.

I, however, was well aware of her existence. Ok Hi's mother had been one of the first women to bring her children to my house for scalp treatments. In warm weather she wore tight, ragged T-shirts that barely contained her breasts, and I doubt that she was unaware of the vibrations she caused by sprawling and stretching on my veranda with her children while I spread ointment on their heads. She would arch her back until the tattered cloth of her T-shirt was ready to split, then change her sitting position to reveal long legs under a voluminous skirt. She also stopped by occasionally to bring fish in payment for my doctoring. In the course of these encounters, I learned that she was ambitious. With money saved from selling makkŏlli and her husband's meager earnings she wanted to start a small business in Inch'ŏn, where she hoped to live a more "cultured" life and to send her children to better schools. The trouble was that, like other fishermen, Kim Ch'angdok drank a great deal, and although he earned fairly good money working on the island boats, most of it was gone by the time he got back to Sŏkp'o.

One morning in July, two handsome thirty-foot junk-rigged fishing boats of a type that I had never seen before were pulled up on the sand in front of Ok Hi's mother's house. Given the usual rhythm of existence in the village, this was something of an event. Sometimes severe storms brought big, lumbering engine-powered boats seeking refuge into the harbor, but nothing as sleek and attractive as these sailboats had ever turned up before. Eager to get a closer look, I headed down for the beach.

It was hot, and as I walked past the houses, night soil that had just recently been poured over young cabbage plants and other greens gave off its peculiarly intense, sweetish smell. Metallic, golden flies swarmed along the path, and swallows darted past my head. The two boats were even more impressive when I looked at them up close, running my hands over the hulls and gear. No paint or varnish had been used, but the gunwales, decks, and spars had a hand-rubbed oiled texture that shone dully in the sunlight. The boats were less crudely built and more carefully maintained than those from this part of the coast.

Below the waterline, tar or pitch covered the bottom just as on the local boats, but even here care had been taken to draw a crisp stripe. Fishing lines were neatly coiled in tubs on deck, and there was a wooden box lined with stones for a charcoal fire aft of the mast. In contrast to the tattered rags used locally, the sails were made of heavy reddish-brown cloth in good condition.

From behind me someone shouted, "Come up here and play for a while!" I turned to see a group of men sitting in the shade of the big pine tree that dominated the hamlet from the top of a grassy knoll behind the beach. It was a lovely spot, just high enough above the rooftops to catch the westerly breeze. Ok Hi's mother's husband, Kim Ch'angdok, was the person who had called. I climbed the knoll and he held out a shiny brass bowl for me and then poured it full of the thin, milky, fermented makkŏlli that was illegally made in villages throughout rural South Korea. It was obviously his party.

Little by little, as we ate pieces of spicy octopus and exchanged bowls of makkŏlli, I learned that the boats were from Mot Som, a small archipelago of rocky islets eighteen miles or so offshore. The formal name (written with Chinese characters 池島) identifies these islands on the map as Chi Do, but the fishermen all used the much more expressive native Korean term, Mot Sŏm, which means "lagoon islands."

Sŏkp'o fishermen, despite a certain amount of swagger and bravado, were well aware of their low occupational and social status in South Korean society. They were not only fishermen, however. They also belonged to the world of farmers and had thoroughly internalized the same Confucian ethics and rules of behavior as their landowning neighbors and relatives. The men from Mot Sŏm and other offshore islands, on the other hand, lived entirely by the sea and associated almost entirely with other fishermen. They designed, built, and cared for their boats with a pride and concern that was unknown on the Ch'ungch'ŏng-do coast. They had no humility about their profession and responded to my questions with enthusiasm, proudly telling me how much faster and more seaworthy their boats were than those made on the mainland. As far as I could tell from the mood of our little drinking party on top of the knoll, Sŏkp'o fishermen agreed, recognizing the superior seamanship and fishing skills of the islanders.

The newer of the two boats belonged to a weather-beaten man in his thirties from Mot Sŏm named Chang Kigwang. Kim Ch'angdok had worked for him at Mot Sŏm for several years, and they were on good terms. The really surprising news was that Kim Ch'angdok spoke as if he was the owner and captain of the other boat. Kim Ch'angdok usually had no money except what his wife gave him from her earnings selling makkŏlli. His reputation in Sŏkp'o was not high, either as an individual or as a fisherman. He had always been just a member of the crew on other people's boats, never captain. But now that her husband was enjoying a new and unaccustomed status as a boat owner, Ok Hi's mother was kept busy running up and down the hill with food and drink.

Capital was even more scarce in Sŏkp'o than other resources, and the envious villagers were intrigued, wondering how Kim Ch'angdok could have borrowed enough money to buy such a boat. Mun Yongbae blurted out what everyone was thinking, "You must have done an awful lot of drinking with Chang Kigwang on Mot Sŏm."

Chang Kigwang himself explained. "We have the boats. There are plenty of fish, but we don't have the men. Kim Ch'angdok can find good crew members here and help me out at Mot Sŏm. So I'm letting him use the boat for a couple of seasons."

The annual croaker fishing season was about to begin offshore, and the rest of the morning was filled with extravagant accounts of the large amounts of money to be made in Mot Sŏm waters. I exchanged bowls of makkŏlli with Chang Kigwang, the equivalent of a mutual self-introduction, and he said, "Everyone knows me at Mot Sŏm. My brothers and I catch lots of fish. We also buy fish from other fishermen and ship the catch in our own boats to Inch'ŏn. We sell fuel oil to the fishing fleet, and we have a ship repair facility. We make lots of money." I couldn't figure out why such a self-proclaimed big shot was spending his time on the beach at Sŏkp'o, so I discounted the talk as typical fisherman's boasting. Later I found out how wrong I was.

During our hours of desultory drinking and eating, the tide had been rising, and when it reached the level of the boats drawn up on the beach, the crews gathered and began to rig them for departure. It was sunny, and there was a strong breeze. I was delighted at being invited to go along on Kim Ch'angdok's boat. Without the slightest idea where we were headed, I just stuck my camera inside my shirt and jumped aboard. It all happened with the puzzling abruptness that sometimes interrupted the slow pace of life in Sŏkp'o.

I heard the phrase paennori several times as we got under way, but "boat play" didn't make any particular sense to me. Now a half dozen Sŏkp'o boats left the beach at about the same time in an atmosphere of excitement and good spirits. It was the only time while in the village that I witnessed boats used for sport. But "sport" here, while highly competitive, was a little different from yacht races at home. The idea was to aim directly at one of the "competitors" and then bear off at the last possible moment, passing as close as possible without causing a collision. Since there were no other rules, and everyone was half drunk, the situation was more chaotic and a good deal more exciting than a crowded racing start in Narragansett Bay. The Mot Sŏm boat was faster and more agile than any of the Sŏkp'o fleet, and Kim Ch'angdok was either inspired or lucky. I got some good pictures.

After an hour or so of paennori and a good deal of incomprehensible (to me) shouting, we stopped trying to sink each other and headed east across the bay on a fast, two-mile reach. The rest of the fleet did the same, and I

Figure 9.1 Boat "play" (*paennori*); author at the helm. (1966)

Figure 9.2 Boat "play"; mixing it up. (1966)

learned that we were going to Sindok, a village that was just visible across the water from Sŏk'p'o on a clear day. A man named Kwŏn Wŏnsang was celebrating his hwangap, or sixtieth birthday, there that afternoon. Mr. Kwŏn was widely known as a wealthy and influential farmer, so this was certain to be an auspicious occasion.

In traditional Korea mortality rates were of course much higher than they are today, and sixty years was regarded as a ripe old age, the fulfillment of a man's life cycle. At sixty a man graduated to the category of elder statesman. He became a dignified ornament to his family, demonstrating the family's industry, harmony, and filial piety. The few who were fortunate enough to reach this age celebrated in the most extravagant way possible.

Mr. Kwŏn was doing things right. From far out in the bay we could see the tents and awnings in front of his house and hear the sound of a drum. The party was, of course, much more than just a celebration of an important rite of passage. It was an assertion of his claim to a prominent position in the community—or in this case, where I estimated there must have been over three hundred guests—in the entire township. When a man of substance turned sixty, the prestige to be gained was in direct proportion to the number of people who could be attracted and overwhelmed by hospitality.

Most of the guests were in their best clothes. Older men wore extremely dignified traditional garments, and nearly all of the married women wore native Korean dresses. Everyone else wore summer clothes (T-shirts, skirts) that were neatly washed and pressed. The women from Sŏkp'o had walked for hours to get to the party, since ancient superstitions strictly prohibited them from traveling in fishing boats. All of us in the water-born Sŏkp'o contingent looked a little shabby compared to the rest of the crowd. Apparently the decision to sail over to the hwangap celebration had been made on the spur of the moment in the midst of boat play.

Mr. Kwŏn, who had obviously been drinking for some hours, held my hand in greeting for about ten minutes in what I assumed was delighted surprise at having attracted a foreigner from across the water. Then he led me unsteadily off to a special part of his big house where county officials, a local politician, the police captain, and very old men were being given particularly elaborate trays of food.

But the old men were mostly toothless and spoke in a thick regional dialect that was almost incomprehensible. The officials affected a learned and lofty style that was often beyond my ordinary, everyday vocabulary. Besides, I had already had enough of sitting in a dark, stuffy room with old men at Teacher Yi's house to last a lifetime. From outside I heard the enticing sounds of a flute accompanied by an hourglass drum and the passionate shouts of onlookers. After half an hour or so of confinement indoors with the elite, I escaped, with the excuse that I wanted to take pictures. It wasn't easy getting away. My companions were determined to demonstrate Korean hospitality and actually pulled me back down to the floor a couple of times when I tried to get up.

Mr. Kwŏn's house and farm stood on a bluff overlooking the bay. Most of the guests, divided strictly into male and female groups, were sitting on reed mats under awnings, and the party was steadily building up a euphoric momentum. *Kisaeng* (professional female entertainers) had been imported from the county seat, and they began to sing and dance to everyone's delight. Ordinary farmers and fishermen all knew about *kisaeng* as a glamorous aspect of the Korean cultural tradition. But *kisaeng* are very expensive. A villager might actually see one in action only once or twice in a lifetime.

Mr. Kwŏn got up and began gyrating among the *kisaeng*. His grotesque version of their graceful classical dancing brought howls of appreciation from the guests. I was busy taking photographs of all the gaudy action when someone roughly jostled my arm and took away the camera. One of the county officials was apparently upset at the idea of a patronizing foreigner taking pictures of undignified country revels. Mr. Kwŏn's wife and son hurried over and restored my camera to me with elaborate apologies. They urged me to take more pictures. It turned out that Mr. Kwŏn had been especially pleased when I arrived at his party precisely because I had brought my camera. So I did my best after that to play the role of official photographer. The *kisaeng* were also eager to have their pictures taken in action, and I even had the pleasure of delivering some prints to them personally when I passed through Sŏsan a few weeks later.

The Sŏkp'o men and women who had trudged all the way around the head of the bay to get to Shin Dok Ri, as well as the guests from other villages, remained segregated by sex, both en route and at the party. The only unmarried young people present were relatives of Mr. Kwŏn along with some of his neighbors who were helping out with the work. For the married women who had come from all over the district, it was a wonderful chance to get together and "play" with relatives and childhood friends. The music continued, and as they drank more makkŏlli, women got up and danced, but always with other women. The only male-female interaction was between the kisaeng and those of us lucky enough to be asked to sit and drink with them.

The eating and drinking went on after dark, with animated chatter, laughter, and the impromptu singing of folk songs. Occasionally an inspired male guest would get up and join in the kisaeng dances. Some had to be led gently away. Others danced well and were cheered by the crowd. Once or twice arguments started to get out of hand, but drinking companions always intervened before real trouble developed.

Finally, a little overwhelmed by all the makkŏlli and food and knowing it would be several hours before we could sail, I went back to the house and slept in an unused room. Kim Ch'angdok woke me up around midnight, and we all staggered down the bluff to where the boat lay on the mud, almost afloat. The breeze had softened and a misty half-moon was just clearing the hills to the south. Everyone's movements in getting underway were automatic. Stowing the anchor, setting the sails, poling out to open water, and shipping the big steering oar were accomplished without any orders and only a little slower than usual. As soon as we were sailing, the crew fell asleep, and when I took the tiller from Kim Ch'angdok, he stretched out, too. I had the whole return trip to myself, looking at the moon and listening to the gentle slap of water against the hull.

The heat of midsummer had taken some of the edge off my scientific ardor. Complexities of lineage structure, informal methods of social control, rational choice alternatives in agriculture, and other social science abstractions seemed less compelling. I began going out fairly regularly on the local boats, fishing for corvina, eel, and skate along the coast. With a tidal range of about twenty-five feet, the whole topography of the bay and the harbor area changed dramatically at high and low water. Since the boats were heavy and slow and sailed reasonably well only in a strong and favorable breeze, tidal currents were at least as important as the wind in getting out to the fishing areas and then returning to the village several hours later. If we left with the last of the morning ebb tide, the channel from the beach was a small stream between high mud banks. When we came back on the flood in the late afternoon, no mud was visible anywhere, and the bay extended miles up the valleys between coastal mountains. If it was nearly high water, we could sail right up onto the beach in front of the fishermen's shacks, and Ok Hi's mother would be out serving makkŏlli and anju even before the fish were hauled out of the hold.

These fishing days, in which every activity was controlled by slow, repetitive rhythms, were infinitely satisfying. The techniques were simple, economical, and efficient, embodying thousands of years of slowly acquired knowledge of the sea. All the tools and artifacts that we used were made by hand, and they had a heft and a weathered patina that was almost as natural as the rocks along the coast.

The most time-consuming and expensive part of long-line fishing was baiting the hundreds of hooks with a kind of tiny anchovy that was caught just off the coves and beaches. The anchovy fishermen used nets, and we would rendezvous with them just after leaving the harbor to obtain bait and have the first drink of the day. We ate the fresh bait as anju. Baiting the hooks took up a good part of the morning, and although I got a little better with practice, I never was able to finish even half as many hooks as the professionals. The fact that I was slow at this as well as most other tasks, meant that my presence in the boat was something of an economic liability, and I desperately hoped for a good catch by way of some sort of supernatural compensation.

After baiting the hooks, we would set out the long lines across the current anywhere from two to five or six miles offshore and then relax for an hour or so with soju, roast sweet potatoes (if it was late in the season), and some kind of dry or salted fish. Then pulling in the lines and taking fish off the hooks took another couple of hours. If we caught a lot of fish, spirits would rise and I would feel welcome on board.

Nothing has ever tasted better to me than the fresh raw and grilled fish with hot sauce, accompanied by more soju that we consumed during return trips after a good day's fishing. The low sun in the west glowed on deeply weathered wooden planks and patched sails. The sea seemed a friendly and bountiful place. When there was a good strong following breeze, the bow wave chuckled, the boat came alive, and for me the trip back into the harbor, past jagged cliffs and ripening rice fields, was over far too soon.

Of course there were other days when it was hot and oily calm and we didn't catch much. Then I felt like some sort of Jonah, abusing the fishermen's hospitality. At the end of a calm day there might be hours of slow sculling back to the beach. No one ever actually complained, but if the fishing was really poor, I was not likely to be invited again on that particular boat.

As the summer went by, I grew more curious about Mot Sŏm. On a clear day if I climbed the 350 feet to the summit of the highest hill near my house, I could just make out a faint mark on the horizon where the islands were. Each time I went out with the fishermen, I wanted to keep on going, instead of always having to turn back at the end of the day.

A few weeks later when Kim Ch'angdok and his boat showed up again in Sŏkp'o, I asked if I could ride with him back to Mot Sŏm. He agreed and told me we would be leaving in a couple of days. But two days later it was blowing so hard out of the southwest that Kim Ch'angdok postponed the departure. It would have been a fast trip with all that wind on our beam, and it certainly seemed to me that the boat was up to it, but Kim Ch'angdok either lacked confidence or was concerned about his foreign passenger. Word of my plans had quickly gotten around the village, and several people, most notably some of my Yi clan "relatives," stopped by and urged me not to go. "Men are lost at sea nearly every year. It is all right for ordinary fishermen to risk their lives, but if something happens to you, there will be all sorts of complications and the reputation of the village as a whole will suffer." Then in a lower voice someone would say, "And besides, Kim Ch'angdok is not an experienced captain."

When we finally left after the wind had moderated, it was not Kim Ch'angdok but his cousin, Kim Ch'angsun, who was in charge. A teenaged cook and Kang Yong Ju, the shaman's son, filled out the crew. Kim Ch'angsun, the captain, was a serious, quiet man who had been a prosperous, well-thought-of fisherman until three years previously. Then, in an argument at sea over damage to his nets by a boat from a neighboring village he had killed a man.

From time to time there was murderous violence in Sŏkp'o, usually as a result of drunken brawls, but occasionally also in bitter fights over property or loss of face. Every effort was made locally to disguise a killing as an accident or illness, with appropriate compensation paid quickly and secretly to the family of the victim. Within the village there was universal agreement that intervention by outside authorities, for any purpose whatsoever, was disastrous, and as a result great social pressure was placed on both parties in a serious dispute to reach agreement. In the case of Kim Ch'angsun, however, the compensation demanded had been too high, and with two different communities involved, it had been impossible to settle the conflict. To everyone's surprise the family of the murdered man carried out its threat and went to the police. Kim Ch'angsun had spent three years in jail.

Recently released, he was trying to regain his former position in the community, and since he was known to be a much better seaman and fisherman than Kim Ch'angdok, we were all pleased to have him as captain. The division of the catch was to be fifty percent for the boat owner, Chang Kigwang's son, thirty percent for the captain, Kim Ch'angsun, fifteen percent for Kang Yong Ju, and only five percent for the cook.

After all the warnings and the postponement, the night before we left was an uneasy one, and I still felt a few qualms as we loaded the boat and poled out through the winding muddy channel at daybreak. With me it's always that way before an ocean passage in a small boat: I study the sky, look at the waves, listen to the wind, and think about all the things that can go wrong. I thought the Koreans also seemed a little subdued. But as soon as we caught the ocean breeze just off the harbor entrance and began to move, the usual pleasure of feeling the sailboat do its work replaced my apprehension.

For three hours we moved along nicely with a good wind under a hazy sun. What bothered me a little was that we were not sailing in quite the right direction. Kim Ch'angsun was silent, and his expression was surly. I did not discuss the boat's heading with him. After all, the Shandung Peninsula of China was only one hundred miles or so off to the west, so we were bound to land somewhere. There was no shelter of any kind on the open deck and, thinking I was tan enough not to need any protection, I slept for a while in just my shorts. When I woke up, the wind had dropped, it was very hot, and I had a painful sunburn.

Ahead of us to the west, masses of heavy clouds rose up from the sea and gradually we were enveloped by a thick fog that mercifully blocked off some of the sun. Still, there was no island. I was beginning to wonder about Korean seat-of-the-pants navigation when suddenly a few boat lengths in front of us a wave broke noisily against rocks, and then we could see misty cliffs rising straight up from the water to disappear into thick clouds overhead. There was little wind, and the boat swept past the rock wall sideways at a frightening speed, sucked to the north by the strong tide. Then to starboard another cliff showed up out of the haze, and it seemed certain that the current would set us directly onto the rocks. I was tensing myself for shipwreck, wondering if I could make it ashore safely, when we shot right through a narrow channel between the two cliffs and out into a large body of calm water. Here the fog lifted, and we could see the other steep, rocky islets that formed Mot Sŏm harbor's protective ring. After drifting for a while we caught the breeze again and headed for a mass of boats clustered off a beach a mile or so away on the other side of the "lagoon." I looked at Kim Ch'angsun. He sat calmly at the tiller, morose as usual, never having moved or said a word.

On the Maine coast we have fog, as well as lots of nasty rocks and strong currents. I sail in the fog when I am caught out and have no choice. Sometimes I'll even deliberately make a passage when the visibility is bad just to test my skill. But I have accurate charts, tide tables, a knotmeter, an accurate watch, and, above all, a carefully adjusted compass. And there is an elaborate system of buoys and fog horns marking the principle dangers along the coast. Kim Ch'angsun had nothing but his own experience. It was a pretty fancy piece of piloting; he hadn't forgotten much in prison.

As we lowered the sails and started sculling towards the beach, other Sŏkp'o men hailed us from some of the big, engine-powered boats that worked out of Inch'ŏn. Kang Yong Ju was our spokesman, shouting out news of relatives and village events across the water.

Standing on the beach as if waiting for us was Song P'algap, a trader from Mohang, the big fishing village south of Sŏkp'o where the bus line ended. With his two young sons he had made the trip the day before when it was blowing really hard. I looked at him and at his boat with new respect. They had brought out cigarettes, liquor, shaving gear, medicines, candy, some simple tools, and spare engine parts to sell to Mot Sŏm fishermen. Since Kim Ch'angdok would be staying in the islands to fish for several weeks, Song P'algap agreed to take me along on his return trip in a few days.

On the broad, steeply sloping pebble beach three or four hundred men mended nets, stretched ropes, repaired small boats, cooked meals, and sat around eating and drinking. A stream of shouted commands, advice, and ribald commentary filled the air. The socializing seemed to be as intense as the work, with no clear separation between the two. Small tenders came and went between the beach and the bigger boats anchored just off it, most of which were rafted up in groups of four or five. All together there must have been more than one hundred engine-powered boats in the harbor. It was a scene full of noise and movement as boats entered and left the lagoon or maneuvered to change position off the beach. The sound of popular music and ragged singing drifted over the water from a few of the boats that had radios.

Leaving our cook in charge of the boat, we all walked up the beach looking for Kim Ch'angdok's island benefactor, Chang Kigwang. Someone shouted greetings to us from nearly every group that we passed: "So Sŏkp'o now has an American fishing partner!" or "Don't waste American help on that lazy Kim Ch'angdok; help us skilled fishermen instead!" or, with some hostility, "There's no PX out here. Will you eat kimch'i and raw fish?" Mostly the fishermen were blunt, friendly, informal, and, above all, curious.

There was no real community on Mot Sŏm. Fishermen either had to camp out on the beach or sleep on their boats. Toilets did not exist. One end of the beach was used for this purpose, with the changing tides taking care of the plumbing. Behind the beach were some warehouses and a small repair shop at the head of a rickety marine railway. Further up the slope, at the base of a cliff, an imposing house with lots of big glass windows seemed strangely out of place. Chang Kigwang and his brothers lived there with their father when they were not out fishing. The old man was in effect king of the island, and it was now evident why Chang Kigwang had said on the beach at Sŏkp'o, "Everyone knows me at Mot Sŏm." The islands were nothing but a base for fishing boats, with the Chang family as the only permanent residents.

We didn't find Chang Kigwang but instead came across his crusty old father standing on the beach, bawling out orders. Nothing was done fast enough or well enough to please him. At his side stood his ten-year-old grandson, ready to run errands, transmit messages, or fetch soju. Old Mr. Chang barely greeted me but then peremptorily ordered me to appear at his house for the evening meal. When Kim Ch'angdok offered to guide me on the assumption that he too was included, Old Mr. Chang bluntly reasserted the island's hierarchy by blurting out, "No, just the American. Do you think I'm running a restaurant for any poor fisherman who lands on this beach?" I was beginning to look back on Sŏkp'o as a place of quiet refinement compared to the rough-and-ready, all-male world of Mot Sŏm.

We had a few hours to spare, since Kim Ch'angdok's boat and nets were all ready for the next day's fishing and required no further work. The crew decided to give me a tour of the island, and we climbed up to a high pass between rocky spires that gave an unrestricted view of the entire archipelago laid out on the surface of the sea like some South Pacific atoll. Except that here there were no luxuriant jungles or waterfalls or sirens in grass skirts. Only a few scattered blades of grass grew among the rocks.

We hiked down the other side of the pass to a curved sandy beach, where Kang Yong Ju joined me for a swim. Neither Kim Ch'angdok nor Kim Ch'angsun knew how to swim, and they laughed at us for imitating fish so incompetently. Afterwards Kang Yong Ju and I ran up and down the beach feeling released, vigorous, and hungry. We bought boiled shrimp and makkŏlli from a poor fisherman who lived in a makeshift tent nearby. He told us he had lost his boat and nets in a storm and now worked for Old Mr. Chang, hoping to get some money together and start again.

Old Mr. Chang's house was made almost entirely of driftwood. The result was a curious rustic-modern style that reminded me of the structures that back-to-the-simple-life ideologues build for themselves in the Vermont woods. The big windows were double panes enclosed in airtight aluminum frames, all made in the USA Old Mr. Chang told me they had been salvaged from the sea, but I guessed they had probably been destined for Seoul hotel construction and had been "salvaged" from the Inch'ŏn docks at night.

That night Old Mr. Chang's daughter, the only woman on the island, served at least seven kinds of seafood, all of it delicious and in enormous quantities. As we ate the old man told me about his disastrous economic situation. This seemed odd, since the fishing, transport, oil supply, and repair operations had all appeared to be humming along nicely at the beach that afternoon. He complained that although he selflessly performed crucial services for the fishing fleets in this desolate outpost, the fishermen took advantage of him mercilessly, and the government demanded outrageous taxes. His real problem, it turned out, was a shortage of capital combined with very high interest rates and a lack of good connections in the Seoul money markets. He delivered his pitch to me with a blustery frankness that jolted me out of my soju-induced semi-stupor. "You won't get anywhere lending money to those backward peasants in Sŏkp'o. My sons and I really know this business. We make money fishing ourselves, and the other fishermen are dependent on us. They have nowhere else to go. Invest your dollars here with me, and we'll both get rich."

Finally, I realized what must have happened. Old Mr. Chang seemed to think I was a rich American with capital to invest, and he wanted a piece of the action. When I protested that I was a scholar with no large sums at my disposal, and that in any case I was only concerned with Sŏkp'o and its problems, he believed me. Certainly the way I looked and the way I reached Mot

Sŏm did not fit in too well with an image of expansive entrepreneurship. His manner became even more peremptory, and I was soon outside, stumbling back in the dark towards the beach.

That night provided me with another good opportunity to reflect on the toughness of Korean fishermen. At night Kim Ch'angdok and his crew did not prepare fir bough beds, as I had been taught to do in wilderness camping. Nor did they crawl into sleeping bags or cover themselves with blankets. They simply lay down on the rocky beach and went to sleep. There was an old piece of canvas on the boat that could be rigged as a kind of tent when it rained, but since it was only foggy, no one had bothered to set it up. I finally wrapped myself in the canvas, after hollowing out slight depressions in the pebbles for my shoulders and rear end. The soju helped, but it was not a restful night, and I was up before things really got going on the beach at about five in the morning.

Once the fires were lit, and the pungent smell of Korean cooking started slicing through the morning mist, it wasn't so bad. Soju for breakfast no longer seemed like such an outlandish idea, and our teenaged cook turned out an acceptable fish stew along with plenty of rice. After eating, I squatted on the beach for a few minutes, savoring the scene and the fact that I was part of it.

As the fog started to lift, we took the masts and sails out of the boat and stowed them on the beach under the canvas. Then we launched the boat and sculled out to an area at one end of the harbor where fifty or sixty other small boats like ours clustered around several motorized trawlers. It was a spectacular spot with a sheer cliff rising hundreds of feet up out of the sea. Mist still clung to the surface of the water, but higher up the rocks gleamed in sunlight. Everyone had friends or relatives on other boats, and all sorts of goods were passed back and forth along with shouts and banter. Mr. Song, the trader from Mohang, was out in his boat doing a lively business.

By nine o'clock, our deck piled high with Old Mr. Chang's nets, we were being towed in a long string of small boats out to the croaker fishing grounds. Six or seven miles northwest of Mot Sŏm we were cast loose. By now the fog was gone, and we spent long, wearisome hours in the hot sun, trying, as far as I could tell, to pull rocks up in the nets from the shallow bottom of the Yellow Sea. There were very few fish. Croaker fishing requires both skill and hard work. On our boat there seemed to be only hard work.

Croakers actually do croak, and at one point in the afternoon Kim Ch'angsun pressed his ear down on the tiller to try and hear the fish. The youngest crew member happened to be standing near him, pissing over the stern into the ocean. A wave came along, slightly disturbing the youth's balance and aim, and a few drops fell on the captain's face. There was a frozen moment of apprehension. Kim Ch'angsun had killed a man in a quarrel over damaged nets, and surely there was no insult greater than this, accidental or not. Slowly the captain lifted his head, straightened up, and wiped his face. Then he grinned and we all laughed uneasily, grateful for the release of tension.

I was as glad to see the sun go down as I was to stop hauling on the nets. There had been too much of both sun and nets for many hours. The cheerful, talkative mood of the morning when we were setting out on a promising new venture had changed. Now I heard only grunts of effort. But no one complained, either about the lack of fish or the physical punishment. Sŏkp'o fishermen were used to the cycle of optimistic expectation, hard work, and disappointment. Perhaps that was their greatest skill: resilience in adversity. I would have preferred some consoling talk about how tired we were and how much my back and shoulders hurt.

We were picked up just before dark, tying onto a long rope behind a trawler. I wondered what would have happened if a storm had come up suddenly or if other circumstances had made it impossible to pick up all the small boats before nightfall. But no one took my questions seriously. They just laughed and told me not to worry. My shipmates, although somewhat subdued, were soon talking and laughing over *soju* and raw fish during the return trip. Here at Mot Sŏm the Sŏkp'o fishermen were elated just because of their participation in the "big time," getting close enough to success to observe from a few yards away the jubilation of the crews on boats that returned heavily laden with fish. Our cargo was mostly torn nets.

The day was over. We could rest, and we had *soju*. For my companions it was enough. But I was not so easily satisfied. I was desperately thirsty and didn't want to get drunk on *soju*, the only liquid on board. And then there was the coming night to think about—fighting a losing battle with the beach fleas and trying to find a way to be comfortable on a pebble bed. I imagined iced drinks, a shower, and clean sheets. After dark I shivered in the chill breeze, even though I was the only one on board with a jacket. Sŏkp'o fishermen had, as far as I could tell, only one outfit: patched pants, a threadbare, long-sleeved cotton undershirt, and bare feet. They wore this when the weather was hot and when it was cold, whether the wind blew or was calm, and whether it rained or not.

But my stoicism had given out. I complained about my thirst and my sunburn. I huddled under the damp nets to get out of the wind. The Koreans probably wondered how America had ever gotten to be such a great and powerful nation.

The next morning was foggy again, and I was up early—stiff, groggy, and still tired—wondering whether suffering on the beach at night and on the boat by day was really the best way to carry out anthropological research. But the rice, pickled cabbage, and a stew of fish and hot bean paste worked its usual miracle, and by seven o'clock I was sketching some of the other crews as they squatted over breakfast fires or worked on their gear.

Chang Kigwang, came by and asked if I'd like to ride with him on one of the trawlers that doubled as mother ships for the small boats. That way I could observe the whole operation. Perhaps Kim Ch'angdok, eager to get rid of whatever malign foreign influences might have antagonized the sea spirits the day before, had spoken to him. I preferred to think that Chang Kigwang was one of the few enlightened souls in the fishing community who took my research seriously. I accepted with pleasure and spent an agreeable, relaxed, and sheltered day at sea, during which I learned endless details not only about croaker fishing skills and technology but also about the financial and administrative complexities of the Inch'ŏn wholesale fish market.

That night the beach was alive with boisterous carousing. Fishermen stumbled back and forth in the dark from one fire to another, drinking with different groups. The night was filled with laughter, singing, loud talk, and quarreling. I thought to myself that except for the cold wind and the fact that we had pebbles instead of sand, it must have been very much like this when pirates gathered with their loot on Caribbean beaches. In spite of the noise sleep came easily. My tired body seemed to have adapted at last to the pebbles.

The next morning I helped Kim Ch'angsun and his crew load the nets and gave the boat a final push off the beach, wishing the crew luck. They hadn't done any better without me on the previous day and now figured optimistically that it must be their turn to find fish.

Alone on the beach I had time to speculate and write in my diary. In spite of the noisy informality of Mot Sŏm beach society, it had become clear that a distinct hierarchy existed among the fishermen. Actually two different systems of rank seemed to be operating simultaneously. One depended on sophistication of equipment and port of origin, with the newest and most powerful boats out of Inch'ŏn taking precedence. Their captains and crews strutted about the beach with special confidence and authority, and other boats tended to give way to them in close encounters on the water. This was by no means always true, however, and some battered old boats bulled their way through the fleet like aging clunkers in American automobile traffic, to the accompaniment of outraged shouts from those who thought they had right of way.

Fishing success determined the other dimension of prestige. Among the smaller boats everyone quickly knew who had caught the most fish, and there were surprisingly detailed estimates of the value of individual shares for every member of a successful or lucky crew. In fact, this was the dominant, even obsessive, topic of conversation most of the time, on shore. Although all the crews were using the same general techniques in the same waters, certain boats consistently did much better than the rest, often by a very large margin.

My fellow crew members accepted the situation as natural, but it bothered me that our Sŏkp'o boat had such a humiliating position at the bottom of both systems of Mot Sŏm ranking. Not for the first time I wondered if there wasn't some way to obtain small diesel engines for the village, so that Sŏkp'o fishermen could upgrade both their technical skills and their profits. I even fantasized about bringing in radar, sonar, and all the fancy hydraulic gadgets that clutter the decks of boats out of New Bedford and Gloucester. Then we could really show off in front of the dazzled Mot Sŏm fishermen!

By midmorning all the boats had gone. Old Mr. Chang continued to stomp up and down the beach with his faithful grandson. Assaulted by both sun and wind, the last of the fog had disappeared, leaving a sharply etched island world of bright sunlight, deep shadows, and soaring, vertical cliff edges. I climbed a high rocky promontory to feel the full force of the wind blowing across the sea from China and to see the endless chaos of brilliant whitecaps in every direction.

Far below I could just make out Song P'algap and his sons getting their boat ready on the beach for the return trip. I scrambled down, picked up my rucksack, and joined them. We had fast sailing across the sheltered water of the lagoon before slipping easily through the gap between the cliffs with a favoring wind and tide. The mountainous islands gave some protection for a half mile or so, and then we were out in the open ocean with big, shimmering walls of green and blue water trying to overwhelm us from astern. The chunky hull rose stolidly up over each surging ridge, and it was only the brilliant foam of a few breaking wave tops that occasionally came aboard and kept things wet. The junk rig was efficient for this downwind sailing, and in a couple of hours we could see the coastal mountains from the tops of the crests.

Nearing the coast, I was surprised to see that we were headed right for Sŏkp'o instead of towards Song P'algap's home port of Mohang five miles to the south. The idea that he would take the time and trouble to sail all the way into the harbor and deliver me to the Big Hamlet was embarrassing. With no engine and unfavorable tides this would add many hours to the passage. I wondered if I would have to put him and his sons up for the night. Then finally I realized with a slight sinking feeling what Mr. Song actually planned to do. Instead of making the long detour into the harbor, he was simply going to drop me off on the deserted rocky coast, after which he would have an easy, fast reach home.

Big waves pounding directly on the exposed shore made it a very tricky operation. Song P'algap's local knowledge was extraordinary, and I wondered if the outlandish maneuver was some sort of standard procedure, carried out countless times through the centuries. He seemed to know precisely which rock was the right one at this exact state of the tide. I shook hands, grabbed my rucksack, and jumped onto a wet, half-submerged ledge in a shower of spray. It took all my strength to fend the boat off until the sails filled and Mr. Song could bear away to the south, smiling and waving as though he had just let me off at the yacht club dock. From my landing place I had to jump three times to other big rocks before reaching the beach. Then there was a short scramble up the cliff and a ten minute walk through the barley fields to my house.

Nothing important had happened during the four-day trip. There had been no real dangers, no triumphs, and no breakthrough insights into how Korean fishermen think and behave. And, of course, no one greeted me with acclaim when I got back to the village. Yet I wonder if my satisfaction wasn't as great as that of any explorer returning from months or years of adventure overseas.

10

The Anthropologist at Work and Play

It was just after breakfast in early fall, and my daughter, Kim, didn't want me to leave the house. As I headed down for the harbor after breakfast, she made a fuss, hanging onto me right at the gap where the brush hedge opened up to the path that led over the ridge to the Fifth Hamlet. Her brother caught the mood and began to cry, also holding onto my pant leg. A group of astonished children on their way to school stopped to watch the strange spectacle in immobilized silence. While trying to disentangle myself, I thought briefly of the advantages of the Korean family system, in which fathers are awesome figures of authority and respect. Kyong Sook finally rescued me by holding onto both squalling children, and I was able to leave for the day's work.

It was a good idea to pay attention to the footing on this path. Sharp stones stuck up here and there through the dirt, and lying right in the middle, were the occasional and surprisingly large turds hastily deposited by small children on their way to school.

The morning was overcast, with a kind of timeless melancholy in the damp air. It was almost high tide, so only a few yards of sand separated the water from the closest fishermen's houses. The nine or ten sailboats of the Sŏkp'o fleet that were still in regular use, and that had been sitting on the mud for hours, were now all afloat on the incoming tide, bobbing around and bumping into each other on their short moorings. Most of them would be going out in an hour or so with the start of the ebb, so I was surprised to see the beach deserted. It was still more surprising to see a big, freshly painted forty-foot trawler lying low in the water a little further offshore. It was this trawler that had attracted me to the harbor. Engine-powered boats rarely entered our isolated bay and then usually only to seek refuge from a storm at sea. But the weather had been calm. What was even more unusual was the boat's sleek, well-maintained look. Along this coast fishermen did not pay much attention to the appearance of their boats. Instead of repainting them regularly, they just daubed the hull with pitch below the waterline. The neat trawler belonged to a different world.

Cheerful sounds of early morning drinking were coming from Kim Ch'angdok's wife's *sulchip* further up the beach, so I knew where everyone was. Alcohol, even very weak alcohol, did not seem quite right, either for the time of day or the state of my stomach. But I told myself that if the *sulchip* was where things were happening in the Big Hamlet, then that was where the anthropologist ought to be. Besides, after my meager breakfast at home, a little fried fish or some other kind of seafood would taste good.

There was the usual hearty welcome as I stuck my head in the drinking shack, and someone quickly got up so I could sit on one of the four stools. Too much obsequious respect at such gatherings had bothered me at first, but by now I was a little corrupted by it, and the stool was much better than squatting in the dirt.

The *sulchip* had only three walls, the eaves and the ancient moldy thatch on top of them hanging far out over the open side facing the bay. The big eaves provided shade on hot summer mornings, while in winter the much lower sun could shine in and give an illusion of warmth. A heavy wooden sill divided the packed-sand-and-mud floor on the inside from the sand and mud outside. The building leaned sharply to the south, and there were lots of places where the mud daubing on the walls had fallen away, showing the wattle construction inside. After a few drinks I always got the peculiar feeling that this place was the creation of a crazed Zen tea master who, in his obsession with the natural and the unpretentious, had finally gone off the deep end. No one drank tea here, however, and on this particular morning Kim Ch'angdok's wife was hustling to keep up with the demand for *makkŏlli* and *soju*.

After a half hour or so and a bowl of *makkŏlli*, I discovered that the skipper of the trawler, Kim Sangman, was originally from Sŏkp'o and had simply decided to stop off and visit family and friends. He was on his way back to Inch'ŏn after a successful fishing expedition to southern waters and was paying for the party. His four crew members were all from other villages and towns along the coast. It was unusual for a local boy to achieve such success, so Kim Sangman was famous. I had heard of him but had never met him. Envied by every man in the *sulchip*, Kim Sangman was getting his money's worth, presiding eloquently over the gathering. He described the ports he had visited, the storms he had encountered, and the vast sums his catch would bring. His familiar talk of the Inch'ŏn waterfront, the enormous wholesale fish market, and the places where the best-looking (and friendliest) women served makkŏlli and soju dazzled the villagers, who smoked my cigarettes, drank Kim Sangman's makkŏlli, and dreamed of making lots of money in far-off places.

Next to me, Mun Ch'ilgap leaned forward and spit slowly on the floor, saying he wished that he, too, had left Sŏkp'o when he was young. "But now it's too late. I have a family, and I have to stay here and live like a caterpillar under a log." Kim Pyŏngwŏn, who was older, laughed derisively. "Do you think you're another Kim Sangman? Lots of young men from Sŏkp'o leave to fish on big boats, but none of them become captains or make any money. They don't learn how to navigate, and they can't fix engines. They just work hard so the boat owners get rich." Kim Sangman agreed. "Most of the money goes to the owner. The rest of us stay poor. No fisherman keeps his money long." Then he poured me more makkŏlli, saying, "But we enjoy life while we can."

I wanted to know how Kim Sangman had broken free of the limitations of a village background and learned the complicated skills of a successful trawler captain. And how had he managed to convince an owner in Inch'ŏn to entrust him with a valuable boat? The best I could come up with to get the conversation headed towards social science was, "Did you go away to sea because you like fishing better than farming?" Everyone laughed, although I wasn't sure why.

He answered, "How could I farm without any land?" There was more laughter, but I kept at it, "If you had ten majigi of rice land [This amounted to about two acres, which was better than the average-size farm, and if the land was fertile and irrigated, it would have been a very substantial farm in Sŏkp'o.], would you stay here instead and be a respectable villager?" Kim Sangman got another laugh by saying, "Don't you think I'm respectable?" Then he looked serious and burst out,

Of course, everyone knows that farming is better than fishing. Look at us. We wear old, dirty clothes. We drink in the morning instead of carrying shit on our backs out to the pepper plants and the spinach the way my brothers and cousins do. We never know when we might drown. We work all night in the wind and the salt spray. We leave our wives behind for weeks at a time and worry that they might take up with someone else while we're gone. When we get back to port we spend all our money on treating ourselves and our friends and the Inch'ŏn women to a good time, instead of sitting sedately in the *sarangbang* smoking pipes and talking about our ancestors. We use bad words whenever we want, we don't show respect to anyone, and we don't keep our faces and hands and feet down in the mud all day.

Everyone was delighted and shouted their approval of this speech, which I vaguely understood to be a kind of macho declaration of the joys and tribulations of the fisherman's way of life.

Ever since first coming to Sŏkp'o, information had been pouring in about the contempt that the established village elite had for fishing and fishermen. Farming, particularly rice farming, was always cited as the preferred occupation. The Yi clan were undeniably the local gentry, and they were all farmers. Landownership was the ultimate badge of rank, and everyone knew that fishermen had less land (often none at all), drank too much, had terrible manners, and showed little respect for their ancestors. It always made me uneasy when something happened to undermine an established "fact" of village life that had already been enshrined in my notebooks.

Although Kim Sangman never answered my question about what he would have done if he owned rice land, I got an explanation of sorts later the same day while talking to one of the teenagers who worked on his boat. "No real fisherman likes farming," he said. "It's slow and monotonous and dirty, and no one in these little fishing villages has enough land to make any money at it anyway. Fishing is hard and dangerous, but when you're lucky, there's a big pile of money all of a sudden."

I asked how he could endure the hard life on the boat month after month. "Don't you get tired and wet and cold and miss living at home and eating your mother's cooking?" The boy surprised me. "No, that's the best part—leaving your home village and getting away from your parents and relatives and all the older people who are always telling you what to do." He added proudly, "I will be fishing all this fall out of Mot Sŏm. Out there I do a man's work; we are treated like men. Compared to my friends at home, I am free."

I persisted, "What happens when you're thirty and have a wife and children and you're still just a deckhand who can't save any money?" He laughed and said, "I don't worry about all that, but I suppose in that case it would be nice to have ten majigi of land to come home to."

The fact that villagers held contradictory attitudes about farming and fishing confronted me again a few weeks later when Teacher Yi reported the results of an assignment he had given his sixth graders, asking them what they wanted to be when they grew up. The boys had put fishing boat captain at the top of the list, followed by schoolteacher, storekeeper, and farmer.

The party broke up and the local fishermen all headed out to sea, riding the ebb tide. I strolled along the shore away from the harbor's small cluster of boats and houses with my stomach pleasantly warmed by makkŏlli, mulling over my new outlook on fishermen's pride. Above the high-water mark there was a clutter of fish skeletons, oyster shells, seaweed, cast-off fishing gear, and the remnants of decaying boats half buried in sand. It was all gently rotting its way back into the landscape, further down on the sloping beach, wet sand gleamed, sleek and gray in the morning haze.

A couple of hundred yards further along the beach, Mun Young Shik (I thought of him as "Old Moon"), his son, his nephew, and a shipbuilder from across the bay were putting the finishing touches on a new boat. Old Moon, who had told my fortune some months before in Teacher Yi's sarangbang, was both a farmer and a fisherman, head of one of the more prosperous households in the Big Hamlet. His deeply creased face, burned very dark by the sun and contrasting sharply with his white crew-cut hair, gave him a strange look in which boyishness was combined with grizzled old age. In his sixties, he was still moderately influential in village affairs and an occasional coffee and whiskey drinker on my veranda. The shipwright had been staying at Mun Young Shik's house for several weeks while he worked, and I had stopped by frequently to watch the transformation of pine logs into a graceful twenty-eight foot seagoing boat. Wood chips flew from the builder's adze, and long, white, sweet-smelling shavings curled up from his plane.

Today Old Moon was performing a kosa, a sort of christening ritual that involved both the propitiation of potentially dangerous gods of the sea and the calling into existence of a particular strong and lucky boat spirit. Kosa is a very general term that is used in all sorts of ritual situations and seems to combine the meanings of consecrate, worship, and placate. As far as I could tell, it always involves the liberal use of makkŏlli and, if possible, specially desirable dishes of food. Although the others were dressed as usual, Old Moon wore clean white clothes. A few raggedy, dirty children, the inevitable audience when anything was happening in Sŏkp'o, watched quietly from a slight distance.

Starting in the bow, Mun Young Shik poured makkŏlli on the clean wood, first all along the starboard side and then to port. At the same time he murmured some sort of incantation. When I asked afterwards what the words were, he brushed my question aside, saying that it should have been done properly by a chŏmjaengi, (a kind of shamanistic fortune-teller), but he was poor and did the best he could on his own. Then he unrolled a reed mat on the sand, insisting that I sit down with him and the shipwright. His son brought makkŏlli and food from the nearby house. When Old Moon poured me a big brimming cup, I refused, saying that the shipwright should drink first. We argued about that for a while, and they finally gave in. Teacher Yi told me later that my instinct had been right, making a favorable impression.

I suppose I qualified as a fellow drinker mostly because I happened to be there at that moment. But I also had my camera with me. Mun Young Shik was happy to have the ceremony for his new boat recorded on film, and he kept pouring generously. The roast eel that was served hot with the makkŏlli was so good that I promised myself we would have more of it at home. Teacher Yi and I usually caught plenty of eels when we were fishing from the rocks, but no one at my house knew how to prepare them properly. I wondered how much coffee and whiskey I would have to give Old Moon before I could send Kyong Sook to his house to learn eel cookery.

At first, our conversation was about the money to be made croaker fishing in late summer. Old Moon planned to send his son, his nephew, and two other young fishermen from Sŏkp'o to the barren offshore islands of Mot Sŏm for six weeks of hard work in the new boat. He talked at length about how much better off they would be there than if exposed to the temptations of Inch'ŏn. Then the problem of obtaining wood for boatbuilding came up, which in turn led to a discussion of illegal tree cutting in the mountains. Both men bitterly denounced county officials, who, according to the fishermen, regularly prevented small landowners from cutting their own trees, while allowing big lumber companies to pillage public land in return for kickbacks. Having previously had almost no success in getting at attitudes towards the government administration, I concentrated on the conversation as closely as the bloated, logy feeling that was creeping over me from the morning's drinking would permit.

The hospitality on these occasions was always so intense and apparently genuine that I never knew when I was supposed to leave. Perhaps this time I stayed too long. Getting up, I staggered a little, telling myself that my legs were numb from sitting so long on the ground cross-legged. When I looked back from fifty yards or so down the path, Old Moon and the shipwright had already disappeared, and Old Moon's son and nephew were devouring what was left of the makkŏlli and food.

My next objective was Yi Pyŏnghyŏk's house over on the other side of the circular arm of the bay that almost completely divided the village at high tide. Yi Pyŏnghyŏk, a cousin of Teacher Yi's and also the village head, had promised me statistics on births, deaths, numbers of households in each lineage, and total population, broken down according to age and sex. This was precious information, and I was ready to pay for it with a bottle of good scotch whiskey carefully stashed away in my knapsack. Since the tide was in, I had to take the long way around via the sandspit path next to the ocean.

As usual, though, there was another diversion, and it was a couple of hours before I actually reached Yi Pyŏnghyŏk's house. Perhaps partly because of my haphazard method and partly because I was just as eager for entertainment as any of the villagers, my research rarely went according to plan. This time, thick smoke rising up behind Teacher Yi's house and the periodic clanging of hammered metal announced that Pirate's forge was operating, so I changed direction and followed the familiar path up past my old sarangbang.

Blacksmithing was another means, in addition to his ownership of land and overbearing manner, by which Pirate could extract a little additional economic gain from his fellow villagers and command their grudging respect. He was the only blacksmith in Sŏkp'o, and about once every two or three weeks he would light up the forge, which was located next to his house in a spacious thatched-roof shed. A light rain had begun to fall, and a small crowd of ten or twelve people had crowded into the shed, enjoying the warmth of the fire and the dramatic spectacle. The usual flock of preschool children, little girls with babies on their backs that were scarcely younger than their older sisters, looked on from between and around the legs of the adults.

Except for the ancient engine in Mun Yong Bae's boat, the forge was probably the most elaborate mechanical contraption in the village. Both the construction and technology were ancient, however. The forge itself was set into a big dome of dried mud, six feet high with a short clay tunnel leading to a smaller dome that housed the bellows. The bellows was made of leather, wood, and bits of wire, and the whole contraption looked more like folk art than machinery.

Since Pirate was too old to swing the big sledgehammer or lift heavy objects, there was a lot of audience participation in the actual blacksmithing. Pirate kept close control over things, however, deciding when the metal was hot enough to be removed from the fire and how it should be tempered. The raw metal was mainly old car springs imported from the city, and from these emerged all sorts of agricultural implements, tools, boat fastenings, and fishing gear, including anchors. For chisels, boat spikes, gaff hooks, or other small objects, Pirate used the tongs and hammer himself, demonstrating his skills before a silently deferential audience. But when others were pounding away on the anvil, the crowd provided a lot of advice and comment, sometimes appreciative, but more often, derisory. Of the younger men who swung the sledge, Carpenter Mun seemed to be the most skillful. He was obviously at home in the forge, and I imagined that after a lifetime of watching Pirate at work, he probably knew as much about blacksmithing as the old man.

It was good entertainment. Urgent, important events were taking place. The bright red metal, the flying sparks, the grunting effort, and the gradual, almost magical shaping of a recognizable object held our attention. I stood there for a couple of hours, feeling strong links with a past when the blacksmith's shop must have been an equally exciting focal point of village life in Europe and America.

Relations between Pirate and his customers and the extent to which they participated in the work unfolded in accordance with rules or customs or habits that were completely mysterious to me. It was as if things had already been rehearsed, or as if the villagers shared some secret, nonlinguistic means of thought transference. No one ever said anything about whose turn it was next, or how much anything cost, or who would hold the tongs and who would do the hammering. When an object was finished, the client would usually wrap it in straw rope because of the heat and soot and leave, saying politely to Pirate, "*chal ssŏsseuu* (I used it [the forge] well)."

That day one brief incident at the forge interrupted the well-worn communal patterns. Yi Sang Baek showed up with a wicker basket full of fish. He was very decidedly no relation to the Sŏkp'o Yis. Yi Sang Baek and his relatives had no aristocratic pretensions. They had arrived suddenly in the village a year or so previously—a family of eleven, comprising not only his own wife and grown son, but two brothers, their wives, and small children. They lived in squalid, temporary straw mat shelters among the sand dunes just above the high water mark at the extreme northern end of the peninsula. There, off a curving beach, they had set up a homemade but nevertheless elaborate fixed net that was far more complex than anything the Sŏkp'o villagers had ever seen. And they were catching fish. Yi Sang Baek was closemouthed about his origins, but it was rumored that after a severe storm had demolished his nets in Chŏlla Province to the south, he had just picked up stakes and headed for the most isolated spot he could find in order to escape heavy debts.

Without money, local relatives, or any social connection at all, the situation of Yi Sang Baek and his relatives in Sŏkp'o was precarious. They went out of their way to be deferential to everyone, asking only to be allowed to continue to net fish at one spot along the coast. The villagers left them pretty much alone. There was suspicion but also tolerance and respect for their superior skills; I had already taken advantage of Yi Sang Baek's eagerness to please, going out in his boat a few times to watch the net in action.

Evidently Yi Sang Baek had asked Pirate to make him some gaff hooks and boat nails, and now he had come to collect them, paying with fish. They had already agreed on a price. Yi Sang Baek pulled several fish out of his basket and laid them on a plank. There was a murmur of appreciation when he put down a fat *urok*, the choicest fish from local waters.

Pirate went over and looked in the basket. He reached in and pulled out two more good-sized fish, adding them to the pile on the plank. Yi Sang Baek was obviously jolted and pointed out in a mild and respectful manner that Pirate was taking far more than the agreed price. Pirate tossed the hooks and nails down disdainfully and picked up the fish. "That's what they're worth." Yi Sang Baek looked around helplessly. There was an uneasy stirring among the crowd. Then a red-faced Carpenter Mun suddenly burst out, "You have made a mistake; that is too many fish for a few hooks and nails." Other spectators agreed in low voices. Pirate glared at Carpenter Mun for a moment, picked up one of the fish, and threw it back in the basket. Before stalking off to his house, Pirate muttered, "Can't you tell the difference between our village people and low-class squatters from Chŏlla Province?"

These sessions at the forge were the only informal gatherings that I can remember in Sŏkp'o where there was never anything to eat or drink. The mood of pleasant tension and camaraderie that always accompanied joint work was certainly present. Perhaps Pirate's stinginess was a factor. Or maybe there was a sensible rule that alcohol and blacksmithing don't mix.

Having had a good deal of experience with a heavy splitting maul in Vermont, I offered to swing the sledgehammer, eager as always to come down off the pedestal labeled "illustrious teacher" and participate. But at the forge there was unanimity. I was not allowed to do more than watch. Teacher Yi told me that the villagers would have felt embarrassed seeing a scholar perform such arduous and dirty work. But T'aemo said afterwards they were probably afraid I might crush someone's fingers or send a piece of red hot metal spinning into the crowd.

It was a short walk from the forge to Yi Pyŏnghyŏk's house, but he was not home. I left the whiskey with his wife. She insisted that I wait for him on the veranda, and although we both knew he probably wouldn't be back soon, I was happy to sit down. I had nothing else to do, and it would be another hour before the tide would let me cross the mudflats on my way back to the Big Hamlet.

Before long, Yi Pyŏnghyŏk's fifteen-year-old daughter appeared with a tray of makkŏlli and anju. "How are you today, sir? I am fine. Isn't this good weather we are having?" In addition to the fact that a light rain was still falling, the startling thing about this statement was that it was in perfectly understandable English. Except for a slight singsong intonation, the girl had almost no accent. I discovered, all in English, that she was living with relatives in Sŏsan and was in her last year at middle school. She had come to Sŏkp'o to visit her parents for a few days. Astonished at being able to communicate, I found out further that her teacher was a Canadian missionary's wife, and that she intended to study English literature and become a teacher herself. This was the only English conversation I ever had in Sŏkp'o. Yi Pyŏnghyŏk's wife was terribly pleased to see us talking without difficulty, and I almost had to use force to stop her preparations for a feast.

It was time to go home and start writing up the day's work. The path led along the edge of rice fields for a couple of hundred yards and then across the mudflats to the Big Hamlet. At the far end of the gap (on the Big Hamlet side) I was just passing the shed that served as dike construction headquarters, when a man called, "Sonsaeng nim!" and hurried out of the shack to catch up with me. I had seen him several times in casual men's groups, but I had never had a chance to talk with him alone. He was slight and handsome, with neither the dark, deeply suntanned skin nor the gnarled hands of the villagers.

"Ŏdi kasimnikka?" he called out. "Where are you going?" It was the standard village greeting transformed into the crisp, formal style and accent that I had learned in Seoul language classes. The soft, drawn out, easygoing vowels of the rural dialect had disappeared. "Chip e kamnida. (I'm going home)." I answered. "Stop and play for a while and then go on with your walk. Let's talk here." He spoke in that assertive Korean style I have never learned to say no to, so I sat down with him on a rough bench outside the shack.

"My name is Han Taegyun, and I am a technical high school graduate," he began. "I work for the county administration in Sŏsan, and I am in charge of the dike construction here." I acknowledged his declaration of personal status with what I hoped was an appropriate exclamation of awed surprise and approval. "Ah, kŭrŏssŭmnikka! (Ah, is that so!)"

The proposed dike across the mouth of the bay would, if it ever was completed and the land reclaimed, more than double the existing rice growing area of the village. The villagers had begun construction work six months before my arrival, but now it was not going well. The project had at first fired everyone's imagination. The impoverished Sŏkp'o peasants thought they were about to be transformed into well-to-do farmers, and nearly everyone had turned out daily for several months to carry rocks and dirt. As a result 100 yards or so of the dike had taken rudimentary shape, poking out tentatively from the shore at both ends. But with twenty-three feet of tidal water racing in and out of the inlet every twelve hours, the stones and dirt were now being washed away as fast as they were dumped in place. Progress was imperceptible, and the villagers were deeply discouraged. A dozen or so men kept at it, but that was only because four pounds of U. S. flour (the dike was a locally administered, American Public Law 480 Food for Peace Act project) were paid out for a day's work, and no other jobs were available. No one even pretended that they were making any progress.

"I will be going back to my house at the county seat in Sŏsan as soon as the dike is finished," Han Taegyun continued. "It is hard living in such a backward, far off place, isn't it?" His wife had set up housekeeping in an abandoned, tumbledown farmhouse nearby, and we had not been talking long before she appeared with a tray on which there were real glasses and a bottle of yakchu, a delicious yellowish wine made from rice that appeared only rarely in the village. Dismayed at first by the idea of still more beer, I somehow managed to force myself into the spirit of the occasion. As we drank, sitting on a bench in the shade of the shack, the young woman made two more trips, each time with a different dish, specially prepared to go with the *yakchu*. All this was astonishing refinement by village standards. The dried shrimp, braised octopus, and some kind of pickled clams were not as good as Mun Young Shik's roasted eel, I thought, but they were obviously fancier and more expensive. My appreciation of all this lavish treatment only resulted in Han's peremptory call for more *makkŏlli*; My heart sank; I would not get away quickly.

"How can an educated person like yourself tolerate the uncouth vulgarity of these fishermen day after day?" Han Taegyun asked. I had no idea what to say to this, managing only the safe cliché, "But they have lots of *insim*." Han persisted in his concern for my well-being and the success of my research. "You should never have left Teacher Yi's house to go and live in the Big Hamlet. That is where all the lowest-class people live. You should avoid the fishermen altogether and talk only to respectable farmers from the Yi lineage. That way you will learn what Korea is really like."

Here it was again—the deep concern that I collect and take with me back to America an idealized version of village life, one that would accord with approved cultural stereotypes. I had already run into this concern not only on my own veranda, but also among professors at Seoul National University.

Han Taegyun continued. "It's not their fault, of course, but people without an education or good family background just do not know how to behave or talk. They do not know good from bad. They have no etiquette. You should spend more time with educated people."

I wondered if this was all Han Taegyun's own personal view. He was beginning to sound like Pirate. Or perhaps I was getting a low-level reflection of gossip at the county seat. In any case, his moralizing rang false. I had twice seen Han Taegyun happily drinking and singing with fishermen in the Big Hamlet, and he was also reputed to be carrying on a clandestine love affair with the wife of one of his neighbors. That afternoon was just one of many occasions when I noticed that town and city people who came "down" to Sŏkp'o were not only likely to emphasize their own social and moral superiority, but that they also tended to exploit the villagers in any way possible.

When I finally left Han Taegyun's shack in the late afternoon, I headed home directly, stumbling now and then over stones in the path. The next morning my mood and my stomach were both sour. Even though the makkŏlli was weak, I had drunk an awful lot of it during the previous twenty-four hours. My real problem, though, was that I had a sociological as well as a physical hangover. My desire for participant observation had run out. Today I did not want to meet and talk to any more farmers or fishermen. I was sick and tired of the struggle to understand them and the struggle to come up with the right words. I didn't want anyone telling me where to go, where to sit, what to eat, what to drink, or what to think about any subject at all. I wanted my autonomy back and some good American distance between me and my fellow man. I decided to go sailing.

Savoring the solitude, I started up the path behind my house. "Ŏdi kahi-yuu?" The familiar, informal greeting seemed to entangle my legs, spoiling the easy freedom of the September morning. I answered vaguely, "Chŏgi, padakka tchok ŭro (Over there, by the shore)," hoping my neighbor from the other side of the ridge wouldn't get curious and want to know more. We went by each other on the narrow path without any more words. He was preoccupied, carrying a heavy fishnet on his pack frame. The standard question had been enough, satisfying the demands of propriety.

My path led up through the pines, over a small saddle on the ridge, and then down a steep hill and across a flat half mile or so of rice fields to a small gravel beach where I kept my boat. The bay sparkled in early sunlight. The tide was right. My boat would be still afloat and the ebb running hard. From the top of the ridge I could see rice ripening in every direction, and off to the west there were glimpses of the ocean wherever notches in the hills gave access to the horizon. In the hamlet at the far edge of the rice fields, thin columns of blue smoke suspended over every roof showed that breakfast fires were still burning.

I waded out and climbed over the gunwale into the boat—a twenty-foot, two-masted junk. Full of water, she pulled heavily at her mooring. Junk is right, I thought, not for the first time, as I bailed vigorously and stuffed strips of oiled rag back between the weathered planks. Everything on the boat was crude, made by hand in the village long ago. Even its few iron fittings had been made at the local forge. Everything was leached out, water-soaked, and sun-washed. With the leaks finally reduced from a steady flow to fast seepage, I raised the masts—just a couple of rough saplings with pulleys lashed at the top—shipped the long steering oar, and cast off. There was no need for sails; the current was enough. I figured three knots, at least, as the tide carried me out into the bay. Away from land the breeze filled in, and I raised the tattered sails.

With a freshening wind on the beam and the favorable tide, my boat must have been making seven knots over the bottom. An old scarred pine branch served as tiller. The rough grain of the bare boards felt good under my bare feet. I was sailing. It was enough. I was happy.

11

Contraband

From my cottage in the pines up on the hill, the village was even lovelier than usual in the golden autumn light, with the sea wind blowing waves in the ripening rice fields and the coastline a series of jagged cliffs fading away southward to misty islands in the distance. Directly below me an elaborately irregular network of footpaths connected the houses, their thatched roofs as natural in this landscape as mushrooms are in the woods at home. To the east, the village bordered a broad, sheltered bay with fiord-like fingers reaching deep into the mountains of South Ch'ungch'ŏng Province. Here a dozen or so small junk-rigged fishing boats were pulled up on the beach in front of a row of *sulchip* and fishermen's shacks. A few yards further out in the bay two larger, engine-powered boats heeled over awkwardly in the mud as the tide ebbed. Fishermen worked on their boats or mended nets on the beach, farmers labored in their tiny fields, and a group of women gossiped while washing clothes at the well. In another hour or so as the sun approached the horizon of the western sea, the women would be gone, and bluish smoke would rise from every chimney for as long as it took to cook the evening rice.

Not only was this panorama endlessly pleasing to look at, but it also provided a kind of living diorama of rural life. I could observe everyone's comings and goings, and when the wind was right, even listen in a little to voices raised in laughter, quarreling, or the scolding of children.

But lately I was no longer captivated by it all. Perhaps the wind made me restless. God knows, I was getting tuned to natural rhythms. But six weeks had gone by since I had seen my wife. Kim and Richie had left for Seoul to be with their mother, and I wanted to join them. The research could wait; I was desperate to get away.

Figure 11.1 Looking south across the salt pans down the coast from my house; Yellow Sea is on the right. (1966)

Usually the trip to Seoul, by bus and train, took nine hours. The first two, on foot, were pleasant enough, but after that the lurching, crowded country buses, the long waits in provincial towns, and the slowly meandering train seemed to take forever. On this occasion all I could think of was getting to the city as fast as possible. A much better alternative, I thought, would be the passage by sea to the port of Inch'ŏn—a spectacular cruise along the coast and through the islands. This took about six hours, and from there Seoul was only three quarters of an hour away by bus or train. So I had asked around among the fishermen to try and get a ride, either on one of the two Sŏkp'o boats that had engines or on a boat passing through from further down the coast. Mun Yongbae, whose luck at fishing was terrible, had recently decided to use his boat, *Samhae Ho* (Three Seas), to transport fish catches and fresh oysters directly to the big metropolitan fish markets where prices were much higher.

One night, a little past midnight, I was wakened by a pounding on my shutter and the breathless shout of a boy who had run up the hill, "Sŏnsaengnim, the *Samhae Ho* is leaving for Inch'ŏn! It is leaving soon!" Although the stars were out, the night was dark and cold with a wind blowing hard out of the north. I lit a candle and thrashed around in the narrow room putting the bedding away, getting out my long underwear, and cramming notebook, camera, sketch pad, and an extra sweater into a knapsack. As I hurried down the hill in the dark, I was muttering to myself, "Always these surprises; why the hell couldn't they have told me about this yesterday?"

Being suddenly stirred awake in the night, the menace of the cold wind, and my apprehension about going to sea in a leaky old lumbering boat all combined to put me in a nasty mood. Only gradually and with some effort, as I stumbled across the rocks and tidal pools towards the landing, was I able to shift back into my proper role—that of the observer, trying to figure out what was going on around me.

What I saw was surprising. Three bonfires were lit on the long strand of rocks that served as a jetty at low tide. Some fifty or sixty people, including women and children, were milling around in the firelight. Compared to the normal bucolic tranquility of Sŏkp'o, the atmosphere here approached pandemonium. Excited children called out from the water's edge, while anxious mothers tried to force them back onto higher ground through sheer lung power. Work chants, a series of peremptory commands, equally peremptory counter-commands, insults, and laughter added to the furor as a long line of youths and men passed heavy crates from hand to hand toward the boat. A flash of bright light, a couple of sharp explosions, and then an insistent, heavy thumping noise from the *Samhae Ho* proved that its ancient engine could still be made to work. Children crowding around to peer into the engine room, where the only electric light in the village dimly illuminated the rusty machinery, were pushed aside with wildly shouted threats that seemed to frighten no one, as the crates were loaded into the hold.

Abruptly I felt foolish, realizing that I was probably the only person in the entire village who hadn't known the boat was leaving with the last of the early morning ebb tide. Someone had thoughtfully remembered to send a messenger to wake me in spite of the hamlet's general preoccupation. My good spirits returned.

As the number of crates increased, the boat settled lower in the water. The engine's thumping grew still more spasmodic and eventually died. Bonfires burned down, children were collected, and the crowd gradually went home. Finally, in addition to the crew, there were only six passengers huddled together in the dark, waiting for the "engineer" (kigwansa), Mun Yongbae's younger brother, Mun Yongju, to coax the engine back to life. Things were complicated by the fact that the electric light worked only after the engine got going, and Mun Yongju looked more and more unsure of himself as he fumbled with tools by torch light. The other crew members made sarcastic comments. The captain, Kim Taegon, was becoming impatient, since with the fast ebbing tide the boat would soon be aground. Mun Yongju was losing face.

Finally someone sent for the owner, Mun Yongbae, and after a while the brothers' combined efforts got the thumping started again. It was more than just a noise; it jolted everything on board with each beat. I wondered what we would do if the engine stopped again at sea and watched with regret as Mun Yongbae headed back towards the village. But it was too late for second thoughts. Lines were cast off, and we moved rapidly away from the jetty into nearly total darkness. The Samhae Ho was quickly picked up by the full force of the tide. No lights (except that one in the engine room), no compass, no charts, no radio, and no life jackets. We were putting a lot of faith in an antique engine and the captain's knowledge of the coast.

In this part of the Yellow Sea there is a tidal range of about twenty-five feet, with strong currents that sometimes run as fast as six knots. I stopped worrying about our captain's skill at piloting after we took on two more passengers and several additional crates from another village across the bay to the north. Somehow we left the main channel at just the right moment and chugged far up a long cove in the dark. For the last hundred yards or so a bonfire on shore provided some help, but getting to the point where the light was visible seemed miraculous to me. There followed a small-scale repetition of the previous loading scene, complete with spectators, shouted commands, the vehement rejection of those commands, and a line of men passing crates out to the Samhae Ho. With the tide still running hard out of the rocky inlet, it was a tricky place, and I had to admire Kim Taegon's skillful boat handling. Whether he accomplished it with the help of, or in spite of, the constant, frantic shouting by crew members and spectators was uncertain.

The sea got rougher as we left the shelter of the bay, and spray began flying across the deck. We passengers cowered in the lee of the wheelhouse, covering ourselves with a couple of old fishy tarpaulins. With the boat low in

Figure 11.2 Photo of the passengers on the Samhae Ho. This is the boat that we took to Inch'ŏn. (1966)

the water, an occasional wave slopped over the gunwale, so the decks were always wet. A child cried more or less continuously, and from time to time someone was noisily seasick over the side. A crew member who had been jammed into the tiny wheelhouse with the captain came out, lifted up the tarp, and invited me to more sheltered quarters. Down below I sat cross-legged on a reed mat next to the engine, along with the engineer and two other members of the crew. Here it was warm, light, and very noisy. We had taken off our shoes, since the greasy mat symbolized a room, and soon glasses of *soju* were being exchanged along with pieces of dried squid. Conversation was almost impossible because of the sound of the engine.

I was somewhat embarrassed by this special treatment and felt that I should have been sharing the sufferings of the other passengers on deck. I did not, however, want to reject the offered hospitality and possibly offend my hosts. Besides, here was a chance to become more intimate, drinking together in close quarters while we shared the camaraderie of the sea. But soon the effects of the *soju*, combined with the motion of the boat and the smell of fuel oil and unwashed feet, drove me back up on deck. I barely had time to put on my shoes.

Outside it was just beginning to get light, and the fresh air quickly settled my stomach. For a while we were in the lee of a large island where the sea was temporarily almost calm, and in the half-light, bedraggled passengers crawled out from under the canvas onto the deck. For them the advantage of traveling by sea was that it saved money, but after the rigors of the night, some of the women remarked that next time they would go by bus.

The engine broke down only once. We wallowed in the rough seas for more than an hour, while the tide carried us steadily to the north. Someone remarked that if we continued to drift, we might be mistaken for a spy ship and picked up by the North Koreans. Serious discussion followed to the effect that most likely everyone would be shot because of the American on board, and a couple of the women began to look at me out of the corners of their eyes with real hostility. Finally, it was the teenaged cook who fixed the engine, not the engineer, Mun Yongju.

With the thumping going again and the boat heading east instead of north, everyone's morale improved; although we were still cold and wet. When the sun came up and the wind dropped, a lavish communal breakfast emerged from the mass of bundles under the tarpaulin. A charcoal fire was lit, and the passengers, who a couple of hours before had more or less resigned themselves to death at sea, began to enjoy life again with a good deal of gusto. In addition to oyster soup and rice, there were several kinds of pickled cabbage, seasoned spinach, squash fried in egg batter, and all sorts of fish, octopus, and shellfish—raw, roasted, dried, salted, and pickled. Someone gave me chopsticks and urged me to eat. Mun Yongju stuck his head out and called me down below for more soju. This was anthropological field work at its best.

In watching the shipboard routine, I was surprised by how little authority the captain had over the rest of the crew. Kim Taegon, although only in his early thirties, was said to be skilled and lucky, both in catching fish and avoiding shipwreck. As a heavy drinker and womanizer, his personal reputation in Sŏkp'o was not particularly good, but he was a somewhat glamorous figure to many young people (both male and female). Spending much of his time at sea or in Inch'ŏn, he had managed to slough off most of the constraints of village life. He wore dark sunglasses and tight jeans, and he acted insolently to his elders in a way that would never have been tolerated had he been a local youth still dependent on an authoritarian father. Nearly everyone in Sŏkp'o had enough skill on boats to be a crew member. But competent captains were rare, and most of them had left to work out of Inch'ŏn or Pusan. In Kim Taegon's case, whether it was because of his personal qualities or as a result of Korean nautical tradition, there seemed to be no real respect for his role as captain. Possibly all the shouting and apparent tension was just a matter of verbal style or a way of letting off steam. The crew actually functioned reasonably well through long association, mutual tolerance, and goodwill. Even Mun Yongju, who had always seemed gloomy and quiet in the village, where he was resentfully dependent on his domineering older brother, became expansive and talkative at sea. He joined in the laughter, even when the jokes were about his incompetence as an engineer.

With just ten or twelve miles left to go before the entrance to Inch'ŏn Harbor, all sorts of ships began to converge in the increasingly sheltered, island-studded waters. A slim Republic of Korea Navy corvette knifed through the sparkling seas, bringing cries of patriotic admiration from the passengers. An American sailor on the bridge of an immense US military cargo ship gave me a startled return wave as we passed. Freighters from all over the world were steaming in and out of the harbor entrance. Deep-sea fishing boats heading out for Samoa or the Indian Ocean went by with brightly colored flags and banners from their departing rituals still festooning the rigging. The numbers of slow, disheveled homegrown boats like ours along with the still slower sailing junks increased enormously as we neared the coast.

A big freighter from Antwerp was passing us to windward when suddenly pieces of wood began raining over its side. Two-by-fours, planks, and sheets of torn plywood caught the sunlight as they fell, splashing into the water only a couple of hundred yards away from us. Kim Taegon changed course for the debris, and the crew all turned out on deck without any orders being given and without any of the noise and excitement that had accompanied the loading operation the night before.

They quickly snagged the wood and hauled it aboard. Within twenty minutes our decks were covered with scrap lumber, and we resumed course, the passengers now confined to a small open space in the stern. As the crew busily pounded nails out of the boards and straightened them, the engineer brought out a really big bottle (about a half-gallon) of *soju* and began roasting pieces of meat over the charcoal fire. Again they cordially invited me to join in the feast.

The mystery of the raining wood was easily cleared up. As ships carrying crated merchandise neared the harbor, their crews stripped off the boards and threw them overboard in preparation for unloading. For rural Koreans, both the wood and the nails represented a substantial windfall, and some boats actually spent all or most of their time cruising these waters with scrap wood as their objective rather than fish.

As we settled down to celebrate our latest catch with food and drink, I was confronted with another mystery—the appearance of sizable amounts of pork roasting over a charcoal brazier on the deck of the *Samhae Ho*. In the 1960s a South Korean peasant or fisherman from a poor village ate pork only five or six times a year on very special occasions. Well-off farmers might kill a pig for a daughter's wedding, a parent's funeral, or a man's *hwan'gap* (sixtieth birthday celebration), and at such times all the kinsmen and neighbors could share in the feast. All this pork roasting away for a midmorning snack on Mun Yongbae's old boat off the Inch'ŏn harbor entrance was truly puzzling. My questions produced only smiles and the answer, "Please eat and drink a lot." With an appetite reinforced by an adventurous night and the still-brisk sea breeze, I happily complied.

By the time we reached the long, dredged channel that leads to the inner harbor at Inch'on, the *soju*, sunlight, pork, and salt air had all contributed to building a euphoric mood. Eager to act out the intrepid ethnographer, I stood proudly in the bow like some weird figurehead. There were hundreds of fishing boats of all shapes and sizes in the inner harbor, lined up three and four deep against the quays or shuttling back and forth across the big, landlocked basin. From their decks shouted greetings, farewells, jokes, and insults competed with the sound of engines. To my deep satisfaction I attracted a good deal of attention, responding with cool self-assurance to the waves, shouted greetings, and whistles of fishermen on nearby boats. An American MP on an Army landing craft did an elaborate double take. It was a triumphant arrival.

There seemed to be no urgency about unloading the crates in the hold, and before long I found myself sauntering along the quay with the entire crew, headed for town. Since I was on my way to Seoul to rejoin my family, I asked about buses and trains, but my companions told me not to worry; they would personally see that I got home all right, and in the meantime we had to eat. In Korea once you are included as a member of a group, particularly a convivial group looking for amusement, it is sometimes impossible to assert your own individual will against the consensus without being both rude and ridiculous. Knowing, too, how important it is to keep accounts straight by reciprocating favors, I offered to buy lunch for the crew in return for my passage and all the soju and roast pork I had consumed. Simple food was unbelievably cheap at hundreds of small outdoor stands, restaurants, and sulchip on the waterfront. My offer to treat the crew provoked not only smiles of approval but a lot of discussion. Kim Taegon and his cousin, Kim Taejin, moved a few yards away from our group and talked things over earnestly in low voices.

They reached agreement, and we headed off in a different direction. The restaurant, which as it turned out belonged to a relative of the two cousins from Ch'ollip'o, was slightly more imposing than what I had in mind. The food there was plentiful, delicious, and accompanied by a lot more soju.

At some point in the afternoon the combination of strong drink and lack of sleep caught up with me, and I felt an overpowering need to take a nap. In most provincial Korean restaurants guests sit on a floor covered with oiled paper so that going to sleep is just a matter of changing to a horizontal position. But here there were tables and chairs on a cement floor. When I blurted out that I wanted to lie down (my Korean was fading fast), the captain spoke to his cousin, and a smiling, motherly barmaid was assigned to guide me, or rather push me, up a narrow ladder to a loft. Here there was an oiled paper floor and plenty of bedding. I was asleep almost at once.

Several hours later I woke up with a slight headache to discover that the "lunch" had moved up the ladder to my bedroom. We had lost our teenage ship's cook but had gained four women, who not only served the food and poured yakchu, but as the party ripened, began drinking themselves and moving closer to the happy crew members. I was quickly revived by some oysters in hot sauce and a glass of "medicine," but it wasn't long before I had to climb down the ladder to look for a urinal. The same cheerful, maternal woman who had put me to bed earlier served as guide, taking me by the hand and leading me out back to a flat paved area next to a high cement wall. There had been no windows in the low-ceilinged loft, so I was surprised to discover outdoors that it was already night. Hesitating in the dark, not knowing quite where to aim, I was startled by my companion's deftness in unzipping my fly and preparing me for action. Unfortunately the courtesy seriously interfered with my normal functions, and finally I had to ask the woman to let go and leave me alone. I was by no means a complete stranger to Korean drinking parties with female entertainers, but they had all been more or less elegant affairs in the capital with classical singing and dancing in an atmosphere of refinement and luxury. The fishermen's subculture in Inch'ŏn evidently offered exotic variations.

Back up in the loft it was snug and warm. Clean white paper covered the walls and ceiling without any seams or sharp angles to break the smooth feeling of harmony and well-being. My friendly guide had joined us from downstairs, and the party was generating a glow of sensuous togetherness that I hoped would go on forever. Fresh food and full bottles kept emerging through the trap door at the top of the ladder. At one point I wondered vaguely if I was expected to pay for all this, but it really didn't seem to matter. In any case I had nowhere near enough money with me. The mood of jovial, bountiful hospitality was so genuine that a crass reckoning seemed out of the question. One thing I knew for certain, though—no one in the crew could possibly afford such extravagance.

We moved along in terms of group dynamics to hand games involving rocks, scissors and paper, in which the losers (always female) were obliged to display certain parts of their anatomy. It was evident that I was about to get even with my matronly friend for the incident downstairs when suddenly Kim Taejin, assumed a new authority. He struggled to his feet and announced in a loud, unsteady, but nevertheless commanding voice that the party was over. It was time to leave. I thought there would be protests, but everyone obediently got up and filed down the ladder. The women and girls rearranged their clothes and cheerfully but impersonally said good-bye at the door just as if we'd all stopped by for a quick bowl of noodles.

Two small taxis were waiting outside. I was pushed into the front of the lead taxi, and we all headed back to the harbor at a desperate speed that made me wish fervently I was in the back seat. At the dock where the *Samhae Ho* was moored, our cook, along with several other young men, some of whom I recognized as fishermen from Sŏkp'o, were unloading crates. It was now almost ten o'clock, and with only two hours left before the midnight curfew, I realized that I could never make it home to Seoul in time. No one could move outdoors after midnight in any South Korean city without being picked up by the police, and given the obsessive anxiety in 1966 regarding the possibility of North Korean subversion, there was always some danger of being shot by a trigger-happy policeman.

Sobered up by the cold night air, I wondered where I would spend the night and began somewhat plaintively questioning Mun Yongju, the engineer. He told me to get back in the taxi and go to the Olympus Hotel.

Or, at least that is what I thought he said. Later, I found out he had actually told me to get back in the taxi and tell anyone who asked me, that I was going to the Olympus Hotel. The Olympus was Inch'ŏn's most luxurious hotel, with Western-style rooms and private baths, a nightclub, a gambling casino, a quasi-continental restaurant, and lots of girls. It was the natural place for an American to be heading at that time of night. I figured I had just enough money to pay for a room, thanks to the fact that no one had asked for payment at the restaurant.

But I was not alone in the taxi. Two crates were loaded in the trunk with its lid propped open, while two more were stacked in the back seat along with Mun Yongju and the cook. The taxi was angled sharply down by its stern, and the driver began to complain about the heavy load. Extra money was promised, and off we went. Now it took us a little longer to reach top speed, while the lurching and jolts when the springs hit bottom were much worse. The frantically reckless driving style remained unchanged.

We tore around the city, stopping four times in alleys behind brightly lit, noisy restaurants. At each place men came out to help unload the crates, handing over money or sometimes just an envelope in exchange. Then we drove back to a pick-up point in an empty garage, where the second taxi met us with another load. Thinking about it all afterwards I realized that the taxi driver caught on before I did. Perhaps he knew from the start. At any rate, after we loaded up for the second time, he stopped on a side street, turned off his lights and said it was too dangerous; he would lose his license if we were stopped by the police. My comrades explained excitedly that the police would not interfere with an American going to the Olympus Hotel, and they gave him a sizable wad of bills out of one of the envelopes. After that our progress was only slightly slower but much more dangerous, since we drove with the lights off.

During our empty phase, after delivering the crates, the taxi's lights went back on, and we raced at top speed through the city streets. This attracted no attention, since all taxis did that in the attempt to get as many partygoers as possible home before curfew. It was while we were heavily laden, unlit, and groping about in the back streets that things were tense.

Suddenly as we were moving along in the dark, a brilliant spotlight shone directly in our faces, and two uniformed national policemen with carbines stepped in front of the taxi. Someone poked me from in back, and I obediently rolled down the window and started explaining in my stilted textbook Korean that my only desire was to get to the Olympus Hotel and gamble the night away. Speaking Korean turned out to be the wrong strategy. My partners groaned in the back seat, poking me some more. What they wanted was an impersonation of a typical off-duty GI. In the 1960s the only foreigners who spoke Korean were missionaries, and since I obviously was not a missionary, the policemen's suspicions were now aroused. They set a somewhat nasty tone for the rest of the interview by clicking rounds into the barrels of their carbines and making us get out to show our ID papers. Luckily I had my passport with me.

The policeman in charge spoke the same Ch'ungch'ŏng Province dialect as the villagers, and it turned out he was from a village on Anmyŏn Island about 20 kilometers south of Sŏkp'o. Gradually the menace of his blunt commands eased, and there was even some conversation about how hard it was to make a living in a fishing village. When Mun Yonju handed him one of the envelopes, he called off his partner who had been shining the flashlight on the crates in back, and we parted on fairly good terms. The policeman's last remark was, "Get him to the hotel and go right home. It's against the law to drive without lights."

To this day I have never been to the Olympus Hotel. We returned to the restaurant loft, usurping what had, at this hour, become the dormitory of the women working at the restaurant. There was a little light scuffling as some of the crew or perhaps the women tried to resume earlier friendships, but things soon settled down, and there was only the sound of heavy sleeping. Because of my long afternoon nap, I lay awake in the dark for a while thinking over, or rather savoring, each detail of the past twenty-four hours.

At breakfast the next morning everyone was in high spirits because of the success of the operation the night before. The cook kept imitating my speech to the policemen, while the rest of the crew roared with laughter. No one pretended that my role had been critical, but at least I had joined in and done my best, so I was part of the enterprise. Apparently they had devised the Olympus Hotel ploy on the boat, the main obstacle being my determination to head right for Seoul as soon as we landed. My offer to buy lunch had given them their opportunity to change my plans. After that it was a simple matter to collaborate with the restaurant owner, who was one of the principal clients for the contraband pork, to keep me around until it was too late to get home.

From the villagers' point of view the problem was that although pork prices in the city were high, there were so many middlemen and officials involved in the transportation, butchering, wholesaling, inspection, and certification of meat that no profit was left for the farmer. The economic terms of trade had always been skewed against the rural population. For hundreds, probably thousands, of years Korean peasants had been fair game for those with a little education, status, and authority who lived in the towns and cities. Farming and fishing created the country's wealth, but because of rulers, aristocrats, administrators, landowners, and merchants, the farmers and fishermen lived at bare subsistence levels. There was no legal way to correct the imbalance. But if pork was quietly butchered in the village, carried to Inch'ŏn in a local boat, and sold directly (and secretly) to restaurants run by people who could be trusted, then substantial profits could be made. Everything depended on the cohesion and loyalty of tight local networks, which included kinsmen who had migrated to the city.

In this particular case, even though most of the money would go to the pig raisers and to Mun Yongbae, who had furnished the boat, the crew had all earned more in one night than they normally made in two or three months. The bribe to the policeman and our restaurant bill were substantial, but there was plenty left over. In fact, my comrades insisted on escorting me all the way to Seoul in a taxi.

There were many things I admired about the people of Sŏkp'o. One of them was the tough, good-humored, resilient, and imaginative way in which they tried to make the most of meager resources in an effort to beat the system and alleviate their poverty. Nothing was ever wasted—in this case not even the dubious value of the foreign anthropologist.

12

Fishing II

In addition to the trips to Seoul, I roamed up and down the coast on foot and by boat, visiting other communities. Mohang, six miles to the south, had at least three times as many households as Sŏkp'o and an imposing fleet of fishing boats, almost half of which had engines. The rickety bus from T'aean reached Mohang twice a day. Four miles further south was another big village, P'ado-ri, and from there it was possible to get a ride now and then on a fishing junk that doubled as a ferry to Yaksan-do, an island five or six miles offshore. The first time I went to P'ado-ri early in the summer, a *sulchip* proprietor there spoke of the people of Yaksan-do as if they were primitive savages living at the end of the world. He told me they did not know how to perform *chesa* properly and worshipped sea and mountain gods at a stone shrine on the island's highest peak. A slightly drunken fellow customer broke in loudly to announce that the men from Yaksan-do were better fishermen than those from P'ado-ri, and that he, as well as most of his fishing colleagues, also performed *kosa* to sea and mountain gods as well as local spirits, asking aggressively, "What was wrong with that?"

I was fascinated and went out to Yaksan-do to see for myself, thinking that this must be the place to study ancient forms of animism free from corruptive Confucian influences. Only seventeen families lived on the island, their houses clustered together above the one rocky beach where it was possible to haul boats above the highest tides. There was plenty of unspoiled beauty on Yaksan-do, but I was glad to get off the island. The islanders were blunt and inhospitable, and I had a terrible time understanding their thick accent.

Chollip'o, about halfway between Mohang and Sŏkp'o, was where I usually stopped to rest on my way back from town. The harbor at Chollip'o was much livelier than the one at Sŏkp'o, partly because everything was concentrated in one small area, but mostly because Chollip'o fishermen caught more fish. On one sunny September afternoon I was settled in on the veranda of the *sulchip* just opposite the small Chollip'o breakwater. It felt good to ease the weight of the rucksack off my back, and I could already smell the roasting eel that would accompany my bowl of *makkŏlli*.

On one side of the narrow harbor entrance there was a steeply sloping pebble beach. At the top of the slope on a strip of flat ground, steam and smoke were pouring out of several enormous black cauldrons that were fired by noisy kerosene burners. Each cauldron must have been four feet in diameter. They were full of boiling sea water in which fishermen were blanching anchovies before spreading them out on tarps to dry in the sun. The dried anchovies that came with my *makkŏlli* and eel were crisp and sweet, and I tried not to think about the swarms of flies I could see settling down over the ones that were still drying on the beach.

Out of the late afternoon sun the local fishing fleet began coming in from the sea. The boats were the same size and design as those at Sŏkp'o. What was strikingly different here was that these boats had engines. I learned from my host that only a year or two previously South Korean factories had begun manufacturing small diesel engines under Japanese license, and it seemed that every fishing community along the coast, except Sŏkp'o, was acquiring them. For local fishermen it was a minor revolution. They could go five or six miles offshore instead of two or three, and they could return when they wanted to at the end of the day without having to wait for the flood tide.

Two fish buyers were waiting with beat-up old Army trucks on the hard sand at the water's edge. They had set up scales on the back of their trucks, and as each boat came in to shore, the different varieties of fish were hauled out of the hold, weighed, and thrown into the trucks. These transactions were accompanied by a good deal of noisy arguing and banter, but the whole process went quickly, and sizable wads of money disappeared without delay into the fishermen's pockets.

The contrast between this operation at Chollip'o and fish landings on the beach in the Big Hamlet below my house was dramatic. At Sŏkp'o the wholesalers, instead of being men with trucks, were sturdy women who walked about five miles from Wangbok, an inland town to the east. On their return trip they carried the fish in large baskets balanced on their heads. The scene on the beach when the boats came into Sŏkp'o was always lively, but at first it was puzzling. The women buyers were extremely eager to get hold of the fish, while the fishermen were strangely reluctant to part with them. It took me quite a while to figure out what was going on behind this tense scene. Even though demand for the fish was great, prices in Sŏkp'o were low because of the primitive transportation and small size of the local Wangbok market. Sŏkp'o fishermen were still isolated from the booming national economy. Also, nearly all the local fishermen had borrowed heavily from the buyers and knew that their catch would mostly go just to pay off interest or reduce their debts. And, in any case, each fisherman wanted to keep back a few fish to eat at home or exchange with other villagers. The buyers, knowing that the boats all had a special secret cache, tried threats and cajolery to extract the hidden fish. As a result, negotiations were long and noisy and included insults, jokes, sexual innuendos, feigned outrage, and real shouts of indignation when the women buyers bore down too hard and damaged male sensibilities. Of course, bystanders also participated.

At Chollip'o when the day's fishing ended, a small crowd gathered at the sulchip, anxious to save me from the desolation of having to drink by myself and eager for American cigarettes. They had money to spend and treated me generously.

I asked,

"How can a poor, out-of-the-way village like this one buy so many diesel engines?" (It was accepted conventional wisdom that all villages along this coast were poor).

There was a rush of answers:

"We sell land to Seoul people for summer villas."

"We have relatives in T'aean who want to invest. Fish prices are high. Anyone who can catch fish now can make real money."

"The fishery cooperative lent me money."

"We got together in my lineage and pooled our savings."

When I asked Chollip'o fishermen why no one in Sŏkp'o had engines, the answers were derisive.

"Who would want to buy land way out there at the end of the peninsula where there is no road?"

"The cooperative knows they will never pay back the loans."

"They don't have any rich relatives."

"They don't know anything about engines. They will always be poor and backward. The only people with money in Sŏkp'o don't fish."

Until recently I had not only felt a strong sense of loyal identity with Sŏkp'o and its reputation for human heartedness, but I was even proud of its leaky sailboats, its isolation, and its poverty. But upon hearing this kind of contemptuous talk, my pride changed to discontent, envy, and resentment. Why should Sŏkp'o be left out? It was beginning to get through to me how much the people there, in spite of their apparently cheerful resignation, longed to break out of a stagnant and "lagging behind" way of life. They were bitter at the idea of being left behind, a backwater in a nation that was on the move economically.

The situation was not just stagnant; it was getting worse. There had once been thirty sailboats in the Sŏkp'o fleet, but now there were only thirteen. Overfishing in the waters close to shore had made the old methods obsolete. Catches were no longer even big enough to make it worthwhile to maintain the boats. With no other way to make a living, many fishermen had to leave the village and go to Inch'ŏn, hoping to find work on big, oceangoing boats. Sŏkp'o households could no longer attract brides for their sons. No young woman wanted to move to a poor village at the end of the world. The only real hope for prosperity had been the dike, but no one believed in that anymore.

I had already made modest money contributions to three village projects: a new well; repairs to the ferry landing; and improvements on a small reservoir. While these were all worthy causes, I gave the money not because I was particularly interested in development and change but only because the villagers asked me to help. It seemed necessary to do so in order to maintain good personal relations. What I was really interested in was examining and analyzing the village just as it was, not in trying to change it for the better. I had also been exposed in graduate school to a different point of view, one that required the anthropologist to take urgent action on behalf of the deprived and exploited people he was studying. But at the elite institution I attended, such ideas were looked down on as the rantings of leftist ideologues. Besides, my initial perspective was that the people of Sŏkp'o lived in a kind of paradise.

Inevitably, however, as I learned more about what was really on their minds, I couldn't help but identify with and even adopt their longing for a better life. This shift on my part from uncritical admiration for a traditional way of life to ardent developmental activism, was reluctant and gradual and never complete. Nevertheless it did take place, influencing both my outlook and my preoccupations during the last couple of months in the village. By the beginning of October I was spending less time enjoying the scenery and the psychic rewards of participation in local activities and more worrying about the local economy. My notebooks for this period are full of theorizing about the reasons for the village's backwardness. Was it possible that my neighbors and adoptive kinsmen were less enterprising than other fishermen along the coast? Was there something about village communalism and cohesiveness that interfered with progress? Was lineage loyalty blocking individual entrepreneurship? I had to give a negative answer to all these questions. The people of Sŏkp'o were just as hard-working, just as risk-taking, and just as good seamen as their neighbors down the coast. I accepted their own explanation that all their troubles were due to geographic isolation, lack of good rice land, and shortage of capital. As usual, I found out that things were a lot more complicated than I could ever possibly have imagined.

In mid-September, on my next trip up to Seoul, I met an old friend from Washington by chance on the train. He was now running a foundation that gave out small American grants to Koreans, mostly for scholarly projects, book publishing, and cultural exchange. David was personally interested in economic development, however, and he had the authority to use his money any way he liked. When he asked me about my work in the village, I poured out the whole sad story of the decline of Sŏkp'o's fishing industry. I explained that without access to engines the situation seemed to be hopeless. We both knew there was no way an ordinary Korean peasant could borrow really sizable amounts of money. "Look, Vin, we've got a few thousand dollars left in the budget this year. Why don't you buy them some boat engines?" David said this as casually as if he were offering me a drink.

The prospect was intriguing, even exciting. Running a development project, even a very small one, was the last thing I ever thought I would be doing in Sŏkp'o, but I was becoming increasingly concerned with the well-being of my friends and neighbors. I had stood by helplessly for months observing a degree of scarcity and lack of opportunity that was far more severe than anything I had ever imagined.

On many occasions I had fantasized about transforming things for the better. Suddenly it seemed that I would really be able to do something useful. My role would change from that of prying nuisance to powerful benefactor. I could turn around the whole fishing sector of the village and get it started on the road to prosperity. I could also help correct what I saw as the unfair cultural prejudice against men who fished. I asked, "How much control do you want over how the money is spent?"

"None whatsoever. You can run things exactly as you please. I might come down once and take a look after things get going, and you can help me write up a final report. Otherwise there are no strings attached. Spend the five thousand dollars any way you want, as long as it's for boat engines."

We discussed the project for the rest of the trip. David, who had worked previously for the Agency for International Development, had a lot of ideas about how to organize things. He emphasized the importance of getting the right people involved, of making sure that the village authorities were not left out, and of convincing the community that everyone would benefit. In Seoul, I asked powerful Korean friends for advice. They were used to thinking in terms of tens of millions of dollars in aid money and laughed at the size of my fund. The banker who had first driven me to Mohang asked, "Why don't you go into partnership with the best fisherman in the village and make some money? Then everyone else will follow your lead." I thought it was a joke, and perhaps it was. It was also very good advice, and I wish I had followed it.

By the time I started back for the village a few days later, I had worked out a fairly detailed plan. The fishermen at Chollip'o had told me how much they paid for their engines and how much it cost to get them installed in their boats. They also gave me estimates of fuel and maintenance costs. Sŏkp'o fishermen would have a little farther to go to get out to sea, but the difference would be minor. The main thing, it seemed to me, was that, except for the engines, there would be nothing new to learn. The rest of the fishing equipment and techniques would be the same as before. Diesel fuel could be picked up and the fish unloaded at Chollip'o. I made the calculations over and over and decided there was no reason why Sŏkp'o fishermen could not make a profit. In spite of what actually happened, I still think this reasoning was perfectly sound.

My idea was to establish a village development fund under the direction of the village head and a small council of the most responsible and influential citizens (yuji). Initially the fund would be used to lend each of five fishermen one thousand dollars, which was about 70 percent of the cost of an engine and installation. Each borrower would then have to come up with the remaining 30 percent, to make sure that he had a responsible stake in the success of the enterprise. The interest rate of 20 percent would be extremely low by local standards (50–60 sixty percent was normal), and since the fund belonged to the entire village, there would be, I thought, enormous social pressure on the recipients to pay back their loans. Gradually, according to this scheme, as money accumulated in the village fund, it would be used for other development projects as decided by the governing council. It all seemed simple, promising, and foolproof. Current living standards would improve, while at the same time establishing momentum towards future development.

I returned to Sŏkp'o from Seoul and immediately went to see Teacher Yi, full of enthusiastic optimism and certain that everyone would be overjoyed with my plan. Teacher Yi was not quite as delighted as I expected. He remarked prophetically, "Everyone will want the money, even people who don't fish." I answered, "But this is just a start. Once the fishermen start making a profit, everyone will benefit."

Teacher Yi peered at me through his big round spectacles. "Why don't you use the money to help finish the dike or build a reservoir? Sŏkp'o needs those things more than boat engines." So, even my friend and hero, Teacher Yi, was prejudiced against fishing! I protested, "But they're making good money catching fish at Chollip'o, Mohang, and P'ado-ri. Here you have the skills and experience but it's all going to waste. All the fishermen will become poor farm laborers, or they'll have to leave for Inch'ŏn. Is that good for the village?"

Teacher Yi laughed. "You must be the only scholar in the world who feels so strongly about boats and fishing. Let's go talk it over with the village head." We walked along the edge of the mudflats on our way to Yi Pyŏnghyŏk's house at the opposite end of the Yi Hamlet. In the kitchen gardens close to the houses, women were weeding vegetables. They all rose and bowed to us deferentially. Teacher Yi also bowed and returned the greetings. Some men who were out in the mudflats digging for octopus shouted out to us, asking about my trip to Seoul. It was good to be back.

Yi Pyŏnghyŏk didn't seem all that pleased either, although he made a rather formal and flowery declaration of gratitude for my concern and efforts on behalf of the village. What chiefly bothered him, I found out later, was the prospect of the long-drawn-out and difficult negotiations that would be required to set up the committee, award the loans, and supervise the fund. He knew better than anyone else what a delicate job it was balancing all the variables so that no lineage or hamlet felt it had been unfairly treated. As farmers, neither he nor any of the other Yis would gain anything, and he was already

Figure 12.1 Low tide showing mud as far as one can see. (1966)

so badly overburdened with administrative duties that he didn't have time to work in his own fields.

But I was delighted with my plan; it never occurred to me that it might not work. I brushed aside the hesitancy of Yi Pyŏnghyŏk and Teacher Yi. Like so many others, I had been seduced by community development ideology in graduate school. Over and over again we had read or been told that the most crucial ingredients for success in a rural development project like this were cooperation, the determination to change things for the better, self-reliance, and unselfish dedication by individuals to a community goal. Certainly the villagers of Sŏkp'o had all these qualities. Sŏkp'o was a place where people worked together and got along with each other because they shared common ideals.

As an anthropologist I admired ancient village institutions and patterns of behavior. I made the mistake of assuming they would function as well in the administration of an innovative economic enterprise as they did in maintaining harmony and upholding Confucian standards of morality. This assumption was just plain wrong.

In Sŏkp'o important decisions involving the entire village were reached through a gradual process of consensus building. "Elections" were not held until everyone knew what the results would be. Some people, however, were much more influential than others in determining the consensus. A poor man from a small inconsequential lineage could, and often did, state his personal views loudly and vehemently in formal village meetings as well as in informal conversations. But his arguments, however well or forcefully expressed, did not really count unless they coincided with the opinions of the yuji. The yuji comprised an informal group of eight to ten of the highest ranking, wealthiest, and best-educated household heads. They might never all meet together to discuss a particular issue, but gradually, through a series of conversations in each other's *sarangbang* the "real" consensus was shaped. The job of the village head was not only to help forge the decisions through *sarangbang* discussions, but also to make sure that the village "consensus" was formally ratified at larger village meetings.

Unfortunately for my project, the Sŏkp'o *yuji* were all landowners who didn't think much of fishing and couldn't understand why my money wasn't being targeted for a more noble purpose such as building a road, a meeting hall, or an irrigation project. Since capital was so scarce, they were determined, if possible, to get some control of the money. The people I had in mind as loan recipients were younger, energetic men with proven fishing skills. Most of them owned land and did some farming but preferred fishing because of the opportunity it provided for quick profits. They were restless and dissatisfied, looking for new opportunities. Some of them would be the *yuji* of the future. There were also, of course, several poor boat owners who would have been happy to install small engines and follow the lead of the Chŏllip'o fishermen. But they had no money of their own to put up, and their status and influence wasn't great enough to allow them to participate in what was becoming an event of political and ritual importance.

Not only was I convinced that the plan should be administered by the *yuji* working through traditional institutions, but I also insisted on an official meeting at which the village head would formally announce the program, introduce the recipients of the loans, and explain the financial details. It seemed to me that some sort of public declaration by the beneficiaries would ensure that they would stick to the agreement and not misuse the money. It also seemed appropriate to tell everyone that in the long run the money would be used, not just to enrich five borrowers but to benefit the entire village.

The meeting was scheduled for two o'clock at the school house on an afternoon in early October. At about a quarter before two Yi Pyŏnghyŏk, the village head, and Kim Hwa Jin, a capable and energetic fisherman in his thirties whom I strongly favored as a loan candidate, showed up at my house. I greeted them, grateful for their courtesy in coming to pick me up. But as I was putting on my shoes to join them and walk down the hill they were taking theirs off and settling themselves comfortably on the veranda.

"There's no hurry," said the village head. "It takes a little while to collect everyone, and we can see from here when it's time to go down." Since he would be running the meeting, I took my shoes off again, got back up on the porch, and asked Kyong Sook to bring us some coffee. I turned to Kim Hwa Jin, "Well, are you going to buy a boat?"

"No, I'm too busy with the anchovy fishing. And besides, with my oldest son starting middle school, I don't want to take on any new responsibilities." This was a real surprise, since he had told me the week before that he was eager to invest. "I'm still young," he continued. "Kim Wŏn'gil has more experience and will use the money well."

I had been out with Kim Wŏn'gil on his boat. He was an easygoing man of about fifty who had plenty of land and fished more as a hobby than because he needed extra income. A couple of months before he had remarked that he was ready to give up fishing completely and devote himself to farming. He was a neighbor and relative of Kim Hwa Jin's. It was disappointing news; I felt that a more hard-driving and younger man such as Kim Hwa Jin would be better, both at learning to operate an engine and at competing in the larger economy beyond the village boundaries.

Impulsively I protested to the village head.

"But I hoped Kim Hwa Jin would be one of the new boat owners. We need men like him to make the scheme work."

"Well, it's all been discussed at length and everything is settled." He answered. "It's too late to change anything now."

Then I asked who else would get the loans, and the answers reinforced the sinking feeling I'd had on hearing about Kim Wŏn'gil. "From the Yi clan there's Yi Changgyu and from the Big Hamlet Kim Ŭigon and Mun Hyong Bae. And then from the Sixth Hamlet there's Kim Ju Won." Yi listed the other four names with an air of having satisfactorily accomplished a difficult task.

It was awful. Except for Mun Hyong Bae none of them were practical, hardheaded go-getters. And Mun's reputation for probity was pretty shaky. If these men shared any quality, it was that of being expansive dreamers and talkers rather than doers. They also shared another attribute. None could be called *yuji*, but they were all closely related to *yuji*, as younger brothers or cousins or in one case as a nephew. They were the chosen instruments of the village establishment—"chosen" in order to acquire control of the money, or at least a say in how it would be spent.

I was dismayed by what seemed to me to be sabotage of any possibility of establishing a flourishing modern fishing economy in the village. Personal merit and fishing ability had not been considered at all in making the choices. Instead kinship ties, seniority, and personal connections had been decisive.

"But everyone knows Yi Changgyu is lazy and extravagant and spoiled." I tried to say. When I got worked up and spoke quickly and emphatically, my Korean became somewhat incoherent. Koreans can tell I am upset at such moments, but they usually can't figure out why.

On this occasion, however, Kim Hwa Jin realized at least that I wasn't saying anything kind about Yi Changgyu, so he pulled me aside and in a sort of stage whisper said, "Remember, he is the nephew of the village head." Yi Changgyu was the archetypical example of the son of a well-to-do farmer who had been overeducated and overexposed to town ways in his youth, so that he was useless in the village. He hadn't learned anything at school of practical value, but his station was now too lofty for him to engage in manual labor. In this particular case Yi Changgyu's father had died young and Yi Changgyu had been given everything he asked for by a doting grandfather, who remained household head long after he should have retired. Largely as a result of the cost of Yi Changgyu's schooling and his drinking and womanizing in nearby towns, the family had fallen on hard times. Probably his powerful Yi clan relatives had thought this would be a good way to pay off his debts and get him involved in something productive. After Kim Hwa Jin's warning, I dropped the subject of Yi Changgyu and started in on Kim Ŭigon.

"Kim Ŭigon is much too poor to put up any of his own money." I said. "Besides, he drinks too much and he is known to be unreliable in money matters." I knew this first hand from my real estate dealings with him.

This time the village head tried to calm me down. "We have found someone who will lend him the additional money. Kim Ŭigon knows boats and used to be a good fisherman. He has just had an awful lot of bad luck. Besides, I thought you wanted him to get a loan. He told me that you insisted on his being one of the five." I was too jolted by this to say anything.

When the village head left the porch briefly to urinate on the ashes piled up behind the house for this purpose, Kim Hwa Jin said, "He too is a first cousin of the village head. Kim Ŭigon's mother was his paternal aunt." I began to look at the quiet, mild-mannered Yi Pyŏnghyŏk with new respect, as a latter-day Machiavellian of considerable talent. I had no special objection to Kim Ju Won, the other borrower, whom I didn't know well, but there was nothing that came to mind, in particular to recommend him either. He seemed to have been chosen mainly so that every hamlet would be represented.

It was now three o'clock, and we could see a small crowd starting to form at the schoolhouse. As we walked down the path, I tried to fight off the gloomy realization that my development project was doomed. At the bottom of the hill we ran into a thick cloud of mosquito-like flying things making a whine so loud that talk was impossible. A little further on women at the well looked up from their washing and asked, "Where are you going?" They knew, but they gave us the standard greeting anyway.

Only about thirty men, or a little less than one-third of all the household heads, had shown up. Most farmers weren't interested, and many of the poorer fishermen had not bothered to come, knowing that everything had already been decided, and that in any case they were excluded from the loans. The village head seemed annoyed: he had urged everyone to show up as a sign of solid community support for economic development.

Yi Changgyu, the Yi clan's choice, was much better dressed than anyone else at the meeting. He had brought two friends with him from town, and they all stayed together throughout the meeting joking and laughing as though they were spectators at an amusing performance. The village head asked him to sit up front with the other borrowers, but Yi Changgyu stayed with his friends in the rear, keeping up a noisy and disturbing chatter.

Mun Hyong Bae wasn't even present, and he had to be sent for. When he finally arrived, he explained that he was already negotiating with some men from Inch'ŏn for the purchase of a boat. It was obvious that the negotiations had been accompanied by several pots of makkŏlli. In the meantime, Yi Changgyu and his friends had disappeared, and they had to be summoned from a waterfront sulchip. When he came back, Yi Changgyu, who was about thirty-five years old, insisted on stopping and talking cordially and loudly to a couple of the younger household heads, deliberately delaying the meeting. I was not only discouraged about how badly things were going, but also shocked at this violation of propriety. Yi Changgyu and his friends remained contemptuous, interrupting the proceedings with jokes and irrelevant remarks. At first there was laughter, but soon the group's mood changed, and two men rose to denounce Yi Changgyu as a disgrace to the village, suggesting that if he was not interested, others could use the money. This public censure was effective and Yi Changgyu quieted down.

The meeting went on and on, filled with acrimonious debate. A lot of those present felt the same way I did about Kim Ŭigon and couldn't understand why he had been picked as a loan recipient. Although no one actually came right out and called him a lazy drunkard, some of the remarks came perilously close.

"Kim Ŭigon never succeeded at anything before. Why do you think he is going to do any better this time? He's older now and drinks even more. I think he's going to do worse." Mun P'algap was not on good terms with Kim Ŭigon, and in any case he liked to pontificate in public.

The village head felt obliged to defend the official choice. "As you all know, Kim Ŭigon worked on Japanese boats during the war. He has more experience on big boats with engines than anyone else here."

Mun P'algap wanted the last word. "But all he did was cook or haul on nets. He wasn't the engineer. He'll run his boat on the rocks the first time he takes it out at night."

Kim Ŭigon got to his feet, his face even darker than usual. He then made a long harangue, dredging up all sorts of half-forgotten incidents that were damaging, not only to Mun P'algap, but also to the reputation of the whole Mun lineage. "Tell us about what you and your brothers did when the North Korean Army came and occupied Sŏkp'o!" This was inflammatory stuff, and the village head broke in, hastily directing the discussion in other directions.

I was surprised at the degree of hostility expressed. Except for drunken brawls, direct face-to-face insults were extremely rare in Sŏkp'o. And yet when I asked about it later, saying that I was afraid at the time there was going to be physical violence, Teacher Yi didn't seem to think anything extraordinary had happened. "That's just the way we conduct our meetings. They didn't mean anything serious by what they said. It's good to get everything out in the open." I sympathized more now with the village head's initial reluctance to get involved. Both Yi Changgyu and Mun Hyung Bae were unwilling at first to come forward and publicly declare their willingness to abide by the conditions of the loan. Mun Hyung Bae said,

> America has been giving lots of aid to South Korea for many years now. Finally a little bit has come all the way down to Sŏkp'o. Why do we need to get all mixed up in this "village fund" business? If the money is to go to me, just give it to me and don't bother with a lot of petty restrictions.

Yi Changgyu was more explicit. "I'm the one who takes the risk and does the hard work. Why should I be responsible to the whole village for this money?"

At this point those *yuji* who were present, as well as the village head, began to bear down. They insisted that the loan conditions were absolutely firm and scolded Mun Hyong Bae and Yi Changgyu for their lack of respect and gratitude. Yi Pyŏnghyŏk complained that the entire community had lost face before a foreigner because of their drunken behavior. Others joined in the denunciation. The loan recipients, who desperately wanted the money and who, in any case, had no leverage, signed the agreement.

For me it had been a terrible afternoon. The wrong men were borrowing "my" money, and they seemed determined to carry out impossibly grandiose schemes. They all wanted to jump instantly into the big time, going far off-shore in big boats. My plan was in shambles. No one wanted to buy a small diesel engine and install it in one of the boats that were currently in use. During the weeks that followed all of the borrowers except Kim Wŏn'gil bought boats. Unfortunately, with the money available the only boats they could find in the thirty-five to forty foot range were ancient and in nearly sinking condition with engines that dated from the Japanese colonial period. Word got around quickly that Sŏkp'o fishermen had money, and everyone along the coast with an unseaworthy wreck limped into the harbor trying to sell it. Knowing very little about boats this size, the prospective owners were dazzled, not only by the impressive bulk of these antiques, but also by the terrible noise and smoke of their engines. *Makkŏlli* flowed abundantly at the waterfront for many days while ownership was changing hands, after which the delighted sellers quickly got out of town, leaving the new owners to cope with rotting hulls and balky machinery.

Kim Wŏn'gil never did buy a boat. He held onto the money as a prospective buyer for nearly six months before being forced by public opinion (and the *yuji*) to return it to the village fund. It was rumored that he had done quite well as a money lender during the intervening period. A couple of years later, when I made my first return trip to Sŏkp'o, the village head proudly showed me the new orchard of chestnut trees that had been planted using Kim Wŏn'gil's money.

The four who bought boats did not prosper. Yi Changgyu, with no money of his own, had borrowed from the two high school classmates who accompanied him to the meeting. He was ashamed of being from such a poor and backward place, and at the meeting he wanted to demonstrate to his friends the social distance that existed between himself and the village establishment, as well as the fact that he was not really subject to local authority. It seemed sad that most Sŏkp'o men not only understood Yi Changgyu's motives, but even shared his low evaluation of themselves and their community. On the other hand there was outrage when Yi Changgyu simply took off with his boat for Inch'ŏn and didn't come back. He was regarded as having absconded with village property and no longer had the "face" to return home. There were reports from the Sŏkp'o network in Inch'ŏn that after living well for a while on the proceeds of a quick resale, Yi Changgyu had nothing left and was forced into various kinds of sleazy occupations on the waterfront. It was a cruel blow to his grandfather.

Instead of fishing, Kim Ŭigon used his boat for trading, carrying fish and other goods between Inch'ŏn and villages all along the coast. Although there was a need for such transportation, in Kim Ŭigon's case it was a losing proposition. He relished the role of captain and boat owner, especially the long negotiations in the *sulchip* over the purchase and sale of cargo. On these occasions he would regularly get drunk and have to be carried back to the boat, more or less unconscious. Inevitably Kim Ŭigon became somewhat dependent on his oldest son, who gradually took over responsibility for maintaining and piloting the boat. For some months they tried to carry on the trading business with Kim Ŭigon spending most of his income on *makkŏlli* and food ashore. Finally the young man, in total frustration, started leaving his father behind whenever he passed out, managing the boat himself with the help of his twelve-year-old younger brother. There were monumental family battles over this violation of filial piety. But waking up stranded and without money in strange harbors made a strong impression on Kim Ŭigon. Although he didn't stop drinking, he stopped going to sea. The son eventually sold the boat, bought a smaller one (with a diesel engine), and began to make money fishing.

Mun Hyong Bae's boat was in as bad condition as any of the others, but he managed to mobilize his relatives to help keep it afloat and operating. A brother-in-law with a reputation as a successful captain on Inch'ŏn boats came back to take charge, while Mun Hyong Bae's younger brother became an engineer through on-the-job training. Most important, a cousin, the only boat carpenter in the village with any skill, replaced most of the planking. But Mun Hyung Bae kept reaching too high, involving himself in increasingly ambitious but risky projects. A few of these succeeded, but most of the time they failed, and finally he had to sell the boat along with some of his land to pay off creditors.

The fifth person to get a loan, Kim Ju Won, was the only one who engaged full time in fishing. He seemed to be doing all right until the end of the good weather in early November. Then a major southwest storm came through. Instead of tapering off after a couple of days of high wind and rain as expected, the gale intensified until the sound of waves breaking against the rocky coast reverberated everywhere throughout the village. Storm winds flattened the maturing rice plants wherever fields were directly exposed to the south and west, and at high tide waves surged across the sandspit, making Sŏkp'o an island. A big section of the unfinished dike simply disappeared. Fishermen hauled their boats higher and higher right into the front yards of the shacks along the harbor.

We rolled down the reed blinds that Kim Ŭigon had insisted I attach to the eaves of my roof, and they provided some protection. Still, with the wind and rain driving in directly off the ocean against our exposed site, it was impossible to use the veranda. And with the blinds down the interior of the house was not only damp but dark and claustrophobic. Escaping from this confinement, I roamed the cliffs to watch the big lumpy green swells explode against the rocks, with plumes of spray shooting up in some places as high as one hundred feet. Our coastal world trembled. Returning home wet and cold, I hugged the hot floor under a comforter, while my clothes dried. Extravagantly, we kept the kitchen fire going to warm the floors and dry things out.

In the late afternoon of the fourth day of the storm a small crowd of twenty-five or thirty people gathered by the boats, even though there was no letup in the wind and rain. I stumbled and slid down my muddy path to find out what

Figure 12.2 The roof was damaged in a southwest storm, and the men are hurrying to complete repairs before bad weather returns. (November, 1966).

was going on. A woman sat by herself on the coarse pebbles at the top of the beach clutching a huge gourd to her stomach and chest as if it was a baby. She rocked back and forth, wailing in the stereotypical manner that Koreans use to mourn the dead. It must have been going on for hours, because her voice was getting hard and raspy—the ugly notes giving the wailing an unholy sound. Her small children clung to her, trying to get some attention, but she ignored them. Earlier in the day the torn body of her husband, Kim Pom Sol, had washed ashore on the windward side of the sandspit, still lashed to what was left of a boat's gunwale. Kim Pom Sol was now laid out in his shack just behind where the new widow was wailing.

Several of us stood under the deep eaves of another, nearby house, watching the sheets of rain go by almost horizontally and listening to the wailing. Chunks of thatch partially torn loose by the wind stood here and there on every roof, and some of the more conscientious villagers were already up on top of their houses in the driving rain lashing things down. Many of the gourds that normally grow on the roofs and ripen in the fall, had been torn loose from the thatch and fallen to the ground. The dead man's wife was embracing one of these. After a while her children stopped crying and pulling at her clothes and began rummaging around inside the kitchen looking for something to eat. She continued to wail.

In the shelter under the eaves of the adjoining houses other groups formed and dispersed restlessly. Most of the men were subdued, but a few talked excitedly and in loud voices about the dangers of the sea. There was one break in the mood of grim tension. Someone mentioned that Kim Pom Sol was an awful mess when they found him, and Kang Young Ju remarked, "He wasn't such a pretty sight even before." Everyone laughed. It was true that Kim Pom Sol had lost a leg in Manchuria as a conscript in the Japanese armies and did not wash often. He had been bald with a scraggly beard, often drunk, and he had made more or less constant, offensive advances to the wives of his neighbors. He had close kin but no close friends. He would not be missed. The uneasy laughter died away quickly. Two other men from Sŏkp'o had been with Kim Pom Sol fishing off Mot Sŏm, and now there was no hope that anyone could have survived. The owner and captain was Kim Ju Won. Because of my development project he and his crew had gone to sea late in the season in a leaky old boat.

Even in the sheltered harbor there were sizable waves. The tide was so high that although the boats were hauled as far as possible up the beach, they were still half afloat, knocking into each other with dull mournful thumps. With the heavy overcast, dusk came early, and no one noticed the slow, ungainly ferry sculled by a single oar at the stern until it was just off the beach. When I saw the body stretched out in it, I realized that this was what we had all been standing there waiting for.

A young woman with a baby on her back came running and staggering down towards the water. She waded out towards the boat crying out wildly— a sound totally different from the ritualized wailing that continued higher up on the beach. Another woman waded out after her and took the baby, just as it was starting to get wet with the surf. Then a man grabbed her roughly and dragged her back to the beach, but she continued to cry out, fighting to get free. The man shouted at her. "It is not your baby's father's body. It is Kim Ju Won." Finally she understood and collapsed on the beach sobbing. A woman threw a blanket over her and helped her to her feet. T'aemo explained to me, "It is Kim Ju Won's body, not that of her husband. It is her brother-in-law who pulled her back. They don't want to see her crying in public, when there is no corpse."

The baby's father's body was never found, and that was the greatest tragedy of the shipwreck for the people of Sŏkp'o. Without the body it was impossible to carry out a proper funeral and burial. The ghost would never be at peace. Kim Pom Sol's wife returned to her native village, but the two other widows remained in Sŏkp'o, raising their children in their husbands' lineages. Whenever I met one of them on a village path, I shrank back inside my own mind, imagining their hatred. But they always dropped their eyes politely, murmured the usual greeting, and passed on by, just as the other women did.

On balance I suppose my development project did the village more economic harm than good. If the loss of life at sea is considered, there is no doubt but that it was a disaster. Two years later, when I returned to Sŏkp'o for a brief visit, however, there were three powered fishing boats—after five years the fleet had increased to seven. Perhaps the flurry of big boat catastrophes had somehow stimulated interest and dispersed knowledge in ways that contributed to village fishing after all.

An unforeseen result of the loan plan was a stone monument erected in my honor, complete with my name, date of birth, residence in America (Putney, Vermont), and the date on which it was dedicated in Sŏkp'o. All this is carved in both Korean and English. Perhaps in a couple of thousand years

Figure 12.3 Stone commemoration of the author's time in Korea; photo taken in 1966. On my return to Sŏkp'o twenty-five years later in 1992, the stele was still upright but badly overgrown.

the inscription will help befuddled linguists reconstruct whichever language has been lost in the meantime. The monument was still standing in 1992.

The dedication ceremony was easily the most notable social event of the year, since it was attended by the county magistrate (*kunsu*). The *kunsu* was a person of almost unimaginably lofty status in a place like Sŏkp'o. He was accompanied by several aides, some of whom were in uniform. I had no coat and tie, so Teacher Yi lent me his, which was much too big. Someone put a large artificial flower in the button hole. There were even congratulatory wreaths brought all the way from Sŏsan. Teacher Yi, without a jacket, could not participate and had to stand with the other spectators. After several speeches, including one by me, we all ate and drank a great deal. My chief impression at the time was that the village children, many of whom had become quite familiar, even sassy at times, suddenly went back to being shy and respectful, just as on the first day I walked into the village.

There aren't many people who can take their children to visit a personal stele, but my pride is a little diluted by a certain ambivalence regarding the actual services performed. This uneasy feeling is reinforced by the fact that the stele is shaped almost exactly like an old New England gravestone.

13

Go Peacefully; Stay Peacefully

A spell of cold weather in early December brought five or six inches of wet snow. It was a dramatic change, and the children were happy at first, dimly remembering winter vacations in Vermont. The snow quickly turned to slush and then to mud, which together with low clouds and a bitter wind off the ocean forced us to crowd together inside on the hot floor. The first twelve inches of air just above the floor stayed pretty warm, but from the waist up (while sitting on the floor) the air inside was about as cold as it was outdoors. We used firewood and candles extravagantly by Sŏkp'o standards, and our sliding glass door let plenty of light into one room at least. But the villagers' houses, with paper windows, small oil lamps for light, and only meager amounts of wood for fires, were dim, cold, and dreary.

Bad weather reinforced the tendency of Sŏkp'o's adult males to gather together in small convivial groups. Confronted with the challenge of much more free time than usual, they consoled themselves with makkŏlli or soju, in someone's sarangbang, in the store, or in a sulchip. A certain amount of quasi-surreptitious gambling also took place in these settings. Both traditional ethics and government regulations prohibited gambling as detrimental to public morality. Nevertheless, a kind of permanent floating card game went on in winter in one or another of the meeting places of the Big Hamlet. If I wanted company and was at all thirsty, all I had to do was saunter down the hill, wander about for a while, and then home in on the noise. Impassioned oratory, laughter, angry shouts, and the cries that accompanied the winning cards made it easy to find each day's gathering. The first time I blundered into one of these sessions the men made a half-hearted move to hide the money and cards, more, I supposed, for form's sake than because anyone really felt guilty or threatened. The players quickly got used to me, however, and urged

Figure 13.1 Looking east over the Big Hamlet. My house is in the clump of trees in the middle of the photo. (1966)

me to join in, competing eagerly to teach me the rules. I slowed the game down quite a bit and was never really able to master the physical skills—the exaggerated body language and the wild shout of triumph as the winner slammed down his final card on top of the pile. On the other hand, since I contentedly lost considerable (by village standards) amounts of money, I suppose I was something of an asset to the group whenever I played cards. Certainly the men of the Big Hamlet (and their wives who served us rice beer and *anju*) always made me feel welcome. From their point of view I was a neighbor and unless I had important work to do elsewhere, was a teetotaler, or puritanically opposed to gambling, it was appropriate that I should be part of one of these groups. What really bothered them apparently was the thought of my sitting all alone in my house with only the children for company, or wandering by myself along the coast.

These men from the Big Hamlet were mostly my age or a little younger, and partly, I suppose, for that reason the tone of their gatherings was different from that of the sessions in Teacher Yi's *sarangbang* that I remembered from eight months before. Some things, of course, were the same: the ripe body smell and everyone's ability to sit cross-legged for interminable hours. This open-ended obliviousness to the passage of time had, for me, almost mythic proportions, clearly marking off a boundary between Sŏkp'o and the modern world. On the other hand, it seemed to me that the floors of the Big Hamlet were colder and the dim daylight that filtered through the paper-covered doors was gloomier than the lamplight and deep shadows on the evenings when Pirate and his colleagues had invaded my bedroom. Perhaps, in addition to age, different class traditions had an effect as well. In any case, the conversation now was a good deal livelier, and I understood more of it. Instead of tomb sites, lineage affairs, farming, and the cosmos, my younger neighbors of the Big Hamlet spent their time talking about economic development, money-making schemes, fishing, migration to town, and sex. A lot of the jokes and innuendos were incomprehensible to me until I persuaded a reluctant T'aemo to give me a couple of remedial vocabulary lessons in local dialect terms for the female anatomy and certain basic body functions.

One dark December afternoon, after a few convivial rounds of makkŏlli, Kang Yong Ju's older cousin, Kang Yong Sik, hit me playfully on the shoulder, asking, "How do you manage when your wife is away in Seoul all the time?" When I was upright again (my cross-legged stance was never really stable) he continued. "A certain fisherman's wife right here in this neighborhood was willing enough. You should have grabbed your chance when her husband was away at Mot Sŏm." There was a lot of laughter, and I got by with a clumsy remark to the effect that Sŏkp'o fishermen were so tough I was afraid to fool around with their wives. It was the first time they had ever included me directly in this kind of conversation.

After some more boisterous talk about how often a man needed a woman and the associated problems of working in the offshore islands or on deep-sea fishing boats, Mun Ch'ilgap, the unfilial son from the "fight factory" below my house, defended the tone of the conversation, speaking directly to me. "We know all about Confucian etiquette and proper behavior, just as much as the Yis do. But we don't need it anymore. Who wants to sit around all the time worrying about who can say what, who should drink first, and who can smoke in front of whom? Korea is changing and we should throw away all those useless old customs."

In early December I began to think about winding up my research and heading home. Hi Young and the children wanted to get away. They had all had enough of the simple rural pleasures, and the children especially were eager to spend Christmas with their mother. But I planned to stay in Sŏkp'o and join in the New Year's festivities which, because of the lunar calendar, would not take place until late January and early February. Everyone told me that this was the high point of the year, a two-week period of continuous good feeling during which the villagers feasted, visited one another's houses, and got together to observe all sorts of old customs and rituals. In mid-December my wife came down and took the children back with her to Seoul. It was unthinkable that I could keep house on my own, so poor Hi Young had to stay behind.

After seeing my family off on the bus at Mohang, I walked home against a cold north wind off the sea that made my eyes water. At Chollip'o blowing sand stung my face. No one was outdoors. On the path to Sŏkp'o high above the waves I thought about the work that remained to be done over the next month or so. Quite abruptly I realized that my thesis topic, about which I had had all sorts of confusion and doubt, was taking shape on its own, almost without conscious effort or direction on my part. I had enough information in my head and in my notebooks to write a structural analysis of Sŏkp'o as a cohesive, self-reliant, and stable community, a place where some hundreds of people successfully followed ancient formulas to live together with goodwill, in isolated poverty. It seemed to me that the New Year's celebrations would be an ideal time to pursue my investigation of the "anatomy of solidarity" in Sŏkp'o.

But the villagers themselves that winter were not talking much about traditional harmony and morality. It was change and progress that dominated the conversation in *sulchip* and *sarangbang*, focusing mainly on two topics. The subject that generated the most intense controversy was the unfinished dike project. Earlier in the year the villagers had given up on the dike, discouraged at finding that their resources were too feeble to block the tides. Recently a distant relative of Teacher Yi's, an engineer from Seoul, agreed to take on the job in return for one-third of the eighty or so acres of potential rice land that would be reclaimed from tidal mud.

Because of all the volunteer work on the dike that they had already carried out, the villagers considered themselves to be experts on construction costs. Day after day the arguments continued, as groups of men, bundled up against the cold, sat together in dim interiors enthusiastically shouting out enormous numbers and arguing about whether Teacher Yi's relative was asking for too big a share of the reclaimed land.

No one opposed the other development project. In October, when the village head had gone up to Seoul to take possession of the five thousand dollars for fishing boat engines, the Korean office manager at the foundation also offered him a big diesel generator left over from another project that the foundation wanted to get rid of. For Yi Pyŏnghyŏk, his kinsmen, and most of the rest of Sŏkp'o residents as well, the idea of installing electricity in the village was far more compelling than the purchase of a few fishing boats. Not only were they convinced that their lives would be transformed, but the idea that they would have lights before any of the other surrounding villages, where the residents habitually looked down on Sŏkp'o, was extremely alluring. I began to see my year in Sŏkp'o as coinciding with a momentous dividing line, a threshold period marking the beginning of the end of the villagers' traditional passive resignation. Real existence is never that neat, of course, and change of one kind or another had been going on more or less continuously in the South Korean countryside for a long time.

Nevertheless, in 1966 important economic, generational, and psychological shifts were taking place. I felt that in writing my dissertation I had a clear choice. Either I could focus on the decline of old values and customs amid the struggle of villagers to adapt to new ideas and ways of doing things, or I could take advantage of my good luck in having gotten a good, hard, last look at a way of life still closely linked to a distant past. In the future, all of the anthropological research on South Korea would have to deal primarily with change and adaptation. There would be plenty of time to study progress. But for now I wanted to focus on Korea's pre-modern legacy, with its overriding concern for community and social harmony.

I expected to spend a relaxed month or so sorting out any loose ends remaining from my various research efforts. Then there would be the New Year's festivities, after which I could leave in an atmosphere of general good feeling. But early in January I received a telegram from the professor at home who was responsible for guiding my study. He wrote that I had been doing field work long enough, and he urged me to wind up the research and return by the first of February in order to be his teaching assistant for a course on primitive society. This was flattering, a good opportunity, and given the hierarchical nature of graduate school, close to a command. My slow and graceful exit from Sŏkp'o was suddenly out of the question. In order to get my family home, find a place to live, and get settled by February first, I would have to leave at once.

I asked around and found out that Mun Hyung Bae's old boat would be making the trip to Inch'ŏn in a few days, as soon as the wind moderated. He was willing to take me and Hi Young and our belongings as deck cargo. I worried about how Hi Young would cope with a six- or seven-hour ocean voyage on deck in midwinter, but she was so eager to rejoin her family in Seoul that even this prospect seemed inviting.

The last few days in Sŏkp'o were hectic and anxious, filled with a mixture of regret that the great adventure was about to end and a certain amount of pleasant anticipation of the new challenges and opportunities at home. In Korean good-byes, the person who stays behind says, "Go peacefully," while the one who leaves says, "Stay peacefully." Perhaps most people don't think of the meaning of the words when they use these conventional phrases, but as I spoke and heard them over and over again, I couldn't help but think there was nothing peaceful about the way I was suddenly leaving the village. On another level I knew that change was imminent in the South Korean countryside, and alongside my hopes for Sŏkp'o's future prosperity, I also felt a profoundly ambivalent desire that the community should stay (peacefully) just the way it was when I had first encountered it. It was not just that I admired the tranquility, mutual trust, and conviviality of Sŏkp'o society. I had also gotten used to a cozy and comfortable set of relationships in which I was the apprentice villager; while the people I was close to had been my coaches, doing their job with patience, humor, and goodwill.

A farewell dinner, songbyŏrhoe (literally, "sending off, separation gathering"), at Teacher Yi's house started out with some formality when all five of his children lined up solemnly to wish me a peaceful farewell. Even his normally obstreperous three-year-old daughter bowed and recited her lines. After dinner we moved to the same sarangbang where I had started out my life in Sŏkp'o. Teacher Yi insisted on opening the bottle of whiskey I had brought him, even though I protested, telling him it was for his own private use. It didn't last long after Pirate and three or four other elders from the Yi clan joined us. Later some Yi cousins of my generation also stopped by. Yi Byong Hui got one of the biggest laughs of the evening when he boldly asked Pirate whether he was giving a songbyŏrhoe for me. Everyone knew that Pirate had exploited me for whiskey and tobacco, and also that he was much too stingy to give anything back by hosting a party. Jokes about my faithlessness in having deserted all my Yi relatives to go and live among the Kims, Muns, and

Kangs were also popular. When the whiskey was gone, an apparently endless series of pots of makkŏlli took its place. I have vivid memories of the aura of boisterous goodwill and companionship that filled Teacher Yi's sarangbang that evening, but none of how I got back to the Big Hamlet.

T'aemo's family did me the extraordinary honor of killing a chicken for a midday feast two days before we were scheduled to leave, and that night still another songbyŏrhoe took place at Carpenter Mun's house. People of various lineages came from all over the village. The crowd spilled out of his sarang-bang into the rest of the house and, in spite of the cold, even into the court-yard. Throughout those last two days, there were too many hands to shake, too many bows, and too much makkŏlli. I did manage to break free for a few hours to make a last solitary tour of the coves, cliffs, and beaches. From the top of the highest hill I spent a long time looking out to sea and up and down the endless coastline. I told my neighbors that after all the drinking, I needed to clear my head.

There remained one final commitment, and that was easily taken care of. I invited Kim Pŏbyong and four or five of my nearest neighbors for a last meeting of the coffee drinkers. As usual, a few others also stopped by, so we had to take turns using the cups. At this gathering I was able to make it clear in front of witnesses that Kim Pŏbyong would move from his shack next to the funeral bier to my house and that he could use it for as long as he wanted to.

And that was it. Packing our few belongings was simple enough, and when the time came, just as when we all had arrived by boat in June, there was a small crowd on hand to help us carry our things down to the jetty. Propelled by a fast ebb tide and Mun's steadily thumping engine, we headed off, accompanied by shouts and waves. The houses of the Big Hamlet and the figures on the jetty rapidly diminished in size and then suddenly disappeared behind the headland as we turned west for the harbor entrance. The Yellow Sea was pale gray and icily calm, without a distinct horizon to separate it from the sky. The familiar shapes of Sŏkp'o's hills above the water remained in sight for another hour or so. I remember them still.

14

Re-encounter

I am on my way back to Sŏkp'o twenty-five years later; it is September 1992.[1] The crumbling road high above the sea has been fixed up enough so that buses and trucks can use it safely. Seven regular buses a day connect Sŏkp'o with T'aean. From the seaward window of the bus I can look almost ninety feet straight down and see waves breaking against the rocks. Distant islands on the western horizon still beckon mysteriously. A couple of miles offshore a big tanker heads north. I remember the two-masted junk with tattered brown sails that was working its way slowly but steadily to windward when I first came this way on foot so many years ago.

As we jounce noisily along, nearing the last shoulder of the mountain, my chest tightens, and my eyes fill. I let myself go, welcoming the unexpectedly strong emotion. Abruptly we are around the last bend, and I can see the entire village in the afternoon sunlight, with surf breaking on the beach and rocky coast beyond, a cluster of boats in front of the Big Hamlet, and the wooded hills building up to a high saddle behind my house. The light reflects brilliantly off the water in the sheltered bay. At first glance it is all unchanged, as beautiful as ever. The bus heads steeply down, and I watch eagerly for the place where the path to Teacher Yi's house drops off the road down into the pines. I know that the new and imposing grassy tomb with a marble slab in front, just where I used to start my climb up the mountain before breakfast, belongs to T'aemo's father. T'aemo told me about it before I left home.

Down on the flat, as we enter the village, crossing what used to be the sandspit, I am suddenly disoriented. The changes are overwhelming. On the right the whole big circular arm of the bay that used to come up to the sandspit and that was mud at low tide, is now ripening rice fields. Everywhere concrete utility poles have sprouted, with myriad wires stringing off of them in all directions. Houses are now mostly made of cement block, covered with brown or white stucco, and the roofs are brightly colored tile, metal, or some sort of corrugated composition. Rutted dirt roads have replaced the footpaths. Trash lies about everywhere, not collected or piled up at all, but just casually discarded, wherever the plastic bottle, candy wrapper, torn fish net, broken pail, eel trap, engine part, cement bag, or tin can ceased to be of use.

After honking its way through the middle of the Big Hamlet, the bus makes its final stop just below my house. I climb the narrow footpath that still provides a shortcut up the hill, wondering who will be there, and how he or she will feel about my return. My house is now surrounded by a cement block wall with a rusty iron gate, so I have to bang on it, shattering the afternoon quiet. Dogs bark from nearby houses. A stocky, pleasant-faced young woman opens the gate and greets me simply. She is a daughter-in law of Kim Ŭigon, wife of his second son, Kim In Nam. She serves me a cup of instant coffee on the veranda, and we talk easily. Thinking that some tension might exist regarding their occupation of the house, I am relieved by this casual welcome. I had some reservations about moving in with Kim Ŭigon's family, but Teacher Yi insisted I should stay here while in Sŏkp'o. It would be strange, he said, if I didn't live in my own house.

The day before, on my way down to Sŏkp'o from Seoul, I had stopped at Sŏsan to see Teacher Yi. Sŏsan, formerly a dusty, somnolent county seat of 20,000 people, has now, with a population of 100,000, been promoted to the status of city. Teacher Yi and I met at the cozy coffee shop near the bus terminal, and it seemed to me that he had changed very little—a big, shy, awkward man who has perhaps finally begun to realize his own worth. As we walked to his house, we talked only about ordinary things, and I found no way to break through his cordial formality and return to the old intimacy. In contrast to this meeting in contemporary, bustling downtown Sŏsan, my memories of our meals together in his *sarangbang* and of swimming off the rocks belonged in a legendary past.

Today Teacher Yi is vice-principal of a large primary school. Having progressed as far as it is possible for someone with only a high school diploma to go in the educational system, he seems to have achieved all his (and his wife's) ambitions. Their five children are educated, and the couple lives in a convenient, modern house near Teacher Yi's school with their eldest son, daughter-in-law, and two respectful grandchildren. Teacher Yi's beaming wife proudly showed off her fancy household appliances and tiled bathroom. We laughed at my memories of her squatting in the dark on the dirt floor of her Sŏkp'o kitchen, lighting a wood fire for the evening meal. I was amazed when Teacher Yi telephoned directly to my old house in Sŏkp'o to tell Kim Ŭigon's widow that I could arrive the next day.

It is curious the way the old contrast between my two most valued informants, Teacher Yi and T'aemo, resurfaced over the question of finding a room in the village. T'aemo now lives in the United States, and I have seen a good deal of him through the years. My wife and I were go-betweens for his marriage, so there is a continuing warm relationship, and we have a sort of godparent status toward his children. When he heard I was going back to Sŏkp'o he called Christian friends there and set everything up so that I could stay with a middle-aged couple whose children had left for the city. His friend's home had plenty of room and had been modernized with central heating, and T'aemo knew it would be clean and quiet. In the meantime, ignorant of T'aemo's efforts on my behalf, I had written to Teacher Yi asking him to arrange something. Teacher Yi's approach to the problem was quite different: he thought primarily in terms of kinship loyalties and reciprocal obligations. Kim Ŭigon was his cousin on his mother's side, and he knew that the widow and her family were having financial troubles. It might not be much, but I would provide them with some additional income. Besides, it was my house, and Kim Ŭigon's son is certainly obligated to me after using it all these years. As it turns out, I made the same mistake that I did twenty-five years earlier—when I followed Teacher Yi's advice about having Kim Ŭigon help me build my house.

From my veranda in Sŏkp'o I used to be able to keep track of almost everything that was going on in the Big Hamlet. Now there is nothing to see except the cement block wall. Actually, by stretching my neck, I can look over the top of the wall and see a little strip of the ocean and a rocky headland where the waves break. I can also hear the voices of people walking up the road in front of the house as in the past, but I can no longer see them go by. Some of my most faithful coffee drinkers are dead, and others have left the village. As I sit here, images of the past come to mind. It would be good to see Kim Pŏbyong's sturdy figure trudging up the path again with his straw hat at a rakish angle. I would even be pleased to welcome Pirate back with a brimming glass of whiskey. Kang Yong Ju always livened things up when he stopped by, while Kim Aji brought dignity to my veranda. But now they are all gone.

The yard in front of the veranda and within the wall is covered over with several translucent, corrugated plastic panels extending out from the roof to create an outdoor, cement-floored space protected from the rain. It is a practical arrangement but very ugly. My delicate little thatched-roof cottage on the hillside, open to the sun and to the whole sweeping panorama of ocean, hamlets, rice fields, and bay, has been transformed into a dark, enclosed fortress, shutting itself away as much as possible from the world outside. Mentally, I relinquished possession. I still have the deed, but the house is no longer mine.

Kim Ŭigon's daughter-in-law tells me to call her "Haeri's Mother." Haeri is her oldest child, Kim Pŏbyong's great-granddaughter. Haeri's Mother shows me where I will sleep. Ten years or so ago Kim Ŭigon, some time before he died, added on two rooms to the house. I will use the room of the third and fourth sons, both of whom are away on deep-sea fishing boats. Their room is a narrow, dark rectangle with a small window high up at the east end. From it I can look out over the harbor and across the bay to far-off mountains. Most of the space in the room is taken up by a TV set and a stereo, in addition to wardrobes and drawers full of clothes and bedding. A gaudy calendar from the fishery cooperative and several certificates of achievement in the martial arts decorate the walls.

Sunlight and a fresh breeze from the ocean lure me outside. After traveling ten thousand miles to get here, I am curiously reluctant to go down into the Big Hamlet and look up old friends. It seems more important to renew my acquaintance with the hills and the coastline. Picking up my sketchbook and pencil, I revert to old habits and decide to hike all the way around the village's coastline. The path in front of the house that led over the ridge to the north and then steeply down to the Fifth Hamlet and its rice fields beyond is now a narrow Jeep road. I follow that until a footpath leads off to the rocky beach along the bay. Beside an enormous pile of old shells an elderly woman squats, opening oysters with great dexterity. She calls out as I approach.

"So you've come back! You don't remember me. I'm an old widow now. You used to go out fishing in my husband's boat. He has been dead for twelve years."

She doesn't give her husband's name, but I remember. This is the spot where I kept my boat, right in front of Kim . . . I think it was Kim Song Kyu's house. Now the house is gone. I used to give him pipe tobacco to look after my boat, and he would take me fishing occasionally. I'm not entirely sure,

Figure 14.1 These are oyster racks, the source of contemporary prosperity. (1992)

but I take a chance, "You're husband was Kim Song Kyu, and your house used to be right here."

She is pleased. "That's right. You remember. Now we live over there." She points to an imposing white stucco house with a bright blue tiled roof. "Here comes my son. Do you remember him, too?"

A chunky man in his fifties approaches from the mudflats on a three wheeled farm tractor. I don't remember the son, of course. He was just another village youth twenty-five years ago. He is towing a trailer piled high with dark, wet oysters. There never used to be oysters this big in Sŏkp'o. I learn that now they are cultivated on racks out in the bay.

I naturally assume that mother and son will stop work and invite me to their house for something to eat and drink, and I start thinking a little impatiently of excuses to get away. I want to get on with my walk, and it's too early to start drinking. But there is no invitation. They keep on working. As I continue on my way, I have the feeling that something is missing. Perhaps I wouldn't have minded a bowl of makkŏlli and some fish or oysters after all.

I follow the road between the rice fields towards the northern tip of the peninsula. Over there is where the great kut at Kim Aji's house took place, when the young men sang for hours into my tape recorder. And those rocks offshore beyond the point mark the place where I sailed my boat to get flat stones for the outdoor oven T'aemo helped me build.

Two small boys are playing in the afternoon sunlight. One has a shiny tricycle, and the other a red plastic car with pedals. They stare for a moment and then ignore me, returning to their struggles to overcome the deep ruts in the road. Their clothes are neither torn nor particularly dirty. Their noses are not running. There are no scabs on their faces or crusty scales on their scalps. I could be in a middle-class Seoul suburb.

I climb up over the sandy pass that separates the most northern, most isolated, and poorest hamlet from the rest of the village. The line of utility poles finally stops here. The few houses are small and mud colored, and except for their composition roofs, they are like the ones I remember. But now every roof has a TV antenna, and I can see washing machines and refrigerators on the verandas or just inside the kitchen doors. There is a small pickup truck parked behind the last house. The road ends at the beach, and I walk on the hard sand toward the last headland at the harbor entrance. Beyond, cliffs plunge into the Yellow Sea. There are no more houses. Here progress has stopped, perhaps even reversed itself with the gradual depopulation of the countryside. The bluffs and hills are more heavily forested than before. There has been almost no lumber harvesting for twenty-five years. A few garlic and pepper fields are still in cultivation between the beach and the hills, but the small terraced rice fields that used to follow every water course have been abandoned and are overgrown with weeds.

Rounding the point, I look out toward the islands to the northwest. Astonishingly, the ocean is crowded with big, motionless freighters and tankers. I can count twenty-six ships, apparently anchored within a couple of kilometers of the coast and extending over a distance of more than ten miles. I can think of no explanation that makes sense. We are sixty-five miles from Inch'ŏn, the nearest major port. The only other person in this landscape is a man working in one of the garlic fields. I walk over and find that he is Kim Ŭigon's second cousin. After greetings and reminiscences, I ask about the ships.

"Oh, it's the big, new harbor and petrochemical complex at Taesan, fifteen kilometers up the coast," He explains." They didn't build enough dock space, and now too many ships are trying to get in there with cargo from overseas. Sometimes they have to anchor out at sea and wait for a week. When it's cloudy, you can see the reflection of all the factory lights in the sky at night."

As far as I knew there had never been any industry at all in this part of South Korea. Now all of a sudden a sleepy fishing town to the north had apparently been transformed into a major industrial center. I ask if it has affected Sŏkp'o at all. Kim Ŭigon's cousin is emphatic. "It's going to ruin the fishing. They dump oil in the water and fish catches are going down. Some of us are already selling our boats."

For more than twenty years, while engaged in research projects in other parts of the country, I had observed South Korea's rapid industrialization. On each trip through the years I encountered more factories, more highways, more high-tension lines, more cars and trucks, more urban shacks (p'anjach'un), and more glittering high-rise buildings. Pollution, environmental degradation, numbers of industrial accidents, and urban crowding had more than kept up with the fantastic economic growth. But it had always been somewhere else, not Sŏkp'o.

When Kim Ŭigon's cousin wanders off to work in another one of his fields, I follow the curve of the beach for another hundred yards or so to where a twenty-foot boat has been left stranded at high tide, with its long sculling oar angled up-out of the stern. The design is almost identical with the old wreck I bought from the shaman, and the unpainted timbers have the same pale, salt-washed gleam in the sunlight. I sit down and sketch. A quarter of a mile beyond the boat, where the tide is coming in, there are long rows of oyster racks sprouting up out of the shallow water. On the far side of the bay beyond is a brilliant white beach.

A half hour later Kim Ŭigon's cousin comes back to look at my sketch. "The boat is pretty good, but you can't tell that's sand over there across the water." It's true. The two mile-long beach is an obvious feature of the landscape, but my drawing just vaguely indicates some kind of shore. He continues, "Samsung (South Korea's largest industrial conglomerate) has bought up that whole area and will build a big summer resort there, even bigger than Mallip'o."

I remember the older generation's disapproval of mixed bathing at Mallip'o and ask, "What do Sŏkp'o people think of having a beach resort just across the bay?"

"Everyone is pleased, of course. There will be a lot of jobs for young people, and then they won't have to leave for the city. It will also bring some culture to this area."

"What kind of culture?" I ask. "Women in bathing suits?"

He laughs and thinks for a moment. "Our young men and women will meet educated people and learn city ways. We might even have a movie theater and all sorts of shops." Laughing again he said, "Maybe my granddaughter will marry Yi Byung Chul's (Samsung's founder's) great grandson!"

Kim Ŭigon's cousin has a pot for makkŏlli and some covered bowls on his packboard, but he doesn't offer me anything; perhaps they are empty. I continue my tour of the peninsula. At the furthest point of land, by the harbor entrance, an imposing coastal defense post sits high above the sea. A solitary soldier is doing exercises on the roof. I remember my jealous antagonism when the first coastal defense detachment of ten men showed up twenty-five years ago. As far as I was concerned, Sŏkp'o was my own private discovery, and I didn't want to share it with any other outsiders.

Now a maze of barbed wire and several bluntly worded warning signs keep me away from the defense post. Continuing south along the coast, I follow a military road that skirts the top of the cliffs. A high, barbed wire fence on the seaward side is rusty, and there are frequent large holes where people (probably women on their way to gather oysters) have passed through in spite of the signs. Pine trees frame views of the coves, beaches, headlands, and islands. I stop again to sketch. The drawing, a view looking down the coast to the south, is a good one. I remember this time to mass all my darks together, so the effect of shade and sunlight is dramatic.

The sound of an engine gives me warning, and I slip into the thick undergrowth to spy on a small truck full of soldiers as it goes by. One of them throws a soft drink can into the ditch. Childishly elated, I jump out from my hiding place after the truck has disappeared and practically skip along the road for a couple of kilometers, until it comes down out of the wooded hills by the promontory where the funeral bier and Kim Pŏbyong's shack used to be. There is nothing at all here now. I keep thinking of Kim Pŏbyong with regret. He would be over one hundred now.

Where the old sandspit used to be, another heavy barbed wire fence and more bluntly worded signs forbid access to the beach, but again several holes and well-worn paths defy the military regulations. A large sign announces a curfew from 10:00 p.m. until 5:00 a.m. Just to the north before the salt pans, there is a new (since 1966) hamlet comprising: a school, a store belonging to the village head's younger brother, a church, three fishermen's houses, two summer villas owned by university professors from Seoul, and a well-tended, engraved stone monument commemorating benevolent deeds performed by an American anthropologist twenty-five years ago. Only the monument is familiar. It has my name on it in both English letters and Korean characters. I am gratified that it is still standing, but the fact that it looks exactly like a tombstone still makes me slightly uneasy. I remember what a struggle it was to memorize my speech when the county magistrate came all the way from Sŏsan to dedicate the monument. Nearby, the buildings of the new school are freshly painted a light tan color, and there is a large playground surrounded by poplars.

I wander into Yi Byong Jin's store. He greets me pleasantly and quietly, calling me hyŏngnim (older brother, or in this case older cousin), as if I had been gone a few days instead of a generation. He asks me to come inside and gives me a small can of lemon soda from his refrigerator. We talk for a while and I ask if business is good.

"Hardly anyone stops by here except school children and people from my own lineage. The stores near your house next to the bus terminal sell much more than I do. Still, people have money to spend, and I can get by." No one ever made such an upbeat economic statement when I was in Sŏkp'o before.

Next I ask about the curfew, and Yi Byong Jin says, "People here don't pay any attention to it, and the soldiers never try to enforce it. They either stay out on the point by themselves or take the first bus they can get into T'aean. The village has formally petitioned the coastal defense commander to take down the barbed wire. No one is worried about an attack from the sea by North Koreans these days."

Thinking that now is as good a time as any to start my research, I ask, "Do people in Sŏkp'o still have insim (human heartedness) and practice hyŏptong (cooperation) the way they used to when I was here before?"

Yi Byong Jin smiles (I can't really tell if his tone is derisive). "No one talks much about insim these days. We are all busy with our own affairs. We used to have to work together just to get by. Now we work separately to make money."

Naturally, I ask if the changes are for the better, and he answers with feeling. "We are so much better off now, no one wants to go back to the old ways. Old people complain about the lack of good manners and the decline in morality, but we don't worry about those things anymore. Everyone wants to make as much money as possible to buy things. We don't get together with our relatives and neighbors so much anymore."

From the sandspit it isn't far to the Yi lineage neighborhood, and I decide to visit more of my fictive kinfolk. There seem to be fewer Yi households than before. A few small children are playing in the paths, and some older women, who are weeding kitchen gardens, smile and bow from a distance. But no one else is around. None of my cousins, nephews, brothers, or uncles is home, so I wander back towards the Big Hamlet across the long dike and the new rice fields behind it. It is a handsome sight—about seventy to eighty acres of ripening (it really is golden!) grain, the ultimate symbol of rural prosperity.

My head is full of questions: Who got how much of the new rice fields, and how was it all decided? Are the owners of all those big, engine-powered boats on the beach in front of the Big Hamlet making money? Who is most prosperous these days? Do members of the Yi lineage still stick to farming and keep themselves a little aloof from the rest of the village? With no Teacher Yi or T'aemo to go to, I don't know where to start. The idea of blurting out all these questions in a casual men's group makes me uneasy. I wonder what kind of informant Kim In Nam (Kim Ŭigon's second son) will be. He is either my landlord or my tenant, depending on how one looks at things. I suppose by now he has squatter's rights. I vaguely remember him as a teenager. Will he be like his easygoing grandfather, Kim Pŏbyong, or his drunken father, Kim Ŭigon?

My legs are tired after the long hike, and I walk past the few stores of the Big Hamlet, wondering where to stop and rest. Before in this neighborhood there were always elders, just hanging around looking for a chance to be sociable. Anyone with enough money for a pot of makkŏlli could mobilize an instant party. Now there is no one. A group of men building a new house nearby are finishing up for the day, but they have been hired by a contractor and are not even from Sŏkp'o. A few fishermen work on their boats. I still feel like a tourist, an outsider. Nothing has happened yet to pull me back into the past and provide a sense of the community I remember. The old relaxed feeling that time, work, and making money do not matter as much as good manners and cordiality seems to be gone.

A hoarse voice that I dimly remember calls out, "Respected Teacher!" I turn and there is Mun Yongbae, sitting in a shop by the side of the road with a baby in his lap. The other side of the shop room opens up directly onto the beach, and I can look right through to the boats, and the bay beyond. He hasn't changed all that much from when I gave him sulfathiazole for his eye. Perhaps he looks a little better now with graying hair. He proudly introduces

Figure 14.2 Sŏkp'o's motorized fleet twenty-five years later. (1992)

me. "This is my grandson. She is the mother." He points to a pretty, solid young woman who is busy at the other end of the store. "This is my eating place." Mun Yongbae was always one of the most energetic, although least successful, entrepreneurs in the village. Now it is strange to see him placidly babysitting, while his daughter-in-law works. He certainly never paid any attention to his own children when they were small.

"Have a beer and some noodles." He doesn't wait for my answer but opens a large bottle of beer, and the baby's mother starts to cook. It is already late afternoon, and this will spoil my appetite for supper. But I give in, welcoming the old feeling of powerlessness in the face of coercive hospitality. He talks on and on about his latest business venture—raising fish as part of a government program to try and restock the coastal fisheries. Apparently the income is substantial, but since Mun Yongbae has had to make large investments in fish tanks, pumps, and water filtering systems he is, as usual, heavily in debt. I keep drinking and gradually lose track of the conversation as it gets more and more technical. It doesn't seem like the right time to try and get answers to my questions about the rice fields.

Someone I don't know comes in and orders *soju* and roast eel. I watch and smell the grilling eel enviously, thinking, that's what I will order next time. When the man leaves, I ask Mun Yongbae if his customer is from Sŏkp'o. He answers, "He only moved here five or six years ago, but he is doing well and has his own boat."

I am surprised. "I thought the fishing was no good anymore and owners were selling their boats."

Mun Yongbae answers, "It is true that every year we catch fewer fish, but Inch'ŏn prices are so high that anyone who is skilled or lucky can still make money." And then with real satisfaction, "There's no end to the demand of city people for oysters. If you work hard, you can get rich. People from other places who used to look down on us now want to live here." This is really surprising news. I am so used to thinking of Sŏkp'o as an impoverished backwater avoided by the rest of the world that I wonder at first if Mun Yongbae is just expressing local pride.

He won't let me pay for the beer, but accepts money for the noodles. I ask how many *sulchip* there are now in the village, and Yongbae says disdainfully, "We don't have *sulchip* any more, just stores and restaurants."

When I get back up the hill to "my" house, Kim Ŭigon's widow is there, and her three grandchildren are home from school. I remember her as a sort of tragic figure, sullen and worn out, but she has turned into a cheerful, healthy, and energetic old lady. The children are inquisitive and charming. Soon I am drawing pictures with the second granddaughter, Haejin. I draw her younger brother, and she fills in the outlines with color. Haeri, her older sister, insists on taking extravagant poses but won't keep still for more than a minute or so. Haejin delights me by asking, "Can anyone in Korea or America draw better than you?"

Kim In Nam doesn't show up until the next day, having spent the night partying with friends in T'aean. He is as handsome as his grandfather, Kim Pŏbyong, but apparently drinks like his father, Kim Ŭigon. He arrives home in a bad mood, quarrels with his wife, ignores the children, and seems ill-at-ease with me. I just don't feel at home here the way I did in Teacher Yi's *sarangbang*, even though this was once my own house. Let's face it; the cooking is terrible, and the toilet shed is dirty and far away. These things seem to bother me more than they used to. Haeri's Mother, who is from a farm village in North Ch'ungch'ŏng Province where the customs are different, makes everything too salty and uses too much red pepper. There is plenty of fish, but it seems always to be the leftovers: less desirable species that were half-crushed on deck or torn in the nets. And they are nearly always cooked as a kind of stew, with everything—heads, bones, guts, fins—all disintegrating in the pot together.

Because Kim Ŭigon's cement block wall shuts off the view from my veranda, I often climb up behind the house and sit on the edge of a small soybean field looking out over the village. The ajumŏni (literally "aunt" but used as a polite term for any older woman) from the house that owns the field has finished harvesting the soybeans and clearing away the dried-up plants, so no one else comes up here or cares that I use this place for an observation platform. I sit here quite a lot, to sketch, or just to try and sort out the meaning of what has happened to me and to Sŏkp'o in twenty-five years. Before breakfast it is where I do exercises, looking east to salute the sun. In the distance I can just barely make out Kwon Won Sang's house (where we attended the big sixtieth birthday party) across the bay. I wonder if he is still alive. To the right of the house there is a notch leading into the mountains, and the sunrise produces all sorts of spectacular lighting effects on each succeeding range. Both the new moon and Jupiter have been in the east at dawn for the past few days. Water and mudflats gleam with a special soft radiance in the early light.

As the days and weeks pass, I look for ways to reestablish my place in the village. Below my house in the Big Hamlet, fishermen drink soju and gamble at the tiny store that has replaced one of the old sulchip near the beach. If I want to, I can sit in and listen to their jokes and gossip. But they are all a lot younger than I, and the soju is harsh in my throat. Instead of roasted eel or pickled octopus, the only anju are peanuts and rice crackers in cellophane bags. Wandering about the village, I find that it is not as difficult as it used to be to avoid makkŏlli at odd hours or rice at lunchtime. No one summons me peremptorily to eat or drink on his veranda. No one asks me to share makkŏlli in the fields. If I am hungry during the day I buy a bowl of noodles at Mun Yongbae's shop.

A serious problem for me is that there is no one I can really talk to, no one to replace Teacher Yi and T'aemo. My Korean thrives as long as the informant is sympathetic and imaginative, but if my questions or comments elicit only uncomprehending stares, I give up quickly. In Kim In Nam's household there are few smiles and not much conversation, except among the children and their grandmother. Kim In Nam hardly ever has a word for the children and communicates by blunt commands and grunts. Rarely in the house, except for silent meals, he is either fishing, working on his boat, drinking at the store, or off in T'aean drinking with friends. Haeri's Mother is far from being intimidated, however. She has a noisy, rapid-fire delivery that is unusual in this part of South Korea, and we are all constantly aware of just what is on her mind.

I spend a fair amount of time talking with Haeri's Mother when everyone else has left the house, and I gradually learn more about this family. Until last year she and her husband lived in T'aean with the children, and he went to sea on a big, offshore fishing boat for weeks at a time. But when Kim In Nam's youngest brother left home to work in the city, their mother was all alone, so Kim In Nam came back to the village to be with her, and fish from his own twenty-eight foot boat. Actually, it isn't his boat; he has to pay over $2,000 to rent it for the six-month season. Haeri's Mother recognizes that she is lucky to have an affable and competent mother-in-law, but she liked her life better in T'aean where she had a place of her own and more free time, because her husband was often away at sea.

Kim in Nam and his wife go out fishing together on his boat whenever the weather permits. There are five such husband-and-wife boat teams in the village, with the women all in their thirties. Twenty-five years ago women were not allowed on fishing boats at all, even to clean them out. Haeri's Mother does not like to fish, and she feels overworked at home because the fishing takes up so much time. She tells me that at first she thought it would be nice to work closely together with her husband on a small boat, but actually it is exhausting and he constantly shouts at her because she doesn't do things exactly right. And now in the fall, since it is getting colder and rougher out at sea, she gets seasick besides. They have caught very little during the last few days ("not even enough to pay for the diesel fuel") and blame it on all the ship traffic offshore. The mood in the household is gloomier than usual, and speech comes only in short, sharp, irritated bursts.

This is not an atmosphere in which I can ask questions easily and then follow up on them or let the conversation go wherever it will. Little by little, though, I learn about household finances from Haeri's Mother and grandmother. They talk jokingly about borrowing money from me. Their account of the family budget makes quite a story. A good deal of money is coming in from fishing and oystering, but much more is going out. The family is deeply in debt, while Kim In Nam continues to spend recklessly. Another one of Kim Ŭigon's sons, was hospitalized and unsuccessfully operated on after being badly injured in a drunken brawl. The family had to borrow heavily to pay for a second operation in Seoul. Kim Ŭigon's youngest son, who recently moved to T'aean from Sŏkp'o, has a black belt in Taekwondo. When he gets in a fight, he always wins, but at the moment two of his victims are suing for bodily injury. "Bad luck" has haunted this family ever since Kim Pŏbyong married the woman of his choice and now the fish are disappearing.

Until just a couple of years ago local fishermen were making a lot of money. Their boats, varying in length from twenty-five to forty feet, have diesel truck engines. Now that South Korea has big modern factories making cars, trucks, and buses for export all over the world, powerful, reliable, and inexpensive diesel engines are readily available. The boats are still heavy and crude and are built more or less along the lines of prewar Japanese designs. Engine installations are crude, too, but everything seems to work. There is nothing elegant about these boats or the way they are handled. When they get going, their bow and stern waves are impressive, and there is a lot of noise and smoke. Each morning as fishermen get under way and maneuver just off the beach at the Big Hamlet, they shout, gun their engines, and don't always avoid collisions. It all seems very much like the provincial bus terminal scenes that I remember from T'aean and Sŏsan in the 1960s.

Local fishermen attribute the recent decline in fish catches to pollution, but over-fishing is probably a more important reason. Most of the choice species that were caught twenty-five years ago have disappeared, and today eels are the main source of income. As long as there are still fish of any kind, however, urban demand is so great that profits are good. After paying for diesel fuel, the crew's share, bait, and boat maintenance, a boat owner can make between seventy-five and one hundred dollars a day, and some days much more than that. The government is paying substantial compensation to local fishermen for pollution damage from the new industrial complex and the accompanying increased ship traffic. Those fishermen who sell their boats and get out of the business completely receive twice as much compensation as those who continue to fish. It seems to be an enlightened way to reduce overfishing.

Haeri's Grandmother does most of the agricultural work in this house-hold, usually working by herself, and since the family still has some land (enough to provide about two-thirds of the rice and perhaps half the vegeta-bles needed), she is busy farming a good deal of the time. When she is not farming and when Haeri's Mother is not fishing, they are both opening oys-ters, earning the equivalent of about six dollars an hour. This is very good pay, even by city standards.

Intensive commercialization of the oyster fishery, that is to say, raising selected varieties under more or less controlled conditions for regular harvest, began in Sŏkp'o only after I left the village. First T'aemo and then Yi Byung Un, the fishnet entrepreneur, were instrumental in promoting improved methods for cashing in on the new crop. Today each family has its own oyster racks out in the bay, and the men regularly bring in enormous loads by boat and by cart. Every woman in the village spends a good part of her time open-ing oysters. It is the main source of Sŏkp'o's new prosperity. They gather in congenial, small groups near the water, and the sound of their conversation is as continuous as that of their picks digging into the shells.

All over the world, wherever ancient peoples lived along the sea coasts, shell mounds have been a favorite place for archeologists to poke around looking for artifacts left by primitive hunters and gatherers. Some of these old shell heaps are of considerable size, and I had always assumed that they must have piled up very slowly over hundreds or even thousands of years. But in Sŏkp'o, after only twenty years of oyster farming, big mounds of shells, some as high as fifteen feet, are piled up here and there along the shore. The heaps would be still higher, except that the villagers use crushed shells to fill in pot holes and ruts in the roads. The people of Sŏkp'o sell all the big cultivated oysters to buyers from the city, preferring to eat the tiny ones that women still gather from the rocks at low tide.

Haeri's Mother says that villages further inland where people are entirely dependent on agriculture are having a very tough time. Young people con-tinue to leave for the city, and most of the farming is being done by old men and women. Here in Sŏkp'o migration to the city also continues, but because of the money that can be made fishing and oystering, there is less poverty, and the exodus is less dramatic. With the completion of the dike, Sŏkp'o has plenty of rice land and can feed itself, while the fishing and oystering bring in cash. So I am discovering that Mun Yongbae was right. Sŏkp'o is now a comparatively rich village. Quite a few young people, finding a disappointing dead-end in the city, have come back. Twenty-five years ago when work was scarce and there were too many mouths to feed, it was a relief for most families when children left for the city. Today everyone's labor is precious.

The broad top of the dike, for the first hundred yards or so nearest the Big Hamlet, is a favorite spot for shucking oysters. There are nearly always groups of women squatting next to piles of shells. Whenever I pass by, older women smile and greet me without interrupting the rhythm of their work. Teenage girls still keep their heads down when the stranger stops to chat, but young women in their twenties stare at me boldly. Nearly all the younger women have migrated from the village, returning home to visit, some for a few days or weeks or months and others for a year or more. Disillusioned by life in factory dormitories, low-paying jobs, or unsuccessful love affairs, they have found an agreeably secure, temporary haven at home where they can make good money opening oysters. They say that they will eventually go back to the city, but for now it is pleasant to sit out of the wind in the sun talking with friends and relatives. Without exception, they intend to marry someone in town, educate their children in urban schools, and move up into the lower reaches of the middle class.

On each successive, sunlit October day the yellow-gold ripening rice contrasts more intensely with the much darker tones of wind-ruffled water and pine-covered hills. It is still a pleasant habit when I first get up, after splashing water on my face, to go outside the gate and brush my teeth while contemplating the whole panorama of bay, mountains, ocean, hamlets, boats, and fields of grain. From my house on the slope above the Big Hamlet I look directly across at the eighty or ninety acres of new rice land that was reclaimed twelve years ago when the dike was finally completed. Absolutely flat and divided into geometrically perfect rectangles, rice fields like these are an unusual sight in this part of South Korea. Everywhere else in Sŏkp'o, paddy fields are small and curved, stepping up and down the contours in graceful terraces.

This morning I wake up to hear a high-pitched, distant hum, which while obviously made by machinery, is quite different from the familiar sounds of boat engines, small tractors, or the bus. For some reason I am late, and every-one has left the house except Haeri's Grandmother. When she brings my breakfast tray to the veranda, I ask about the noise, and she points over the wall to the rice fields in the distance, saying with some satisfaction, "It is Yi Chang Sun's combine. There is lots of rice to harvest." I get to my feet, put on my glasses, and peer over the wall. Three quarters of a mile away, just this side of the Yi lineage neighborhood, a tiny orange-and-white cube moves slowly through the rice. Evidently that is the combine. I have never seen a combine at work except for the giant machines in movies of Kansas or Saskatchewan. The Sŏkp'o version doesn't seem to be on that scale at all, but it obviously requires investigation. After crossing the dike and walking along the edge of the reservoir in front of the Yi neighborhood for a few hundred yards, I reach a small crowd of ten or twelve people watching the combine harvest Yi Byong Hui's fields. A short, sturdy man of about fifty, Yi Byong Hui, is throwing forty-five kilogram bags of rice with easy skill, from the edge of the field where the machine has stacked them into a cart. The son of my fictive second cousin, he was one of the young men I knew fairly well twenty-five years ago, and we are on cordial terms. Most of the crowd are older men. The machine is very compact, a rectangular steel box on caterpillar tracks, and it does its work—cutting, threshing, and bagging the unhulled rice (p'ye)—with uncanny efficiency. Yi Byong Hui tells me that the machinery is manufactured in Korea under Japanese license. The owner of the combine, Yi Chang Sun, another second cousin, drives it from a tiny seat on top, and a mechanic walks along beside in constant attendance. The combine methodically engorges the rice plants, leaving straw on the ground behind it in neat rows. Two men follow with hand sickles, cutting rice that the combine can't get at in the comers of the field, or where it makes its 180-degree turns. These bundles are shoved by hand into the orange maw.

Outside the straight edges of most of the reclaimed land, a few smaller, irregularly shaped fields border the brackish ponds near the dike or the edge of the reservoir. Here women and teenagers are harvesting the rice by hand. The harvesters stay bent over for what seems an excruciatingly long time, cutting the stalks neatly and efficiently. But it is terribly slow compared to the work done by the combine, which is now operating for its second year.

When Yi Byong Hui stops to rest, I ask him about his rice crop. He replies. "It is a bumper crop. I will have about sixty-five or seventy bags of polished rice [ssal]." This is an enormous amount of rice by the Sŏkp'o standards that I remember from the past, but he speaks without any particular pride or enthusiasm. Haeri's Grandmother will get only about nine bags from her few

Figure 14.3 Rice harvester/combine. (1992)

Figure 14.4 One of Sŏkp'o's "rich" men. He sent his son to college in Seoul. (1992)

fields this year, and she seems far more satisfied with her harvest than Yi Byong Hui is with his. I congratulate him on owning so much rice land.

A bystander says, "Yes, Yi Byong Hui is the rice King of Sŏkp'o," and everyone laughs. I am puzzled by the laughter. If there was one thing that I learned unequivocally during my year in Sŏkp'o a generation ago, it was that rice was the ultimate standard of rural wealth, prestige, and nearly all other satisfactions. Having too much rice was a concept that just did not exist.

And yet Yi Byong Hui seems almost rueful in talking about his big harvest. "Suji matchi anŭnda" (The figures don't work out), he says. I was to hear this sorrowful cliché many more times from other rice growers and even from agricultural economists in Seoul before leaving Korea. Yi Byong Hui continues, "I can buy all the rice I need to eat for a month with the money I get from just one day's haul of octopus. Growing rice is a waste of time."

I can't help asking, "Then why do most people keep on growing rice?"

Just then Yi Byong Hui's wife arrives balancing an enormous tray on her head, on top of which is a big cloth-wrapped bundle. The bundle contains most of the ingredients for an outdoor harvest picnic feast for ten people, and soon we are sitting on the ground exchanging bowls of makkŏlli. The younger men sit in the same circle, drinking soju and smoking boldly right in front of us. I appear to be the only one who is offended by these bad manners. I ignore them. Fish, octopus, and oysters accompany the rice, kimch'i, lettuce, and hot bean paste. This is the way I have nostalgically remembered Sŏkp'o all these years. Here I am, back in the bosom of my adoptive lineage, coping cheerfully with the challenges of field work and using skills that have not deserted me during all the intervening years.

Yi Byong Hui does not forget my question. After we have eaten for a while, and when the constant motion of the bowls of makkŏlli has slowed somewhat, he says, "All my life I have grown rice. Everyone here has always thought that growing rice is the most important thing we can do. The government has been urging us to grow more rice for as long as I can remember. We have the irrigated rice fields, and we have the skills. Now we get yields that are just as high as those in Japan. What else can we do? We lose even more money raising cattle, pigs, or chickens."

The conversation is depressing, and I don't pursue it. This is a happy occasion. The most important event in the agricultural cycle is being successfully completed and is celebrated by tradition. No one will go hungry. Yi

Figure 14.5 Impromptu *makkŏlli* party on path between the Fourth and Fifth hamlets. This one ended up with solo dancing by the woman at extreme left.

Byong Hui's large veranda will groan under the weight of all those bags of rice. Perhaps it is best to ignore the fact that all this effort has very little positive economic meaning. Yi Byong Hui brightens up a little when I ask him how he can make ends meet.

"Octopus," he says. "I am the best octopus catcher in Sŏkp'o. I can make 90,000 *wŏn* a day [about $70.00], and that is how I put all my children through college."

The feast is over, and Yi Byong Hui's wife trudges back up the hill with a much smaller bundle on her head than when she arrived an hour ago. His nephew starts up the three-wheel tractor and begins towing a small trailer loaded with bags of rice. He will have to make at least ten trips with the trailer before all the rice is safely stored. The combine grinds its way slowly across the bare stubble towards the old sandspit, where someone else's rice fields are ready for harvesting. Yi Byong Hui picks up his shovel, his bucket, and his rubber boots. He walks with me as far as the dike and then branches off in the direction of the mudflats. It is low tide, and he is going after octopus.

No matter what aspect of village life I look into, change seems to be more characteristic than continuity. From the edge of "my" soybean field the sound of wind in the pines and of distant waves on the rocks is the same as always, and the shouts of men guiding their oxen have not changed. The shrill voices of children released from school carry all the way across the fields and salt pans just as before. But a lot of the other sounds are new. I can regularly distinguish four (five when the combine is in use) different engine noises: three-wheeled tractors, boats, motorcycles, and trucks or buses. Snatches of TV or radio programs come up the hill from the store below my house where the bus line ends. At our house at least one and often two TV sets are on continuously from 6 p.m. until bedtime. But the most insistent, and to me most obnoxious noise, is that of dogs barking. Most households in Sŏkp'o have two or more dogs. Some have fifteen. All these dogs are in cages, and at some time during the day or night they take turns barking—when a stranger walks by the house, when challenged by provocative howling from another hamlet, or simply to lament a nasty existence.

Twenty-five years ago no one had a dog. Any scraps that were left over went to the family pig. Pigs were important, raised to supply meat for special occasions such as weddings, funerals, parental death days, or a sixtieth birthday celebration. But now that Sŏkp'o participates in the national economy, it no longer makes economic sense to raise pigs. When pork is needed, it can be bought in town. Raising dogs for city markets, however, is a profitable enterprise. Kim In Nam bought young dogs for 50,000 wŏn each (about $60.00), and he expects to sell them for ten times that amount when they are fully grown next year. With the emphasis on fattening the dogs as fast as possible, the cages are too small to allow any real exercise. It is surprising how many different breeds there are, just in the Big Hamlet. At some houses the dogs are big and fierce and especially noisy, while at others they whimper and try desperately to make friends with any passerby. The Kim Ŭigon household had two dogs caged next to the outhouse a few meters down the hill, so there was no way to avoid them. Each day they seem to think they can persuade me to take them on as pets. Each day I have to turn them down.

Most of the obvious changes in Sŏkp'o are for the better. To take one particularly dramatic example, childhood has been transformed. Infant mortality was, of course, always high in the past. Accordingly, to ensure that someone would care for them in old age and that the bloodline would continue, each household head had as many children as possible. As in most other parts of the world, when the worst epidemics began to be controlled (in Korea's case during the early nineteenth century), the rural population exploded. Without economic development this rapid population increase meant steadily intensifying poverty for each subsequent generation. In 1966, ragged, dirty children were everywhere. Mothers cared as best they could for the latest baby, but as soon as it was weaned and replaced by another, the tiny boys and girls were very much on their own, perhaps under the casual eye of a slightly older sister. There seemed to be no separate children's world, no games, toys, or other entertainments. Children hovered silently on the edge of village life, gawking curiously at the adult world from their bare-foot condition on its fringes. Any unusual event attracted them instantly as spectators. Adults mostly shouted at them, scolded them when the children did something wrong, or demanded the performance of chores. Children never talked back. They were apprentice human beings, learning their roles by watching the villagers perform. Parental love was taken for granted in the Confucian scheme of things. There was no need to express it publicly. Subsistence life was grim, and people acted accordingly.

Today, not only are the children well dressed and well supplied with toys, they have an entirely new self-confidence and sense of their own importance. They demand attention and talk back to their parents and grandparents. Outdoors, they are absorbed in their games and pay little attention to grown-ups. Even at Kim In Nam's house, with his surly pres-ence, the children happily chatter, laugh, and roughhouse from early morn-ing until they fall asleep at night. Nothing like this existed twenty-five years ago. The change is revolutionary and, it seems to me, challenges the whole structure of values and family relationships.

I ask Haeri's Grandmother about it, and she laughs philosophically. "It is not the way we brought up our children. But that is the way they do it now. I feel I must change and not interfere. These are different times, and the old ways are out of date." She laughs again. "Perhaps it is all your fault for teaching us new customs. I still remember how you used to carry your son around all the time on your shoulders. We thought you acted like a woman and had no sense of shame."

In spite of all the changes, I am surprised at how easily people discard beliefs and customs that are inconvenient or unfashionable. For example, respect for parents and elders is no longer the dominant value that it was a generation ago. Of course, it's not tested the way it used to be either, since most teenagers leave home to get jobs in town, just at the age when parental domination used to bear down so heavily. In the three cases that I've observed so far, where sons are in their twenties and still living nearby, the relationship with their fathers is a good deal more easygoing than I remember. A lot of the stiffness and elaborately formal etiquette, amounting almost to father-son mutual avoidance, seems to have been sloughed off. Nevertheless, those households that are not Christian (more than two-thirds of the village) continue to perform ancestor worship ceremonies, so the ritual aspect of filial piety is still going strong.

Kim Hwa Jin, an old coffee drinker and anchovy-fishing friend from the Fifth Hamlet, invites me to attend his father's commemoration service. The ceremony is similar to what I remember, except that the Kim lineage, which used to do these things much more simply and crudely, now rivals the ritual polish of the Yis. The calligraphy of the summons to the spirit has an appropriately classical flair, and the women have piled sacrificial food on trays in much greater abundance than in the past. Members of the lineage, which is a different branch of Kims from Kim Ŭigon lineage, are pleased to be gathered together in this show of cordial solidarity and tangible wealth. There is the same mixture of reverence and informality that I remember from the past.

But even in such a traditional context, change is apparent. Kim Hwa Jin's house is big and recently remodeled. He proudly shows me the computerized controls for his new poira (boiler) central heating system. It has tiny blue, red, and white lights to show the various states of operation. I don't tell anyone that I heat my house with wood stoves in Vermont. We bow deeply many times, and my joints protest slightly. The heating system works. Although the late October evening is cool, the room is just a little too warm for my sweater.

After the ritual is over, at about 1:00 a.m., there is respectful talk about Kim Hwa Jin's father, and then we devour the feast. The proper fishes—yellowtail (pangŏ), croaker (chogi), and snapper (tomi)—are no longer caught in coastal waters, so Kim Hwa Jin has had to buy them in town. There is lots of good yellow medicinal yakchu though. As always, Kim Hwa Jin doesn't drink but loosens up in perfect synchronization with the degree of inebriation of his guests. He offers me yakchu more than once, but not with the same forceful intensity as in the past. People notice that I drink a good deal less than I did twenty-five years ago, and someone comments approvingly that indeed one must be more careful in old age. I am discovering that many other families live a good deal better than we do at Kim In Nam's house. I recapture for a moment the old satisfactions of being drawn in and enveloped by communal hospitality and goodwill.

Kim Hwa Jin, who has always been cynical about supernatural and ritual matters, tells me in a conspiratorial aside,

> Every year our chesa gets more elaborate as we have more money to spend, and we become more careful about doing everything just right. I go along with all this because my wife and younger brother insist on it. The women like to demonstrate how well they follow the old customs, even though they have to do most of the work. Also, they want to show the Christians that our traditions and morality are just as good as theirs.

The village's Christian church is twelve years old, but it is new to me. Covered with gray stucco, the building is almost aggressively plain on the outside. A small tower on the roof is topped by two powerful loudspeakers and a white wooden cross. I find some comfort in the fact that the cross is not outlined in neon lights as in most Korean towns and cities. The tower also contains some sort of electronic device that simulates the playing of hymns by bells. It sounds mechanical, and the notes are a little flat. The hymns start very early on Sunday mornings, and throughout most of the village there is no way to escape them. Attached to the church is a low building that is used for various activities, and the pastor's residence is just across a small churchyard. The congregation keeps everything, including a late-model van, meticulously maintained. Sŏkp'o Christians have an advantage over the other villagers. In an emergency they can go to town in the van.

One Sunday afternoon I pass by the church compound some hours after the service is over and find the churchyard still crowded. Some older women stand together talking by the gate, and we exchange greetings. I can hear the choir practicing inside the chapel. Ten or twelve younger women are holding a meeting on the veranda of the building next to it, and teenagers of both sexes lounge about, some of them going in and out of the buildings on purposeful errands. Small children call out shrilly as they dart here and there, using the women's legs and skirts for turning points in an endless game of tag. Everyone has on good clean clothes, and the adults all carry Bibles. Most of the married women have their hair done in tight frizzled permanents. It is not at all becoming, and for some reason they look dowdier in their Sunday best than when they are opening oysters during the week.

One woman, however, still has the sleek, pulled-back traditional hairstyle, with a large silver pin thrust through a knot at the nape of her neck. She is in her sixties and looks much more stylish in her traditional Korean clothes than the others. I remember her vividly and am startled to see her here in the church-yard. It is Kyong Hi's Mother, the ajumŏni who used to run a sulchip below my house near the harbor. On several occasions we could hear the screams and shouts from my veranda when she got drunk and abused her customers. Also, she was a notorious adulteress, treating her husband with contempt and stalk-ing off openly to spend the night at the house of the manager of the salt pans. Now she is a widow, and the salt pan manager has died as well.

She still has an effusively gregarious manner and pulls me into the church-yard. "Look at our church. Isn't it beautiful?" I don't take off my shoes and go inside, but just peer in through the door. The interior is dim and cool, and the polished floor gleams in subdued light. A young woman is accompanying choir practice at a small organ. There is one stained glass window. It is all much more authentic than I expected. I remember that T'aemo and my sister-in-law, Hi Young, sent a good deal of money from the States to the church when the building was under construction.

The former sulchip ajumŏni drags me to the pastor's house and summons his wife with shouts. "The exalted American guest has arrived." I try to escape, but it is too late. The pastor's wife appears and greets me traditionally, but without much enthusiasm. She is pale and looks tired. Perhaps she has heard that I am not a practicing Christian. Or perhaps it is just that Sunday is a busy day.

The other village women join in as they realize what the sulchip ajumŏni has in mind. They sense a party in the making and compete with each other to inform the pastor's wife of how worthy I am of being treated to entertain-ment. "It is the illustrious teacher's monument that you see every day just down the road. The county chief himself came to dedicate it." "The illustri-ous teacher is famous here for helping the village." "He has come back again after so many years."

The pastor's wife finally resigns herself to the demands of village hospital-ity. She goes off to her kitchen to prepare refreshments. Two of the women go with her to help. After a while they come back with a big tray on which there is a pitcher of juice, some glasses, a plateful of persimmons, and a new package of cookies from the store. The other "aunts," with small cries of approval, drop their shoes off in the dirt and join me around the tray on the veranda.

Almost with nostalgia, I recognize Kim Ŭigon's favorite technique, still in use after so many years. When he was thirsty and at loose ends, he would drag me with him around the village, using my illustrious presence to bully well-to-do households into providing copious quantities of food and drink. Now, the women, delighted with their success and in a party mood, begin to peel the persimmons. Neither I nor the pastor's wife is pleased, but we have been outwitted. The ajumŏni all know that ultimately it is their money that bought the juice, the persimmons, and the cookies. At home they would never think of indulging in such luxuries. We drink and eat in an atmosphere of prim conviviality.

I am surprised by the size and influence of the Christian congregation. In 1966 I assumed that there were no Christians at all in Sŏkp'o. Certainly there was no church. But apparently a handful of women had married in from Christian communities, and they were determined to establish a congregation. T'aemo's mother was one of them.

Twenty-five years ago I was convinced that Sŏkp'o was in good spiritual health—that it was a community where people lived together harmoniously and were generous and tolerant with each other, prizing cooperation and cordial personal relationships above most of the other good things in life. I would not have thought that the villagers needed a new religious code to live by. Now a third of the village belongs to the Christian congregation. The sudden erosion of Confucian customs and values left a gap that is being filled to some extent by Christian doctrine and practice. Except for some older widows, most of the congregation is middle aged or younger. The Christians of Sŏkp'o form a cohesive, close-knit community that, surprisingly, cuts across kinship boundaries. They seem to be the hardest working, least extravagant, and in some ways the most respectable element in the village. In addition to getting together at weddings, funerals, birthdays, and other festive occasions, they regularly visit each other and help out when anyone is sick or in trouble. The members of the congregation give generously to their church, which organizes all sorts of group activities. Perhaps the Yis, still clinging to their yangban origins, are not quite as well represented among the Christians as the other lineages. In any case, as a group the Christians are prospering.

"I don't like the Christian church," says Kim Sang Gun, as he steers his boat easily through the big offshore swells. We have been out fishing beyond the anchored freighters almost as far as Ulsŏm, the first of the big offshore islands. Now, after hauling in a reasonably good catch, we are on our way back to the harbor. The wind on deck is bitterly cold, but crammed in the tiny wheel house we are comfortable enough. Kim Sang Gun was the cook on Kim Changdok's boat when we sailed to Mot Sŏm twenty-five years ago, and we drink soju now with easy familiarity.

"Personally, I don't see why they think they are better than the rest of us. And why should the church take a tenth of all the money I make fishing? And if there is work to do, or the fishing is good, it is silly to sit around all day on Sunday singing hymns and reading the Bible. I am a free man, and I don't want anyone telling me what I can and can't do." He holds up the bottle of soju. "And what's wrong with drinking a little bit now and then, as long as we don't get drunk and beat our wives or get in fights?" He opens the door and summons his young deck hand who squeezes in with us and also has a glass. "But the worst thing the Christians do is to make us show disrespect for our dead parents and grandparents. The Christian minister is wrong to denounce the chesa (ancestor commemoration ceremony)."

I agree with him on all these counts. I ask, "Then why is it that the church is growing so fast in Sŏkp'o?"

The crew member goes back out on deck, and we are silent for a while. Then Kim Sang Gun continues. "I know it sounds strange after what I just said, but we will probably join the church next year. My wife and children want to belong. The Christians are always getting together, not just in church but for picnics, sightseeing trips, and joint singing and praying with congregations in other villages. When I was young we also did everything together with our kin and neighbors—playing together, working together, drinking together, and helping each other out. But now we are by ourselves most of the time. Then he laughs, "Besides, the Christian God seems to be helping his believers more than our ancestors help us."

What preoccupies me more than all the changes that have taken place in Sŏkp'o is the problem of making sense out of my own reactions to them. Twenty-five years ago I was dazzled by the strong sense of community, and I identified emotionally with a fragile, vulnerable, and doomed way of life. Now, for me, some things have changed too fast. I seem to be the one who is suffering from culture shock, not the Sŏkp'o peasants who have abruptly and happily entered the modern world.

To take one example, at the end of an overgrown, faintly familiar path up the ridge behind my house, there is still a small clearing in the pines, but the village shrine is gone; It was a tiny, square, thatched hut with cracks in the slat walls that let the breeze and some light pass through. Although I never went inside, I used to peer through the cracks, and I can remember that except for a small, crudely made wooden box resting on a flat stone in the middle of the dirt floor, the hut was empty. Ordinary villagers stayed away from the shrine, but in ceremonies that were very old (from long before Confucius was even heard of in Korea), ritually purified men pleaded there with local gods at the lunar New Year to protect the village during the coming year. My house was the nearest one in the village to the shrine, and I used to hike up there from time to time, always feeling a pleasantly mysterious sense of connectedness with an ancient world. Now I have an almost proprietary sense of loss. When I ask Haeri's Grandmother what happened, she tells me that three years ago the Christian congregation of Sŏkp'o, led by a zealous minister from outside the village, objected to the earthy and occasionally drunken New Year's rites at the shrine and proposed that it be torn down. Apparently there was a good deal of lively argument at the time, but the Christian minister prevailed.

Already it is late November, and I start thinking about getting back to New England for the Christmas holidays. I wonder if this time when I leave Sŏkp'o, it will be for good. With the cold weather and stronger winds, I find myself spending more and more time outdoors, trying to memorize the landscapes and the way they change with the light and the tides. My meditations, at the soy bean field, on the hilltops, and along the edge of the ocean, seem to have become more positive. Twenty-five years ago fundamental change was what everyone in the village most desperately wanted. And now things have worked out far better than anyone at that time could have imagined. The people of Sŏkp'o (and most other Koreans as well), confronted with new challenges, new pressures, and new opportunities, are creating innovative cultural patterns—fitting themselves into a different kind of world by inventing new ways to live and think. And they do this easily, with toughness and skill. It is something to admire.

I have decided to leave Sŏkp'o on December 10. With only a couple of weeks left, I start to hustle. Hustling means wandering around in search of chance encounters, although the process now is much different than it used to be. In some ways it is easier and more productive, as long as the goal is simply to collect factual information. I meet a lot of people and fill up my notebook with reasonably accurate data. But I have to keep moving. My informants are cheerful and friendly and make a quick stab at responding to my questions. But they don't stop working for long. Everyone is fully aware of the value of his time, and long interruptions are not welcome. The villagers don't complain about how hard life is or make fun of their low station in life at the end of the world the way they used to. No one is ashamed to be from Sŏkp'o these days.

If I bring it up, I can provoke some discussion of the mounting trash problem. But it's obviously not an issue that really matters. No one worries about the environment, except for the decline in coastal fishing. Boat owners and their crews often discuss the pollution of coastal fishing waters, but not in cataclysmic terms. They are proud of South Korea's industrial development and demonstrate a curiously adaptive resilience, where it affects their own lives. A typical reaction is, "If the fishing gets much worse, we can always take the compensation money and set up a small engine-repair (electronics, clothing, retail fish, etc.) shop in town. My wife and children would much rather live in Sŏsan than here."

Although it was in Sŏkp'o, in 1966, that I learned from the villagers about community, I realize, with a slight shock, that now I seem to be the only one who is thinking about collective concerns.

If I am truly honest with myself, I have to admit that my upbeat admiration for change is somewhat forced. What bothers me most and makes this reencounter with Sŏkp'o so troubling, is that I often feel a little alienated and out of place watching what goes on with critical detachment. The people of Sŏkp'o are too busy to open up their houses and their lives the way they used to invite me to share their pleasures, hopes, or despair. No longer emotionally involved in some sort of momentous personal quest, I admit to myself that I am just another anthropologist, carrying out another more or less routine research project. The villagers are just ordinary people, not mythical heroes or villains, and their preoccupations are mundane.

The day before my departure, while crossing the dike from the Big Hamlet on my way to visit the Yi neighborhood, I have to move way over to the edge to make room for a small tractor and trailer to pass by. The trailer is piled high with brush, and an elderly woman is perched precariously on top. Not until the tractor pulls even with where I am standing and stops do I realize that it is Yi Pyŏngun (with his wife up on top of what turns out to be dried-up soybean plants). He is a handsome man in his mid-sixties, the head of the wealthiest household in the Yi lineage. He is also my third cousin. It was at his house that I attended my first *chesa* with Teacher Yi and Kim Ŭigon. Yi Pyŏngun is someone I can talk to easily, and we have already had a few long conversations about how things have changed. Even when I first met Yi Pyŏngun as a fairly young man, he had seemed more thoughtful and articulate than any of the other villagers except Teacher Yi. His father had already been dead for several years, and Yi Pyŏngun was obliged to become a responsible household head at a relatively young age. In the Far East the idea that successful local leaders should play a prominent role in promoting the well-being of the entire community is a deeply embedded part of rural Confucian traditions, and Yi Pyŏngun, although quieter, younger, and less self-assertive than other influential men in Sŏkp'o, took this obligation seriously. He was constantly trying to introduce new farming and fishing methods, not just to make money for himself, but with the explicit purpose of finding and demonstrating innovative ways for the villagers to work their own way out of poverty. No one else was willing to take the risks, so Yi Pyŏngun had to try out his new ideas by investing his own capital. During my first stay in Sŏkp'o, he invested in two schemes, the first was a large semicircular fishnet that was hauled through the surf up onto the beach, the second a chestnut tree plantation, both of which failed. But ten years or so after I left, he had introduced the new technique of growing oysters on racks implanted in the tidal mud. It turned out that the sheltered bay at Sŏkp'o was ideal for this kind of oyster farming, and in just a few years the village economy had been transformed.

His invitation now is a little puzzling, "Why don't you stop and play at my deer ranch. It's just another few kilometers up the bay beyond that point. It is close to noon, and the word "play" has profoundly attractive associations. I am already hungry and certain that if anyone has kept up the old standards of hospitality at mealtimes, it is Yi Pyŏngun. I am also curious to find out what a "deer ranch" is. So I happily accept, following along at a gradually increasing distance behind the tractor.

When I finally catch up with it, parked in front of a new, whitewashed, barn-like building, the soybean plants have been thrown over a chain link fence that encloses about a half-acre of grassland dotted with a few pine trees. And sure enough, inside the fence there are twelve small and skittish deer, eating the husks and stems. One of the deer is white. Yi Pyŏngun comes out of the building and shows me around, explaining that he wants to develop a park where people from the city can come and enjoy the beauties of nature. And then, of course, there is a good market for the fresh antlers that he will be able to harvest each year.

Although we are only three quarters of an hour's walk from his house, Yi Pyŏngun has set up separate living quarters at one end of the new building and is now spending most of his time there. Inside he serves my favorite medicinal alcohol, yakchu, along with roast eel and peanuts. The impromptu meal that follows is the best I've had since returning to Sŏkp'o. We eat quietly, and real conversation starts only as his wife clears away the dishes. I ask him what he thinks about all the changes that have taken place in Sŏkp'o in recent years.

"Good things and bad things have happened. Sŏkp'o itself as a place doesn't count for much anymore in people's thinking." He pauses, lights a cigarette, and continues in a thoughtful, somewhat pontifical tone.

"Young people, whose great-grandfathers I can still remember, are moving away for good, while other people that I've never heard of before are moving into the village. And almost no one expects that his children will go on living here after they grow up. We used to know all about everyone else, and we knew just what to expect. Now people keep more to themselves and don't trust each other the way they used to."

I can see that Yi Pyŏngun has thought a good deal about all this and that he is pleased to have me for an audience. He continues, "We live better, we eat better, we can get medical attention when we need it, and our young people come and go as they please and marry whom they please. We go to T'aean and Sŏsan all the time, both for business reasons and to see friends and relatives. Sŏkp'o is just a place where people own land and houses."

I say, "All that sounds like the kind of development that everyone has wanted all along. What are the bad things that have happened?"

Yi Pyŏngun answers this time with more emotion.

There is nothing secure and permanent in our lives the way there used to be. We can't depend on our relatives and friends when we need help, only on the money we earn. People will do anything for money. When I was young we learned that the most precious thing was the land our ancestors handed down to us—that it was the whole basis of our family's reputation and prosperity, and that we must preserve it above all other things. But now, the land no longer pays, even to grow rice. We don't need the trees anymore on our mountain land for firewood or to build our houses and boats. So my cousins sell their land to rich people from the city, even when it has their ancestors' tombs on it!

I ask, "Do the city people who buy the land do anything with it?"

No. They never even come here again once the sale is finished. The villagers who sell their land think they have it both ways. They have more money than they ever saw before all at once. And the land is still there on the hillside just the way it always was, if they should want to go out and gather ferns or cut some wood. I have not sold any of the land my grandfather and father left to me. I can still stand up and report to them without shame when we have a *chesa*. Unless we maintain our ties with the past and respect our ancestors, there is nothing stable to depend on.

Before I leave, I ask, "What do you think about the destruction of the village shrine?" Yi Pyŏngun laughs. "I am not superstitious. Maybe there are some old village spirits still hanging around. Probably not. If they are still here, they must be weak and lonely and badly nourished."

NOTES

1. I would like to thank the International Cultural Society of Korea (what is now known as the Korea Foundation) for their support of my research and memoir.